Counterfactual History and Bosnia-Herzegovina

Stian Nordengen Christensen

2018
Torkel Opsahl Academic EPublisher
Brussels

This and other publications in the *Publication Series* may be openly accessed and downloaded through the web site http://www.toaep.org/ which uses Persistent URLs for all publications it makes available (such PURLs will not be changed). This publication was published on 11 July 2018.

ISBNs: 978-82-8348-102-0 (print) and 978-82-8348-103-7 (e-book).

For my wife

FOREWORD

The experiences from large-scale armed conflicts shape our thinking about how we should respond in the future, in terms both of international law and international politics. This is certainly true for the armed conflicts in Bosnia and Herzegovina (hereinafter 'Bosnia-Herzegovina') in the 1990s, which were critical for the development of international law and institutions, and for diplomatic and military planning, in the subsequent decades. Many of these developments stem from the notion of historical possibilities: That international armed conflicts could have been prevented or at least that the suffering could have been reduced. If so, then we can prepare better for the future.

It is therefore essential that we have a clear understanding of historical possibilities. Despite this, there is a clear and persistent reluctance among professional historians to consider counterfactual possibilities from a scientific point of view. This book suggests how to increase the understanding of past possibilities in large-scale armed conflicts, though counterfactual analysis. Hopefully, this can lead to more informed decisions on future law and policy options.

This book is based on my doctoral dissertation, completed in 2011. There are several persons deserving of thanks for helping me in this work. First among them is Professor Tor Egil Førland, who guided me through the final stages of writing and provided feedback and suggestions that have led to a significantly improved product. I am also indebted to Professor Øystein Sørensen, Professor Ottar Dahl, Professor Knut Kjeldstadli, Marius Søberg, Kai Yamaguchi, Bård Frydenlund and Nils August Andresen, who all read through the dissertation at various stages and provided suggestions and insights that have doubtlessly improved the quality of the work. I would also like to thank the members of the Ph.D. commission and the independent experts who evaluated this dissertation and provided me with helpful and insightful feedback, namely Finn Erhard Johannesen, Aviezer Tucker, Sabrina P. Ramet, Arne Johan Vetlesen and Susan L. Woodward.

I thank Stig Oppedal for his proof-reading and useful suggestions regarding language and clarity. Staff members at the Department of Archaeology, Conservation and History at the University of Oslo, the Nobel Institute in Oslo, and the Archives of the Royal Norwegian Ministry of Foreign Affairs also deserve credit for their service and assistance. I also thank the Torkel Opsahl Academic EPublisher for its highly professional work in getting the manuscript ready for publication, in particular SIN Ngok Shek and Manek Minhas.

Finally, let me thank my wife, Kristine, for all her love and support, and for her understanding when I have worked with the dissertation through many weekends and evenings. I am incredibly fortunate to have her as my wife.

TABLE OF CONTENTS

PART II

APPROACHING COUNTERFACTUALS

PART III

COUNTERFACTUALS IN THE HISTORIOGRAPHY OF THE WAR IN BOSNIA-HERZEGOVINA IN 1993

ABBREVIATIONS

ArBiH	Army of Government of Bosnia-Herzegovina
CIA	Central Intelligence Agency
EC/EU	European Community/European Union
HV	Croatian Army
HVO	Bosnian Croat forces
ICFY	International Conference on the Former Yugoslavia
ICTY	International Criminal Tribunal for the Former Yugoslavia
IFOR	NATO Implementation Force
JNA	Yugoslav People's Army
MP	Member of Parliament
NATO	North Atlantic Treaty Organization
UN	United Nations
UNPROFOR	UN Protection Force
US	United States of America
VRS	Bosnian Serb Army
WWII	World War II

PART I

INTRODUCTION

1

Introduction

1.1. General Introduction

1.1.1. Aims of this Book

The aim of this book is to explore the questions of if and how counterfactual hypotheses can be labelled scientifically coherent and plausible.

Part II of this book discusses the theoretical foundations for counterfactuals in general, and aims to conclude with a proposal for a set of criteria for scientific coherence and plausibility of counterfactual historical analysis. I take, as a starting point, that although counterfactual thought-experiments are frequently used both in historiography and to inform policy decisions, no comprehensive theory of their scientific coherence exists. This book aims to propose a framework suitable for evaluating whether a given counterfactual hypothesis is closer to scientific inquiry on the one hand, or to unfounded speculation on the other hand. To achieve this, I will also discuss broadly the relation between counterfactual history and historiography in order to clarify the limitations and advantages of counterfactual analysis. Although the proposed framework will not be all-encompassing, my hope is that the book may serve as a resource for more informed debate on counterfactual history and its theory in the future.

Part III of this book discusses three counterfactual hypotheses in the historiography of the wars in Bosnia-Herzegovina in the 1990s. They have been advocated by both historians and contemporary diplomats. The discussion will show how counterfactual analyses are an integral part of the historiography of the war, and that these counterfactual hypotheses have both clear limitations and possibilities that can be clarified through informed use of counterfactual theory, so as to inform the theory of counterfactual history in general.

1.1.2. Definition of a Counterfactual Hypothesis

If a hypothesis is based on one or more antecedents that are clearly untrue, it is counterfactual. A counterfactual hypothesis, in the simpliest form, is: "If A, which is not, then B".

In historiography, counterfactual hypotheses are most commonly used to explain the necessity of specific causes. For example, "if Lenin had died in 1916, which he did not, then the October Revolution would not have happened". This hypothesis, if found to be scientifically coherent and plausible, would underscore Lenin as a necessary factor for the occurrence of the October Revolution. This book discusses other potential pragmatic advantages of counterfactual history.

'Counterfactual history', refers to the practice of using counterfactual hypotheses. There are two counterparts of counterfactual history. One is what I will refer to as *'factual history'*. I use these terms instead of 'counterfactual historiography' and 'factual historiography' because they are simpler, and because the term 'counterfactual history' is generally accepted in the philosophy of history. The labels are complicated, however, by the claim made by some historians that all historiography in fact includes counterfactual thought-experiments. However, it is fair to say that most works of historiography that are published today do not explicitly invoke any method of counterfactual inquiry when explaining historical processes or events. For this reason, I believe the dichotomy of counterfactual and factual history is useful for the discussion within these pages.[1]

The other counterpart is what I refer to as *'unfounded speculation'*. At the extreme end of this category of counterfactual analysis is 'counterfactual fiction' which is alternative or alternate histories without scientific value, and includes an increasingly popular genre of novels. One of its foremost proponents is Harry Turtledove, the author of many works in the genre, including a history of the United States without the Revolutionary War.[2] Drawing a line between this genre and counterfactual history as scientific inquiry is usually fairly simple. The counterfactual fiction of Turtledove and similar authors takes history as its starting point, but it is written first and foremost for the purposes of entertainment and not for the sake of scholarly history.

It is more difficult to differentiate between counterfactual history as scientific inquiry and counterfactual hypotheses as unfounded speculation,

---

1 A similar terminology, comparing "counterfactuals" with the "factual", is used in Richard Ned Lebow (ed.), *Forbidden Fruit, Counterfactuals and International Relations*, Princeton University Press, 2010, see particularly pp. 29–38.

2 Richard Dreyfuss and Harry Turtledove, *The Two Georges: The Novel of an Alternate America*, Tom Doherty Associates, New York, 1996.

when the latter is intended to assert what realistically could have happened. In many cases, historians present counterfactual hypotheses that are uninformed by theory of counterfactuals, thus they are difficult to be assessed on a scientific basis. By setting up criteria for the evaluation of counterfactual hypotheses, this book attempts to provide a framework for assessing whether a given counterfactual hypotheses is closer to one or the other category.

1.1.3. Establishing Relevance: The Munich Counterfactual

Counterfactual hypotheses are important. Counterfactuals are routinely used by ordinary people and policymakers, inspired by regrets or beliefs that better outcomes could have been achieved.[3] In Chapter 1, I argue that counterfactuals are used at least implicitly in all historical causal explanations.[4] Therefore, they have great political significance. The perhaps most well-known example today is the 'Munich counterfactual'. In essence, the common argument is that if the British – or the British in alignment with the French, Americans and Soviets – had strongly opposed the Fascist expansionism of the 1930s, then World War II would have been avoided. The most famous ones concern the appeasement policy carried out by British Prime Minister Neville Chamberlain in Munich in 1938, when Nazi Germany was granted the right to occupy Sudetenland in western Czechoslovakia. Since then, 'Munich' became synonymous with the appeasement policy of the Western governments toward the Fascist states in the 1930s.[5]

The most serious proponents of the Munich counterfactual view will point to instances when Adolf Hitler or Benito Mussolini could have been confronted – usually Czechoslovakia, Rhineland, Saarland, Abyssinia or the various arms control negotiations in the 1930s. They may even argue in favour of specific counterfactual policies, often involving strong threats or the use of armed force against Germany and/or Italy.

---

3 Lebow (ed.), 2010, p. 29, see *supra* note 1.

4 Richard Ned Lebow and Philip E. Tetlock, "Scholars and Causation", in Lebow (ed.), 2010, p. 137, see *supra* note 1.

5 Among those who have published works on the various aspects of the Munich analogy are Jeffrey Record, *Making War, Thinking History: Munich, Vietnam, and Presidential Uses of Force from Korea to Kosovo*, Naval Institute Press, Annapolis, 2002; and KHONG Yuen Foong, *Analogies at War: Korea, Munich, Dien Bien Phu, and the American Decisions of 1965*, Princeton University Press, 1992.

However, one may question whether an investigation into a counterfactual, Munich or other, can yield any outcome which would be scientifically coherent. Counterfactuals seem, for example, to be untestable: since it is impossible to re-run history with an altered policy, we cannot establish objectively what would have happened. In factual history, historians will argue that what actually happened is the proof of his theory. One can argue that this too is pseudo-scientific. A theory that explains a historical process is not necessarily the only theory capable of doing so. Since it is impossible to re-run history, as one would do in a laboratory, factual historical theories cannot be confirmed like those in natural sciences. Still, a factual historical process is certainly more reliable than a hypothetical historical process.

There is no way of directly verifying or falsifying a counterfactual scenario. Why, then, should we bother with exploring counterfactuals? In addition to the potential scientific value added, which I will discuss in Chapter 3, counterfactuals should be explored because of their clear political importance. Jeffrey Record, one of those who have studied the political significance of the Munich counterfactual, concluded, in his 2002 work, that the Munich Accord has played an important role in shaping the thinking of American policy-makers about military interventions abroad in practically every case since World War II.[6] For example, consider this passage from Harry S. Truman's memoirs, recalling his own thoughts when North Korea attacked South Korea on 25 June 1950:[7]

> In my generation, this was not the first occasion when the strong had attacked the weak. I recalled some earlier instances: Manchuria, Ethiopia, Austria. I remembered each time that the democracies failed to act, it had just encouraged the aggressors to keep going ahead. Communism was acting in Korea just as Hitler, Mussolini and the Japanese had acted ten, fifteen and twenty years earlier.

This passage indicates that Truman drew upon the Munich analogy when shaping his plans for intervening in the Korean War. At the very least, he used Munich to justify the American intervention to the general public, in his own memoirs. Even considering the problems of using memoirs as

---

6 Record, 2002, see *supra* note 5.

7 Harry S. Truman, *Years of Trial And Hope*, vol. 2, Hodder and Stroughton, Bungay, 1956, p. 351; Record, 2002, see *supra* note 5.

historical evidence, it is unproblematic to argue that the Munich analogy influenced both the policy of intervention in Korea, and how this intervention was, and is, generally viewed by Americans. The same can be said for many, if not all, other post-World War II American military interventions. The Munich analogy matters because it shapes both policies of military intervention and how decision makers publicly argue in favour of that.

Since no commonly accepted analytical framework of counterfactuals exists, many researchers have gotten away with wildly implausible counterfactuals regarding Munich and World War II in general. I will consider one example of this tradition. In 2002, Johan Galtung was invited to be a consultant on a peace exhibition in the Memorial for Peace Museum in Caen, France. He produced a concept that was almost entirely counterfactual, including an attempt to describe ways in which World War II could have been avoided. He listed five measures which he believed would have prevented World War II:

- Conflict transformation, by revising the Versailles Treaty.
- Massive nonviolence actions by the German people and supported abroad.
- Building peace structure, by strengthening the progressive forces in Germany.
- Building peace culture, by criticising the German/Nazi world-view.
- Encouraging massive conscientious objection.[8]

I will not discuss these arguments in detail, but merely point out that these counterfactuals represent something completely different from serious historical inquiry. Apart from the first argument of revising the Versailles Treaty, these proposed measures have no historical foundation. Rather, they are the result of his own political agenda, which is promoting nonviolence as a means of conflict resolution today.

Counterfactual arguments, whether of Galtung's or Truman's type, will always be used in political debates. Although it should be self-evident to a historically conscious person that Galtung's line of reasoning is flawed, it is probably harder to criticise Truman's. Both, however, have in common

[8] Johan Galtung, "Toward Peaceful Worlds: A Guide to Peace", in *Working Paper,* Centre for Peace Studies, University of Tromsø, Tromsø, 2002.

that there is no clear method for checking the scientific coherence or plausibility of their hypotheses. Their theories cannot even be clarified without entering into a counterfactual analysis. Therefore, it is important to establish a framework for counterfactual inquiry with consensus. This book aspires to propose and test such criteria of scientific coherence and plausibility in counterfactual inquiry.

1.2. Previous Research on Counterfactuals

1.2.1. Counterfactuals in the Philosophy of Science

When discussing counterfactuals in the philosophy of science, David Lewis' *Counterfactuals* (1973) has a special position.[9] Although there have been many accounts dedicated to exploring, or at least touching upon, counterfactuals in publications preceding Lewis', notably Nelson Goodman's *Fact, Fiction and Forecast* (1955),[10] his account is clearly the most quoted and therefore the most important reference work in the philosophy of science. No serious account of counterfactuals in the philosophy of science since 1973 fails to mention Lewis.

In this book, however, I will not devote much attention to Lewis' account. First, my own project is about counterfactual analysis in historiography, not in the philosophy of science in general. It is true that Lewis' theories have, in one way or another, been integrated into the literature dealing specifically with historical counterfactuals, therefore forming part of the mainstream theory. Second, those not included in the mainstream theory on historical counterfactuals are often narrow problems in the philosophy of science, and are not that important to historical theory and practice. For example, Lewis' theory has been criticised, quite rightly, for failing to adequately explain the so-called pre-emptive causation, which is causation by fragile events and indeterministic causation.[11] I aim to steer away from these problems, in order to focus on my primary objective, which is the use of counterfactual analysis for the historian.

---

9 David Lewis, *Counterfactuals*, Basil Blackwell, Oxford, 1986.

10 Nelson Goodman, *Fact, Fiction and Forecast*, Bobbs-Merril, Indianapolis, 1973.

11 See, for example, Murali Ramachandran, "A Counterfactual Analysis of Causation", in *Mind*, 1997, vol. 106, no. 422, pp. 263–277, especially p. 263.

Some would also include Bas van Fraassen, particularly his theory of contrastive explanations, as a major contributor to the theory of counterfactuals in the philosophy of science.[12] However, van Fraassen's contribution in this respect, although undoubtedly important, does not really fall in the category of counterfactuals in the philosophy of science, but rather in the field of explanations in the philosophy of science, and that his treatment of counterfactuals is not broad enough for it to merit comparison with Lewis's *Counterfactuals*.

1.2.2. Counterfactuals in Social Science

There is no authoritative account in the field of counterfactuals in social science that matches the position that Lewis' work has gained in the field of counterfactuals in the philosophy of science. However, there are some works that tend to be quoted in many accounts.The first ones among those seem to be Max Weber's "Objective Possibility and Adequate Causation in Historical Explanation",[13] Jon Elster's *Logic and Society*,[14] James Fearon's "Counterfactuals and Hypothesis Testing in Political Science",[15] and finally Philip E. Tetlock and Aaron Belkin's *Counterfactual Thought Experiments in World Politics*.[16] The last one approaches the subject in ways very similar to my own – attempting to establish criteria for scientifically coherent counterfactuals – but the focus is on social science in general, not on particular history that leads to differing conclusions about the boundaries of counterfactual inquiry, to which I will return in more detail below.

During the course of writing this book, I have been asked why I do not include game theory in it. There are articles published in the field of

12 Bas C. van Fraassen, *The Scientific Image*, Clarendon Press, Oxford, 1980.

13 Max Weber, "Objektive Möglichkeit und Adäquate Verursachung in der Historischen Kausalbetrachtung", in Max Weber, *Gesammelte Aufsätze zur Wissenschaftlehre*, J.C.B. Mohr, Tübingen, 1922, pp. 266–290.

14 Jon Elster, *Logic and Society: Contradictions and Possible Worlds*, John Wiley, Chichester, 1978.

15 James F. Fearon, "Counterfactuals and Hypothesis Testing in Political Science", in *World Politics*, 1991, vol. 43, no. 2, pp. 169–195.

16 Philip E. Tetlock and Aaron Belkin (eds.), *Counterfactual Thought Experiments in World Politics: Logical, Methodological, and Psychological Perspectives*, Princeton University Press, 1996.

counterfactual history that are derived from the perspective of game theory.[17] However, this should be seen as a variant of counterfactual history, not as a separate discipline. Game theory is one of the approaches that have been used to write counterfactual history, but it is not the only one, nor necessarily the best. In this book, I will not dwell on the method of game theory and its various conjunctions with counterfactual history, as I am more concerned with the scientific coherence and plausibility of counterfactual analyses than the method or approach for writing counterfactuals. However, I will comment on the relevance of counterfactuals in historiography and social science respectively in Chapter 1, because of its significance in the scope of scientifically coherent counterfactual inquiry.

1.2.3. Counterfactuals in the Philosophy of History

If the approach to counterfactuals in social science is divided, then the approach in the philosophy of history is anarchic, at best. Many – probably most – accounts lack any comprehensive grasp of the subject, both in regard to counterfactual theory in general, and historical counterfactuals in particular. An example is John Lewis Gaddis' references to counterfactual history in *The Landscape of History* (2002), where he claims that the rules of counterfactual inquiry are these:

> You can't throw multiple counterfactuals into the pot, because it makes it impossible to pinpoint the effects of any of them. You can't experiment with single variables that weren't within the range of the technology or the culture of the times.[18]

Certainly, one could say, on face value, that these two points are reasonable, but, in reality, there are no agreed theories on (1) whether counterfactuals can be combined, and (2) whether technological levels can be counterfactually altered. In fact, the most famous historiographic counterfactual of all times, Robert Fogel's "American history without railroads", alters the level of technology, and this has been heatedly debated ever since.[19] Most importantly, Gaddis' criteria are clearly insufficient in that the fundamental problems of counterfactual analysis in historiography remain

[17] See, for example, Bruce Bueno de Mesquita, "Counterfactuals and International Affairs: Some Insights From Game Theory", in Tetlock and Belkin (eds.), 1996, see *supra* note 16.

[18] John Lewis Gaddis, *The Landscape of History: How Historians Map the Past*, Oxford University Press, 2002, p. 101.

[19] Robert William Fogel, *Railroad and American Economic Growth: Essays in Econometric History*, Johns Hopkins Press, Baltimore, 1964.

untouched: how can one make a scientifically coherent counterfactual statement, when there is no way of showing, or testing, that the counterfactual consequent would have been realised according to the hypothesis? It is not my intention here to disdain that, but I bring up Gaddis' treatment because it is typical, and because Gaddis himself is a famous historian. Such inadequate theoretical treatments are, regrettably, commonplace in counterfactual history. If such superficialities go unchallenged, historical science will suffer. Yet, many of the most well-known philosophers of history barely touch upon the issue of counterfactuals. This is one of the main reasons why I am writing this book.

However, there is a growing amount of what may be called 'informed accounts' of counterfactual history. Most of these draw heavily upon the philosophers I have mentioned above, and particularly on Tetlock/Belkin and Elster. Aviezer Tucker, in his *Our Knowledge of the Past*, is one of those which devote relatively significant space to counterfactuals.[20] Although his account draws together some of the most important conclusions from previous works, it is not comprehensive, nor does it aim to be so.

What seems certain is the rapid growth in volume of theories of counterfactual history, and counterfactual history itself in the last 10–15 years. However, this is not the first time counterfactual history has come to the attention of many mainstream historians. All recent works in the field owe something, positive or negative, to the debate on Robert Fogel's *Railroads and American Economic Growth*,[21] which was hotly debated among scholars in the 1960s and 1970s, and a main reference for Elster, among others. Indeed, it is likely that many historians even today think of Fogel's theories first, when the issue of counterfactual history is brought up. However, Fogel – and what is called 'econometric history' in general – is just one variant of counterfactual history as such. It is in fact problematic to label Fogel's line of counterfactual analysis 'historical', because the premises of the analysis could be interpreted as too removed from history.

Geoffrey Hawthorn's *Plausible Worlds* (1991) is one of the more recent works in counterfactual history that should be mentioned here.[22] His

20 Aviezer Tucker, *Our Knowledge of the Past: A Philosophy of Historiography*, Cambridge University Press, Cambridge, 2004, particularly pp. 227–239.

21 Fogel, 1964, see *supra* note 19.

22 Geoffrey Hawthorn, *Plausible Worlds: Possibility and Understanding in History and the Social Sciences*, Cambridge University Press, Cambridge, 1991.

theories on counterfactuals in history may not be particularly innovative, as they are mostly drawn from Goodman, Lewis and other philosophers, but the three counterfactual cases in *Plausible Worlds* are still among the most quoted. Hawthorn convincingly argues that, for example, the occupation of South Korea by the United States after World War II was not inevitable, which has certain consequences for our understanding of the Korean War in particular and the Cold War in general.

Alexander Demandt's *History That Never Happened* is perhaps the most ambitious account of the theory of counterfactual history to date.[23] Demandt's work is frequently quoted in mainstream literature on counterfactual history. This seems to be the case despite the many shortcomings in Demandt's theories, which I will return in subsequent chapters.

Niall Ferguson's *Virtual History* (1997) is perhaps best known to contemporary readers of history.[24] The reason is primarily the wide circulation of this book, probably because Ferguson is among the most famous professors of history in the world today and a regular contributor to important journals, such as *Foreign Affairs*. *Virtual History* is an anthology with multiple contributors, but it is Ferguson's introductory chapter on theory that concerns us here. In that chapter, he introduces the term 'chaostory', which signifies a form of historiography (that is, counterfactual history) that is open to the seeming indeterminism inherent in some natural sciences, such as chaos theory in mathematics and quantum theory in physics.[25] In fact, Ferguson calls this form of historiography a potential new paradigm, in reference to Thomas Kuhn's famous theory of scientific revolutions.[26] The term seems to be on the verge of entering mainstream counterfactual history. I devote some space to reflect on aspects of the term here, but it seems to me that there are many reasons to approach it with scepticism. Counterfactual history, in being a method of historical inquiry and not a type of historiography, such as materialism or idealism, does not seem to be a paradigm change. Nor is it necessarily fruitful to equate historical inquiry to that of the natural sciences, as chaos theory might not be

---

23 Alexander Demandt, *History That Never Happened: A Treatise on the Question, What Would Have Happened If...?*, McFarland, Jefferson, North Carolina, 1993.

24 Niall Ferguson (ed.), *Virtual History: Alternatives and Counterfactuals*, Picador, London, 1997.

25 *Ibid.*, p. 90.

26 Thomas Kuhn, *The Structure of Scientific Revolutions*, University of Chicago Press, Chicago, 1962.

the best guide for understanding human actions and societies. I will return to this in Chapter 2.

In this book, I also draw on some Norwegian historians, notably Ottar Dahl and Øystein Sørensen. If measured solely by the number of references to their works by other scholars, of course they cannot be put in the same class as the other thinkers mentioned here. This may be because both write in Norwegian, which naturally limits the circulation of their works. However, they have published books and articles with interesting viewpoints not found in mainstream philosophy. I have therefore tried to point out those viewpoints where appropriate.

The relative poverty of theory on counterfactual history may be one of the reasons why a great deal of attention was paid to E.H. Carr's *What is History* in counterfactual history writings.[27] A remarkable number of the historians and philosophers I have mentioned here discuss Carr when dealing with historical counterfactuals: Ferguson,[28] Hawthorn,[29] Sørensen[30] and Fearon,[31] to mention some.[32] Most popular in the 'Carr debate' is the discussion of a sentence in Pascal's *Pensées*: "Cleopatra's nose: had it been shorter, the whole aspect of the world would have been altered".[33] This counterfactual statement is among the most quoted in the theory of counterfactual history, which is why I have chosen to offer my own viewpoints and the debate on that in this book.

The most important work of reference for this book, however, is Tetlock and Belkin's *Counterfactual Thought Experiments in World Politics*. To me, the most urgently needed matter in counterfactual history is not a method of writing, nor ideas for new topics, but awareness about potential

27 E.H. Carr, *What is History? The George Macaulay Trevelyan Lectures delivered in the University of Cambridge January–March 1961*, Macmillan, London, 1986.

28 Fergusson (ed.), 1997, pp. 12–17, see *supra* note 24.

29 Hawthorn, 1991, pp. 8–9, see *supra* note 22.

30 Øystein Sørensen, *Historien om det som ikke skjedde: Kontrafaktisk historie* [History That Did Not Happen], Aschehoug, Oslo, 2004.

31 Fearon, 1991, p. 191, see *supra* note 15.

32 In addition, see Elazar Weinryb, "Historiographic Counterfactuals", in Aviezer Tucker (ed.), *A Companion to the Philosophy of History and Historiography*, Blackwell, Chichester, 2009, p. 109; Gaddis, 2002, pp. 91–93, see *supra* note 18; Martin Bunzl, "Counterfactual History: A User's Guide", in *The American Historical Review*, 2004, vol. 109, no. 3, p. 845.

33 Blaise Pascal, *Pensées*, Section II, fragment 162.

criteria for evaluating the scientific coherence and plausibility of counterfactual analyses in historiography. To my mind, this is the most important contribution of Tetlock and Belkin's work, as they attempt to set up such criteria. I will attempt to clarify the strengths and weaknesses of Tetlock and Belkin's approach, and endeavour to suggest appropriate revisions, clarifications or additions to the list of criteria they present.

1.2.4. A Note on Theories of Scientific Explanations and Demarcation

Many historians regard counterfactual history lying outside the scope of inquiry of the scholarly discipline of history.[34] Therefore, it is useful to draw on the philosophy for demarcation between sciences and pseudosciences.[35] However, this is problematic because the debate on demarcation is as old as the philosophy of science itself, and the complex conjunctions between epistemology and philosophy of science make demarcation a very challenging matter.

In the course of writing this book, I tried to obtain a sufficient overview of the debate on demarcation in the philosophy of science in general, in order to apply relevant aspects of this debate to the theory of counterfactual history. However, it seems that this is not actually possible, because there is no consensus on what constitutes a scientifically coherent explanation. In the twentieth century, the most heatedly debated criteria of scientifically coherent explanations included Karl Popper's theory of demarcation and Carl Gustav Hempel's covering laws.[36] At present, however, there is no consensus on scientific explanations. It seems that most philosophers of science share Wesley Salmon's opinion that defining

34 As mentioned, one work that is often referred to in this regard is Carr, 1986, see *supra* note 27. Another example is David Hackett Fischer, *Historians' Fallacies: Toward a Logic of Historical Thought*, Routledge and Kegan Paul, London, 1971, see particularly p. 19.

35 "Demarcation" is commonly used in the philosophy of science to describe the boundary of science in contrast to pseudoscience or fiction. Examples include the difference between astrology and astronomy or, albeit highly controversial, between theology and science of religion.

36 Karl Popper, *The Logic of Scientific Discovery*, Hutchison, London, 1975; C.G. Hempel, "The Function of General Laws in History", in *Aspects of Scientific Explanation and Other Essays in the Philosophy of Science*, The Free Press, New York, 1965.

scientifically coherent explanations is one of the major unsolved issues in the philosophy of science.[37]

Noting the dissent, I must say that I find Karl Popper's line of thought appealing in analysing the scientific coherence of counterfactual hypotheses. The core of Popper's demarcation is the concept of falsifiability – that a scientifically coherent hypothesis should be at least indirectly testable. Of course, there are many vocal critics of Popper's theories, notably Paul Feyerabend, who argued that it is meaningless to propose general rules of scientific inquiry at all, because there are no unquestionable facts or laws and no means of solving or bypassing Hume's problem of induction.[38] Still, I believe that Popper's demarcation principle, if taken in its most narrow sense of calling for falsifiability, is apt for differentiating between counterfactual history as a scholarly exercise and unfounded speculation, or counterfactual fiction. There is always the issue of evidence in historiography, usually held as crucial even in spite of all the obvious points about how we epistemologically can never know that our explanations are correct. Therefore, I place a great deal of emphasis on Popper's demarcation principle, albeit in a narrow sense of the theory, which will be apparent in the following chapters.

1.2.5. Remaining Dilemmas and Shortcomings in the Existing Literature

I have argued above that it is necessary to approach counterfactual history with an eye to achieve a common understanding of how to separate scientifically coherent hypotheses from what should be labelled 'pseudo-science', and that Tetlock and Belkin's contribution has already made a great effort to set up criteria for judging such scientific coherence. I think it fair to say that their attempt is, to synthesise the bits and pieces of theory on counterfactuals that already existed, and come up with a list of criteria that may provide the basis for further discussion. As I also aspire to con-

37 Wesley C. Salmon, "Scientific Explanation: How We Got from There to Here", in *Causality and Explanation,* Oxford University Press, 1998, p. 316.

38 Paul Feyerabend, *Against Method: Outline of an Anarchistic Theory of Knowledge*, NLB, London, 1975; Paul K Feyerabend, "Realism, Rationalism and Scientific Method", in *Philosophical Papers,* vol. 1, Cambridge University Press, 1981, pp. 204–205.

struct a list of criteria of the scientific coherence and plausibility of counterfactual historical hypotheses, there is a need to indicate which challenges are inherent in Tetlock and Belkin's approach.

First, Tetlock and Belkin's starting point is not counterfactual history, but counterfactuals in world politics. Such starting point takes for granted that it is feasible to speak of counterfactuals in social science, not just in historical science. Concretely, Tetlock and Belkin speak of the difference between 'idiographic' and 'nomothetic' counterfactuals.[39] The idiographic counterfactuals signify those that are case-specific, and the nomothetic signify those that invoke a Hempelian law. They provide the following example of an idiographic counterfactual: given the connection between money supply and inflation, what would have happened if the Russian central bank had a different policy in 1992?[40] They further explain that the nomothetic counterfactual does not concern itself with how the antecedents could have been different, but rather invoke a so-called "miracle cause" – an alteration of the antecedent without specifying how or why this antecedent could have been different – and then attempt to see what the outcome would have been.[41] In the nomothetic counterfactual, "[t]he goal is not historical understanding; rather it is to pursue the logical implications of a theoretical framework".[42] It is therefore something separate from historical inquiry, despite that it is scrutinising a historical case.

However, is it possible at all to speak of counterfactuals that are scientifically coherent in social science, but not in historiography? Should it be scientifically permissible to alter an antecedent without explaining why it is credible that this antecedent could have been different? I will discuss this line of thought in Chapter 1.

Second, Tetlock and Belkin's theory allows for a number of variants of counterfactuals that are more or less separate from historical science in the narrow sense, such as "idiographic-nomothetic counterfactuals" (game theory applied to history), "computer simulation counterfactuals" (pure thought-experiments) and "mental simulations of counterfactual worlds" (designed to show bias and psychological inconsistencies by pointing to

39 Tetlock and Belkin (eds.), 1996, pp. 7–9, see *supra* note 16.

40 *Ibid.*, pp. 8–9

41 *Ibid.*, p. 9.

42 *Ibid.*, p. 9.

counterfactuals).[43] It is unclear whether these variants of counterfactuals are characterised by their pragmatic advantages, "functions" in Tetlock and Belkin's terminology, or types of counterfactuals. The variants are defined by their pragmatic advantages when first introduced, but are also referred to as "styles of counterfactual argumentation" and finally as "ideal-type patterns of counterfactual reasoning" in the same text.[44]

Ideally, I think it would be useful to distinguish between the structure of a counterfactual and its pragmatic advantages. In this sense, the "structure" would refer to how the form of the hypothesis conforms to the criteria of scientific coherence and plausibility, whereas the "pragmatic advantages" would signify the way(s) that the hypothesis provides new and useful insights. I will mainly discuss the pragmatic advantages of counterfactuals in Chapter 4. The structure of counterfactuals, on the other hand, is a topic for the whole book, but mainly in Chapter 2. A significant question is whether there can be more than one ideal structure of a counterfactual. As mentioned, Tetlock and Belkin list five such 'structures' (in my terminology).

Third and most importantly, discussion of criteria for the scientific coherence and plausibility of counterfactuals is the central aim of this book. Tetlock and Belkin have proposed six criteria, which probably are the most widely used criteria in counterfactual history, and also in works published prior to Tetlock and Belkin's work, because it can also be seen as an attempted synthesis of previous theories. I refrain from introducing the concrete criteria at this point, because they all require prior information and/or lengthy explanations. Although a discussion of the criteria of counterfactual history is at the core of what I hope to obtain through this book, I will introduce Tetlock and Belkin's criteria in Chapter 5. Only at that point in this book will it be meaningful to go into the strong and weak points of those criteria, by referring to the more general philosophical discussions in Chapters 2–4. The aim in Chapter 5 is to present a modified list of criteria, which hopefully has even stronger philosophical foundations than Tetlock and Belkin's version.

It will become apparent that my approach to such criteria also differs somewhat from Tetlock and Belkin in regard to terminology. The criteria

43 *Ibid.*, pp. 11–14.

44 *Ibid.*; "Styles of counterfactual argumentation" on p. 7; "functions" on p. 6, and "ideal-type patterns of counterfactual reasoning" in Lebow (ed.), 2010, p. 17, see *supra* note 1.

listed in *Counterfactual Thought Experiments in World Politics* are, according to the authors, actually for "plausibility".[45] I believe it is more fruitful to approach the subject matter with an aim to distinguish between what establishes the 'scientific coherence' and what may show the "plausibility" of a given hypothesis. The 'scientific coherence' of a counterfactual hypothesis should be determined by criteria which the hypothesis must *necessarily* not violate in order to be labelled 'scientific'. "Plausibility", on the other hand, should be determined by criteria that are appropriate for evaluation of the overall reliability of the hypothesis.

1.2.6. Objections to Counterfactual History

Although recent historiography seems to show a gradually increased acceptance of counterfactual hypotheses, I find that those who believe counterfactual history is useful devote most of their theoretical discussions to defending or even excusing counterfactual history against real or perceived critics. In his much-quoted book on counterfactual history, Alexander Demandt introduces his own work with an excuse: "In making it [the book], I say with Luther: 'It may be that I owe my God and the world one more act of folly, and this I am now committing'".[46]

The seemingly defensive approach of many counterfactual theories is, interestingly enough, usually not made in reference to any authoritative work. There are very few published works that consider counterfactual history in depth and conclude by rejecting counterfactual method outright. The strongest criticism seems to revolve around more general perceptions of counterfactual theories as generally irrelevant, uninteresting, unnecessary or too subjective. Some vocal, oft-quoted critics of counterfactual history are David Fischer and, as mentioned, E.H. Carr.[47] In addition, there is the debate about Fogel's economic counterfactuals from the 1960s and 1970s, but that is just a variant of counterfactual history.

I will discuss some of the commonly asserted or likely objections to counterfactual history in Chapter 3. In particular, the debate on value ob-

---

45 Tetlock and Belkin (eds.), 1996, p. 5, see *supra* note 16.

46 Demandt, 1993, p. 2, see *supra* note 23.

47 Fischer, 1971, p. 19, see *supra* note 34; Carr, 1986, see *supra* note 27; Demandt also presents a list of what he conceives to be common or natural objections in Demandt, 1993, pp. 3–8, see *supra* note 23.

jectivity in counterfactual history is a discussion in this category that deserves closer explanation, which I will discuss at length. During the course of writing this book, several have suggested that it might be better to omit this. The reason for this, I believe, is that the issue of value objectivity is part of a broad philosophical debate that would be impossible to encompass in this book. I will not endeavour to do so, and instead will take the view that one should strive for objectivity when providing a scientific explanation as a starting point.

Because counterfactual hypotheses are not solely based on factual events, subjectively influenced explanations may occur more often than in factual history. In historiography in general, where real-world experimentation is nearly always impossible, there is a greater danger of subjectively contaminated explanations than in, say, physics.[48] In counterfactual history, which has even less evidence to build upon than factual history, the danger of subjectivity is even greater. Several scholars have pointed that out, including Tetlock and Belkin.[49] In Chapter 3, I attempt to shed light on this problem and discuss whether methodological measures can be introduced to limit the danger of subjectivity inherent in counterfactuals.

1.3. The Case: Historiography of the War in Bosnia-Herzegovina in 1993

1.3.1. Relevance: Why Bosnia-Herzegovina?

I have selected hypotheses from the historiography of the war in Bosnia-Herzegovina as examples for discussing how counterfactual analysis is used by historians. There are reasons to believe that counterfactual hypotheses are likely to be common in historiography of recent conflicts. It seems only natural for any person who is studying a human tragedy to ask whether this could have been avoided wholly or partly. In other words, it is to search for counterfactual alternatives to actual historical events. For this reason, I

48 Thor Heyerdahl's experiments may arguably be considered examples of how experimentation can be used in historical science, although Heyerdahl's proving that something could be done, however, does not prove it actually did.

49 Tetlock and Belkin (eds.), 1996, p. 32, see *supra* note 16. See also Fergusson (ed.), 1997, p. 11, see *supra* note 24; Carr, 1986, pp. 91–92, see *supra* note 27; and Gregory Mitchell, "Case Studies, Counterfactuals, and Causal Explanations", in *University of Pennsylvania Law Review*, 2004, vol. 152, no. 5, pp. 1562–1564.

believe it is likely that the war in Bosnia-Herzegovina may provide good examples for further scrutiny.

Since counterfactuals have been used in the historiography of the war in Bosnia-Herzegovina, it is important to ask to what extent the accounts of the war clarify that certain hypotheses are counterfactual, and whether this leads to understanding of the limitations of the conclusions that can be drawn. If such clarifications are not explicit, a relevant question is whether the limitations and possibilities of the hypotheses can be seen as implicit and can be inferred.

Another reason to focus on Bosnia-Herzegovina is its importance to contemporary policy development. The accounts of this war, and of what might have been done to stop it, still influences the way Western states think about and handle international conflicts.

Examples from history, both factual and counterfactual, tend to influence policy decisions, and to be used to explain such decisions. For example, we know that the war in Bosnia-Herzegovina coloured the thinking about responding to the crisis in Kosovo in 1999. Not only contemporary journalists looked to Bosnia-Herzegovina to find answers to the present situation, but also President Clinton and NATO's Secretary-General, Javier Solana, who explained in detail how the response to the Bosnian crisis coloured the actions in Kosovo.[50]

However, decision-makers, journalists and researchers may, at times, be too hasty when applying lessons from past conflicts. There is a risk of failing to analyse sufficiently the scientific coherence and plausibility of the conclusions drawn, something which seems particularly to be the case when counterfactuals are invoked. An example is a statement made by Clinton's National Security Advisor, Sandy Berger in 1999, that "we [the United States] waited too long in Bosnia – we [were not going] to wait too long in Kosovo. We have enough evidence to know what would have happened if we didn't act".[51] The implication is that the United States could have acted more quickly and more resolutely in order to resolve the situation in Bosnia-Herzegovina, and that was the reason why the reaction over

---

50 Javier Solana, "NATO: Lessons learned from Bosnia", in *M2 Presswire*, 15 March 1999 (transcribed speech by Dr. Javier Solana at the Instituto De Defensa Nacional, Portugal).

51 Carl M. Cannon, "From Bosnia to Kosovo: To Understand Why President Clinton Approved Military Action in Kosovo, It's Necessary to Understand What Lessons He Drew From Bosnia", in *National Journal*, 3 April 1999.

Kosovo had to be more resolute. However, drawing such a conclusion requires a precise analysis of what evidence backing up the claim that the United States could have resolved the Bosnian crisis at an earlier stage. Such an analysis can be aided by a clear foundation in the theory of counterfactual history, particularly if specific criteria can be provided.

Without specific conditions or evidence, Berger's analogy would be clearly insufficient as a guide for policy decisions. As will become apparent from the case study here, counterfactual argumentation is not only common in politics, but also in scholarly debates about the war in Bosnia-Herzegovina. Counterfactual arguments are, in fact, so commonplace that there is little reason to believe that they will cease to be used, even if philosophers conclude that they have little actual value. This underscores the need to engage in discussions of both counterfactuals in general, and the use of counterfactual hypotheses as guides for future action. Hopefully, the theory presented here may aid in clarifying such arguments by providing guidelines for evaluating the scientific coherence and plausibility of counterfactual hypotheses.

1.3.2. Previous Literature on the War in Bosnia-Herzegovina

There is a vast body of literature on the wars in Bosnia-Herzegovina in the 1990s ('the war'), and it would be impossible for any researcher to account for all, or even most, works written on this war. In 1998, Rusko Matulić published a *Bibliography of Sources on the Region of Former Yugoslavia*, which listed 12,578 published sources on Yugoslavia, including 2,170 under the chapter "Destruction of Yugoslavia (from 1990)".[52] The bibliography was, of course, not comprehensive even when it was published in 1998, and much less today. It is self-evident that no one is able to cover the entire spectrum of published works on the war. One is forced to make some sort of selection.

A general problem in reviewing the literature of the war in Bosnia-Herzegovina is that the scholarly debate is still heavily politicised. There have been many attempts to provide objective accounts of the war, but none seem to have managed to completely avoid charges of partiality. Charges

52 Rusko Matulić, *Bibliography of Sources on the Region of Former Yugoslavia*, East European Monographs, Boulder, 1998.

of bias toward one of the parties in the war are particularly common.[53] As time passes and passions temper, this phenomenon is likely to diminish.

In the first generation of accounts of the war, many of the works are autobiographical, written as by some of the main political actors in the war. Among the most quoted are the autobiographies of Lord David Owen (EC/EU representative and peace mediator), Richard Holbrooke (US Special Envoy), Carl Bildt (EU representative and peace mediator), General Sir Michael Rose (UNPROFOR commander in 1994) and Warren Zimmermann (the last ambassador of the United States to Yugoslavia).[54] These are only a few of the many, as most of the heavily involved actors in the war have published their recollections or opinions in one way or another. Over the years, autobiographical works have been added to the list, as serving politicians have published their memoirs, such as President Bill Clinton, Prime Minister John Major and British Foreign Secretary Douglas Hurd.[55]

The autobiographical works are, of course, coloured by the authors' personal stakes in how the course of the war is interpreted; the accounts are often defensive, as in the case of Lord Owen, or triumphant, as in the case of Holbrooke. Even so, these works continue to influence common perceptions of the war, because of their wide circulation and the credibility, to a varying degree, of the authors.

In this book, I focus particularly on Lord Owen's and Zimmermann's works, because both accounts include clear and important examples of counterfactual hypotheses that I will discuss. Owen argues that the Vance–Owen plan could have stopped the war at an earlier stage, and Zimmermann argues that air strikes could have ended the war sooner.

---

53 The bibliography edited by Quentin Hoare and Noel Malcolm contains many polemic book reviews accusing scholars of "pro-Serb bias", see Quentin Hoare and Noel Malcolm, *Books on Bosnia: A Critical bibliography of works relating to Bosnia-Herzegovina published since 1990 in West European languages*, The Bosnian Institute, London, 1999.

54 David Owen, *Balkan Odyssey*, Harcourt Brace, London, 1995; Richard Holbrooke, *To End a War*, Random House, New York, 1998; Carl Bildt, *Peace Journey: The Struggle for Peace in Bosnia*, Weinfield and Nicholson, London, 1998; Michael Rose, *Fighting for Peace: Bosnia 1994*, The Harvill Press, London, 1998; Warren Zimmermann, *Origins of a Catastrophe: Yugoslavia and Its Destroyers – America's Last Ambassador Tells What Happened and Why*, Random House, New York, 1996.

55 Bill Clinton, *My Life*, Hutchinson, London, 2004; John Major, *The Autobiography*, HarperCollins Publishers, London, 1999; Douglas Hurd, *Memoirs*, Little, Brown & Company, London, 2003.

The first generation of works on the war in Bosnia-Herzegovina also include scholarly accounts of the war, or attempts at such. Many of these were written by people who had personal experience with the war in one way or another, for example those that had worked in Bosnia-Herzegovina. Some of the books are polemic, displaying frustration over the genocide in Bosnia that continued for so long without forceful intervention by the international community. Examples of publications in this category are those by Misha Glenny and James Gow.[56]

In this book, I will discuss Gow's *Triumph of the Lack of Will* (1997) particularly. The book received generally good reviews when it came out.[57] Sabrina P. Ramet calls it "truly one of the very best books dealing with the war in Bosnia and very probably the best blow-by-blow account in English of international diplomacy in that war".[58] More important for the purposes of this book, however, is that it stirred significant debate around its main arguments, which are clear examples of counterfactual hypotheses in the historiography of the war.[59] The central argument in Gow's book is that the Vance–Owen plan could have brought peace to Bosnia in 1993. Gow sides with Lord Owen in this regard, but elaborates more thoroughly on how he believes that this peace plan was a missed opportunity for peace. Although there are many counterfactual hypotheses of this sort in the first generation of works on Bosnia, Gow's is among those that have been debated most.

---

56 Misha Glenny, *The Fall of Yugoslavia: The Third Balkan War*, Penguin, London, 1993; James Gow, *Triumph of the Lack of Will: International Diplomacy and the Yugoslav War*, Hurst, London, 1997.

57 See, for example, Allen C. Lynch, "Triumph of the Lack of Will: International Diplomacy and the Yugoslav War. By James Gow. New York: Columbia University Press, 1997. Xii, 343 pp. Notes. Index. Maps. $29.50, Hard Bound.", in *Slavic Review,* 1998, vol. 57, no. 2, pp. 439–440; Christopher Cviic, "Some Will, Some Triumph", in *The World Today*, 1997, vol. 53, no. 12, p. 322; John M. Fraser, "Review: Cold War Inheritances: Triumph of the Lack of Will", in *International Journal*, 1998, vol. 53, no. 1, pp. 183–185; Cathie Carmichael, Reviews: James Gow, *Triumph of the Lack of Will. International Diplomacy and the Yugoslav War.* London: C. Hurst and Co., 1997, 343 pp., £14.95", in *Europe-Asia Studies*, 1998, vol. 50, no. 3, pp. 560–561.

58 Sabrina P. Ramet, *Thinking about Yugoslavia: Scholarly Debates about the Yugoslav Break-up and the Wars in Bosnia and Kosovo*, Cambridge University Press, 2005, p. 78.

59 Gow's hypotheses are criticised in, among other works, Steven L. Burg and Paul S. Shoup, *The War in Bosnia-Herzegovina: Ethnic Conflict and International Intervention*, M.E. Sharpe, Armonk, 1999; and Brendan Simms, *Unfinest Hour: Britain and the Destruction of Bosnia*, Penguin, London, 2002.

One other account, which might fall in the same category except for its publication date, is Brendan Simms' *Unfinest Hour*, first published in 2001. This is a book which is certainly scholarly and well-researched, but also polemic. I will often refer to Simms' work in this book. The reason is twofold. First, the book reads like an answer to Gow's book and the counterfactual hypotheses in that work. Second, Simms presents his own counterfactual analysis much in line with Zimmermann's line of reasoning, which suggests that a more forceful military approach to the conflict would have put an early end to the war.

Of course, there were also many works that attempt to describe the course of the war in a more non-polemic and detached manner. Among such works in the first generation are Norman Cigar's *Genocide in Bosnia*, Susan Woodward's *Balkan Tragedy,* Reneo Lukic and Allen Lynch's *Europe from the Balkans to the Urals*, and Laura Silber and Allan Little's *The Death of Yugoslavia*, to mention a few.[60] However, these works have also been subjected to certain charges of bias.

In the second generation of works, accounts have been added to the body of works attempting to describe the war in a non-polemic and detached manner. A notable book is Steven Burg and Paul Shoup's *The War in Bosnia-Herzegovina* (1999), which is a significant attempt to produce a comprehensive account of the war.[61] The book received good reviews when it was published and does, in my opinion, still remain valuable.[62] Finally, I

60 Norman Cigar, *Genocide in Bosnia: The "Policy of Ethnic Cleansing"*, Texas A&M University Press, College Station, 1995; Susan Woodward, *Balkan Tragedy: Chaos and Dissolution After the Cold War*, The Brookings Institution, Washington, D.C., 1995; Reneo Lukic and Allen Lynch, *Europe from the Balkans to the Urals: The Disintegration of Yugoslavia and the Soviet Union*, Oxford University Press, Solna, 1996; Laura Silber and Allan Little, *The Death of Yugoslavia*, Penguin, London, 1995.

61 Burg and Shoup, 1999, see *supra* note 59.

62 See, for example, Richard M. Wilcox, "The War in Bosnia-Herzegovina: Ethnic Conlifct and International Intervention", in *Political Science Quarterly*, 1999, no. 3, pp. 521–522; Dan Smith, "Burg, Steven L. & Paul S. Shoup, 2000. *The War in Bosnia-Herzegovina: Ethic Conflict & International Intervention*. Armonk, NY & London: M.E. Sharpe. Xviii + 499 pp. ISBN 1563243091 (paperback)", in *Journal of Peace Research*, 2001, vol. 38, no. 3, p. 407; and Richard M. Swain, "The Journal of Military History.", in *The Journal of Military History,* 2000, vol. 64, no. 1, pp. 264–266.

would like to mention Sabrina P. Ramet's *The Three Yugoslavias*, which provides a detailed and thoroughly researched account of the war.[63]

The existing literature on the war in Bosnia-Herzegovina is still somewhat limited by the availability of sources, but to a diminishing degree. As time passes, more information becomes available as they are declassified or uncovered through processes like the trials before the International Criminal Tribunal for the Former Yugoslavia in The Hague (ICTY).

1.3.3. Sources and Methodological Approach

The case study of this book is not source-driven, but based mainly on historiography. It is not my purpose to present new facts or sources. Rather, the main basis for the case study is published works, either accounts and analyses of the war, or published memoirs. In addition, I make use of contemporary newspaper articles to fill in the details of the events in question.

The reason for this choice of basis is that the case study is intended to be a historiographical study. My analysis is limited to the scrutiny of three counterfactual hypotheses. I attempt to show that they are indeed counterfactual, and to use the criteria from Part II to evaluate the hypotheses' scientific coherence and plausibility. In the evaluation, I draw upon sources such as the mentioned memoirs and newspaper articles, but still rely heavily on published books and articles. This methodological approach means that there are limitations to the conclusions as far as the history of the war is concerned, as opposed to the historiography. I believe the approach is defensible because the focus of the study is on the historiography, or more specifically, examples of counterfactuals in the historiography, of the war in Bosnia-Herzegovina, and not the history of the war as such.

The case study is limited in scope. I only discuss three hypotheses, where the United States government is the primary counterfactual historical actor, the British government is the secondary counterfactual historical actor, and only during a short time span in 1993. Other potential counterfactual actors, such as Russia, France and Germany, are treated more superficially. A more comprehensive account of all involved parties and a more source-driven methodology would have led to stronger conclusions on the plausibility of the three hypotheses. However, I believe that the published sources, accounts and analysis that form the basis for the current discussion

63 Sabrina P. Ramet, *The Three Yugoslavias: State-Building and Legitimation, 1918–2005*, Woodrow Wilson Center Press, Washington, D.C., 2006.

are more than sufficient for achieving the primary aims of this part of this book: To show that counterfactual hypotheses are an integral part of the historiography of the war in Bosnia-Herzegovina, and using counterfactual theory to point out limitations and possibilities of some of the counterfactual approaches to the war that have been used in existing historiography.

With the kind assistance of the publisher, the Torkel Opsahl Academic EPublisher, I have used the diacritical marks in the names of persons and places referred to in Part III, to indicate the phonetic value of letters in the Bosnian-Croat-Serb language.[64]

1.4. The Contents of this Book

1.4.1. The Theory Section

Chapter 2 outlines and discusses the most general philosophical aspects of counterfactuals on theoretical foundations, including the relationship between counterfactuals and philosophical 'truth'; the relation between counterfactuals and common types of historical explanation; the types of counterfactuals; the general counterfactual methodology in practice as compared with theory; and the relevance of counterfactuals in different types of historiography.

The chapter does not aim to discuss exhaustively the issues at hand. Rather, the aim is to present the most relevant aspects of counterfactual thought-experiments. For example, the connection between 'truth', 'scientific coherence' and 'plausibility', could in itself be the topic of a doctoral dissertation. However, they are is merely brought up here as a backdrop for the discussion on method. The same can be said for the topic of historical explanations, which is also brought up in Chapter 2. There is vast literature on the different types of historical explanations, and there are numerous problems with differentiating the four types that are brought up in Chapter 1, which are not mentioned or discussed in this book. Again, the reason is that the types of explanations must be brought up for the sole purpose of providing a backdrop for the discussion of method.

The difference between causes, events and effects of histories, which is discussed in Chapter 2, sets a tone for the entire book. If one can approach

---

64 Other publications have presented similar arguments for the the use of unmarked forms, see, for example, Charles R. Schrader, *The Muslim-Croat Civil War in Central Bosnia: A Military History, 1992–1994*, Texas A&M University Press, College Station, 2003, p. xxi.

consensus on the limitations of counterfactual history in regard to which antecedents, and which and how many consequents can be altered, then he would be much closer to a more precise understanding of the scope of counterfactual history than ever. The conclusions I offer might not be acceptable to all, but they should at least provide a direction for further debate.

The discussion about how counterfactual thought-experiments in historiography are actually formed represents a somewhat new approach in this book. As has already been mentioned, there may be an increased risk of subjectivity in counterfactual history when compared with factual history. I attempt to clarify this by differentiating between the challenges posed by the practice and the theory of counterfactual history respectively. This topic is also discussed further in Chapter 3.

Chapter 2 also briefly mentions different types of historiography and their relation to counterfactuals. There is no intention to list every type of historiography here, but merely to investigate whether the relevance of counterfactuals may vary according to the type of historiography in question.

Chapter 3 discusses some of the most significant problems with, or objections to, counterfactual history, specifically: limitations in counterfactual history as seen from determinist and collectivist viewpoints, the problem of limitless possibilities, the problems of empirical evidence and testability, and the argument that counterfactuals are usually the result of wishful thinking.

The most problematic part of counterfactual analysis is the same as in factual history, that of the impossibility of falsifying an explanation. This issue is discussed in Chapter 3, where I attempt to show that the demand for falsification is met only indirectly in historical inquiry. This is not in itself a new position. What is new, is to claim that both factual and counterfactual history draw on the same line of reasoning to strengthen or weaken hypotheses. If this is the case, then a main objection to counterfactual analysis may need reconsideration.

Chapter 4 discusses the pragmatic advantages of counterfactual history. As a starting point, I take that counterfactuals must be justified by their value added in comparison with factual history. In the chapter, I attempt to sketch out some of the possible categories of pragmatic advantages of counterfactual history, which include both the advance of historical knowledge in itself, and historiography's significance in shaping people's world views and guiding future actions.

It is not the intention in that chapter to provide an exhaustive list of the pragmatic advantages of counterfactual and factual historical inquiry. Certainly, such pragmatic advantages are always case specific. Furthermore, it is natural that historians have different opinions about what is the main pragmatic advantage of their work. However, the chapter does aim to cover the most general and common justifications for practising factual history, and inquires as to whether counterfactual history has value added to them.

Chapter 5 will conclude the theory section. Starting with Tetlock and Belkin's list of criteria, and based on the theoretical discussions in the preceding chapters, the objective there is to present a modified and improved list of criteria for scientific coherence and plausibility of counterfactual history. These criteria are at the core of this book,and will guide the discussion in the section on the war in Bosnia-Herzegovina. Even though the aim is that these criteria shall be comprehensive in regard to counterfactual history, it is unlikely that they will be acceptable to all, especially because unanswered questions will remain, as they nearly always do in matters regarding philosophy of science. However, I hope that the criteria will at least be suitable for improving the basis for a much-needed scholarly debate about such criteria.

1.4.2. The Case Study: Bosnia-Herzegovina and the Vance–Owen Peace Plan

Chapter 6, the first chapter of the case section, briefly describes the factual course of the war in Bosnia-Herzegovina in the 1990s, and introduces the three counterfactual hypotheses that I have selected for further scrutiny. That chapter is intended merely to establish a sufficient framework for the counterfactual hypotheses discussed in Chapters 6 to 8. I have chosen not to enter into the many and complex causes for the war in Bosnia-Herzegovina or the break-up of Yugoslavia in general, or to describe in detail the ethnic cleansing that was performed at the cost of great human suffering. Those are topics of a vast body of literature, and their inclusion would needlessly complicate the matter in this part of the historiography of the war. Rather, the focus of the chapter is the historical events in the first half of 1993 and the peace process tied to the Vance–Owen plan. It is this plan and this time period that serve as the focus through the hypotheses that are discussed in the succeeding chapters.

Chapters 7 to 9 discuss counterfactual hypotheses regarding both actual and counterfactual policies connected with the Clinton administration in the first half of 1993. Each chapter focuses on one of the three hypotheses that I have selected: 'increased US diplomatic pressure', 'progressive implementation' of the Vance–Owen peace plan, and 'early air strikes', respectively. All three hypotheses are based on policy debates that existed during the war and even today. The three hypotheses argue in different ways that the war could have been stopped sooner if specific policy measures had been introduced in 1993.

I discuss the three hypotheses in light of the criteria proposed in Chapter 5. In this way, I hope to clarify the hypotheses' relation to counterfactual theory, and evaluate their respective shortcomings and possibilities. The discussions in all chapters conclude in assessments of the overall plausibility of the hypotheses.

It may seem questionable that in these chapters I discuss the plausibility of the hypotheses after arguing that there may be doubts as to their full compliance with the criteria of scientific coherence, as outlined in Chapter 5. However, I think that doubts about scientific coherence do not require us to reject outright the hypothesis in question. Only if the hypothesis is deemed clearly in breach of the criteria of scientific coherence would a discussion about plausibility be completely unwarranted.

The conclusions regarding the plausibility of the three hypotheses also suffer from the fact that the hypotheses all envisage large-scale and sequential consequences. This is particularly the case with the two latter hypotheses, which both suggest potential effects of counterfactual military intervention in Bosnia-Herzegovina in 1993. It is self-evident that military campaigns involve many risks and uncertainties that cannot be completely clear, until the operations have been completed. Despite these limitations, I consider it important to pursue the discussion of counterfactual eventualities in regard to an early military intervention. If for no other purpose, then at least this would show the limitations of the counterfactual post-war arguments that have been drawn from the historiography of the war in Bosnia-Herzegovina.

Chapter 10 is the final chapter of this book. The chapter serves as a conclusion to the section on the war in Bosnia-Herzegovina, attempting to comment on some of the common features of discussion of the hypotheses in Chapters 6 to 8. The chapter is limited in its scope. It covers only the most general issues in regard to counterfactuals in the historiography of the war, as indicated by the discussion of the three hypotheses. The reason for the limited scope is that the conclusions in the preceding chapters are intended to cover the specific issues concerning the three hypotheses respectively.

Part II

Approaching Counterfactuals in History

2

The Theoretical Foundations of Counterfactual History

This chapter aims to outline the most general problems and issues associated with counterfactual history. More specifically, it will discuss five issues:

1. What is, and should be, the most general philosophical foundations of counterfactuals. In other words, how should a counterfactual hypothesis fit in with traditional explanations in historiography and relate to concepts of truth?
2. What types of counterfactuals can be identified? Can there be unhistorical counterfactual hypotheses in social science?
3. What is the general nature of counterfactual antecedents and consequents, and how does this relate to factual history?
4. How are counterfactual theories actually made, and how does this differ from ideal theory?
5. Is it useful to speak of counterfactuals being scientifically coherent only in certain types of history?

2.1. Counterfactual History: General Philosophical Foundations

2.1.1. Counterfactuals as a Type of Explanation

Richard Ned Lebow has claimed that "all counterfactuals are causal assertions".[1] Is this an accurate claim? There are numerous types of explanations in historiography. McCullagh writes about two main variants of historical causal explanations: "genetic explanations" (why something happened) and

1 Richard Ned Lebow (ed.), *Forbidden Fruit, Counterfactuals and International Relations*, Princeton University Press, 2010, p. 40.

"contrastive explanations" (why something happened as opposed to something else).[2] I addition, he also speaks of "structural explanations" (both how structures influence individual behaviour, and how structures themselves change), "covering law explanations" and "rational explanations" (how an individual's *reasons* cause actions).[3] Other types of explanations in historiography can be mentioned, such as "narrative explanations" (when the emplotment of a series of events is said to be a historical explanation) and "functional explanations" (how processes are explained by pointing to the functions of those same processes).[4] In the following, I intend to focus on these six types: casual, narrative, historical law, functional, structural and rational explanations.

Certainly, others may add to this list. There is neither consensus in the philosophy of science nor in the philosophy of history on what constitutes a scientifically coherent explanation. In fact, Wesley Salmon has argued that "we can relinquish the search for one small number of formal models of scientific explanation that are supposed to have universal applicability".[5] This seems to be a reasonable point. For the purposes of the

---

2 C. Behan McCullagh, *The Truth of History*, Routledge, London, 1998, p. 173; C. Behan McCullagh, *The Logic of History: Putting Postmodernism in Perspective*, Routledge, London, 2004, p. 171. On contrastive explanations, see also H.L.A. Hart and T. Honoré, *Causation in the Law*, Clarendon Press, Oxford, 1985, particularly part I.

3 McCullagh, 2004, p. 184, see *supra* note 2; McCullagh, 1998, pp. 173–176, see *supra* note 2. On "covering laws" in history, see also C.G. Hempel, "The Function of General Laws in History", in *Aspects of Scientific Explanation and Other Essays in the Philosophy of Science*, The Free Press, New York, 1965, pp. 231 and 243. On contrastive explanations, see Bas C. van Fraassen, *The Scientific Image*, Clarendon Press, Oxford, 1980, chapter 5, specifically p. 146.

4 On narrative explanations, see Arthur C. Danto, *Narration and Knowledge: Including the Integral Text of Analytical Philosophy of History*, Columbia University Press, New York, 1985; David Carr, "Narrative Explanation and Its Malcontents", in *History and Theory*, 2008, vol. 47, no. 1, pp. 19–30; David Carr, "Narrative and the Real World: An Argument for Continuity", in Geoffrey Roberts (ed.), *The History and Narrative Reader*, Routledge, London, 2001, pp. 143-156. On functional explanations, see Gerald Allan Cohen, *Karl Marx's Theory of History: A Defence*, Oxford University Press, 2000; Gerald Allan Cohen, "Functional explanation: Reply to Elster", in *Political Studies*, 1982, vol. 28, no. 1, pp. 129–135. Functional explanations are also discussed extensively in *History and Theory Theme Issue: The Return of Science: Evolutionary Ideas and History*, 1999, vol. 38, no. 4, see particularly Joseph Fracchia and R.C. Lewontin, "Does Culture Evolve?", pp. 52–78.

5 Wesley C. Salmon, "Scientific Explanation: How We Got from There to Here", in *Causality and Explanation,* Oxford University Press, 1998, p. 316.

discussion here, I will limit the scope to inquire briefly into how counterfactuals relate to the six types of explanations mentioned above.

Of these six types, it is apparent that causal explanations are where one will find the most counterfactual hypotheses. This follows from the form of the common subjunctive sentence "if it had (not) been that X, then Y". Causal explanations must therefore be central in any theory of counterfactual history. More specifically, when a causal explanation involves the identification of one or more necessary causes, the possibility for counterfactual hypotheses should be particularly evident: If one would theoretically remove a necessary cause from history, the following historical event would not have occurred, or would have been dissimilar to the actual event.

As regards potential counterfactual narrative explanations, I will not dismiss these outright, but nor will I attempt to present a thorough analysis of the subject. In principle, a plausible counterfactual narrative might well serve the same purposes as a counterfactual causal explanation, but this would depend on whether one accepts narrative explanations as scientifically coherent or not. The debate on narrative explanations is extensive, and I will not attempt to address it in this book.[6]

I would also dismiss outright the notion of a counterfactual historical 'law'. The concept of a 'counterfactual law' is useless to historians, whether 'inductive-statistic' or 'deductive-nomological'. A counterfactual historical law, and any counterfactual scenario derived from this law, would be nonsense, similar to saying "if there was no gravity on Earth, then ...". A law cannot apply in only one instance, or it would not be a law. Therefore, changing a historical law cannot be done without changing all previous instances where the same law applied, meaning that large parts of history would also have to be hypothetically altered. This clearly falls outside the scope of any meaningful historical inquiry.

What about counterfactual functional explanations? Could these potentially make sense in a historical debate? Such an approach would require altering a trait of a given phenomenon (either an entity or a process), a trait of which the people who created the phenomenon were not aware but contributed to the phenomenon's continued presence. An example is this: "If the ancient Greek theatre had not had a cathartic function, it would not have

6 See, for example, David Carr, "Narrative Explanation and Its Malcontents", in *History and Theory*, 2008, vol. 47, no. 1, pp. 19–30; Aviezer Tucker, *Our Knowledge of the Past: A Philosophy of Historiography*, Cambridge University Press, 2004, pp. 12–14 and 138–139.

become a significant cultural institution". It is important to observe that such an alteration requires no rationalisation of the alteration itself. In fact, it seems improbable that a counterfactual functional explanation can rationalise the altered antecedent, as such rationalisation seems to require an action as a cause of change, but this violates the premise of a functional explanation. Rather, the counterfactual functional explanation must invoke what has been labelled a 'miracle cause', meaning that there is no discussion of how and why the antecedents could have been different, only a focus on the outcome if the antecedents had been different. Many theoreticians of counterfactuals would allow this, among them Tetlock and Belkin.[7] This is problematic for reasons that I will return to. For now, it is sufficient to point out that the possibility of using counterfactuals in a functional explanation depends on the possibility of invoking 'miracle causes'.

Counterfactuals in structural explanations are difficult, because it is difficult to reduce structural explanations to a single form. As mentioned, McCullagh already needs to differentiate that into two forms. In addition, there are the added problems of so-called 'grand narratives' of history, such as Marxism (materialism), and the debate about collectivism and methodological individualism in historiography.[8] Because these types of historical explanations are complicated, and pose particular problems in regard to counterfactuals, I will discuss them in more detail later in this book. However, at this point I will limit myself to assert that there are reasons to argue that, as a rule, counterfactual history should focus on altering antecedents that are as narrowly specified in nature and in time as possible. This rule is commonly referred to as the 'minimal rewrite rule', and is among Tetlock and Belkin's criteria for scientifically coherent counterfactuals.[9] The more complex the event or entity to be counterfactually altered, the more effort must be spent on rationalising the alteration *and* the greater the risk of drawing the wrong conclusions.

---

7 Philip E. Tetlock and Aaron Belkin (eds.), *Counterfactual Thought Experiments in World Politics: Logical, Methodological, and Psychological Perspectives*, Princeton University Press, 1996, p. 9.

8 On the 'grand narratives', see Jean-Francois Lyotard, *The Postmodern Condition: A Report on Knowledge*, University of Minnesota Press, Minneapolis, 1984; and also McCullagh, 1998, pp. 297–302, see *supra* note 2. On collectivism and methodological individualism, see McCullagh, 1998, pp. 290–297, see *supra* note 2; and John O'Neill (ed.), *Modes of Individualism and Collectivism*, Gregg Revivals, Aldershot, 1992.

9 Tetlock and Belkin (eds.), 1996, p. 18, see *supra* note 7.

In regard to rational explanations, I would argue that this is perhaps the category where counterfactual history makes the most sense. The reason is that counterfactual personal choices can be imagined more easily than changes in structures or causes beyond human control. The premise is of course that the historical actor could have chosen otherwise. The plausibility of this will vary from case to case, as well as with the researcher's personal views of the degree of free will embedded in humans. But if one *can* argue that a significant historical antecedent could have been changed through a choice by a decision maker, then the counterfactual is likely to be more plausible.

There is debate among philosophers of history about rational explanations and whether reasons can be used as causes in a historical explanation.[10] R.G. Collingwood is among the best known proponents of the view that reasons should be part of historical explanations.[11] Donald Davidson has also presented a much-cited defence of the view that reasons can be causes.[12] It is not self-evident that reasons can be causes and how reasons and actions connect. If one does believe, however, that reasons may be part of a scientifically coherent factual historical explanation, then one cannot rule out counterfactual rational hypotheses.

The conclusion seems to be that rational and causal explanations are the most common types of historical explanation where counterfactuals are likely to be used, and also the types where one is most likely to find scientifically coherent and plausible uses of counterfactuals.

2.1.2. Counterfactual or Contrastive Explanations?

At face value, counterfactual and contrastive explanations, in McCullagh's version, seem similar. He writes that contrastive explanations are about giv-

---

10 See, for example, *History and Theory*, 2001, vol. 40, no. 4 (Theme Issue: Agency after Postmodernism).

11 R.G. Collingwood, *The Idea of History*, Oxford University Press, London, 1961, p. 9; also William Dray, *Laws and Explanation in History*, Oxford University Press, 1964.

12 Donald Davidson, "Actions, Reasons and Causes", in A.R. Mele (ed.), *The Philosophy of Action*, Oxford University Press, 1997, pp. 3–21. See also Guiseppina D'Oro, "Two Dogmas of Contemporary Philosophy of Action", in *Journal of the Philosophy of History*, 2007, vol. 1, no. 1, pp. 10–24.

ing enough information to show that the factual outcome was more probable than the other plausible alternatives that did not happen.[13] This is derived from Bas van Fraassen's theory of contrastive explanations, which states that the evaluation of answers must consider whether the given answer is better than other possible answers to the question.[14]

McCullagh's version of contrastive explanation is designed to avoid teleology in historical explanations. The other plausible outcomes in such an explanation are, of course, counterfactual outcomes. However, counterfactual and contrastive inquiries differ in nature. As an example, a counterfactual hypothesis would be to say: "If Brutus had chosen to uphold the bond of friendship with Caesar instead of following his political convictions, then Caesar would not have been assassinated". The contrastive standard would be to ask: "Why is it that Brutus decided to conspire against Caesar instead of aligning with him?", and then explain the factual event as a consequence of Brutus' political convictions outweighing other considerations.

There are certainly similarities between the two. Most importantly, contrastive explanations must consider the plausibility of a counterfactual phenomenon. The continued survival of Caesar is an example of this. Similarly, the counterfactual hypothesis must take the factual effect into consideration. Should Brutus have chosen not to act, it might have led to a different effect from the factual one.

However, the difference is that contrastive explanation does not need to refer to counterfactual antecedents. Rather, it only requires causes that could lead both to the factual and the counterfactual event, but all these causes are factual. Counterfactual hypothesis, on the other hand, requires an alteration of the causes. Furthermore, it is not necessary for the effect to be counterfactual for the hypothesis to be counterfactual as well. For example, it is possible that Caesar would have been assassinated, even without the aid of Brutus. However, if the antecedents are altered, then the whole scenario must be considered a counterfactual. Therefore, McCullagh's contrastive explanation falls outside the scope of counterfactual history as defined as a subjunctive statement about the past.

---

13 McCullagh, 1998, p. 188, see *supra* note 2.

14 van Fraassen, 1980, pp. 146 and 156, see *supra* note 3.

There may be some limited exceptions to this conclusion. Tim de Mey and Erik Weber have argued that counterfactual thought-experiments are indispensable when arriving at weighted explanations of contrasts, or what they call 'more-important-than' explanations.[15] They use an example aiming to explain why a revolution succeeded at time t_2 whereas a previous attempt failed at time t_1. If the question is whether the inflation rate or the army's equipment at times t_1 and t_2 were more important for explaining why only the last revolution succeeded, the historian would be forced to engage in counterfactual thought-experiments. Specifically, one would need to substitute the inflation rate at time t_2 with the similar rate for t_1, and do the same with the army's equipment.[16]

De Mey and Weber's argument seems sound. However, the force of the explanation would depend ultimately on two counterfactual questions: (1) "What if the inflation rate at t_2 had been equal to the rate at t_1?"; and (2) "What if the army's equipment at t_2 had been equal to its equipment at t_1?" It thus seems that the categories of contrastive and counterfactual should be seen as separate methods of historiographical inquiry.

2.1.3. Truth, Scientific Coherence and Plausibility

It is not the aim of counterfactual hypotheses to establish truth. Rather, the aim is to provide meaningful insights. In fact, it is pointless to speak of truth in relation to counterfactuals. A counterfactual hypothesis cannot be true, but must instead be measured as being more or less 'scientifically coherent' and 'plausible'. The scientific coherence of a counterfactual hypothesis is measured against the level of compliance with general rules of logic and scientific standards. The plausibility of counterfactuals is the level of credibility that follows from the quality of evidence and argumentation presented in favour of the given hypothesis.

The difference between truth on the one hand, and 'plausibility' and 'scientific coherence'" on the other, seems to be a source of confusion where counterfactual history is involved. With Leopold von Ranke, historians have claimed in the past that their goal has been to write history "as it actually happened". This idea is founded in the correspondence theory of

15 Tim de Mey and Erik Weber, "Explanation and Thought Experiments in History", in *History and Theory*, 2003, vol. 42, no. 1, pp. 28–38, particularly pp. 37–38.

16 *Ibid.*, p. 37.

truth, meaning that the degree of truth, and scientific value, of historiography is decided by the degree of correspondence to the real world.[17] However, counterfactuals can never correspond with reality, since they, by definition, never happened. In other words, counterfactuals must be seen, by any account or definition, as untrue.

However, that all counterfactuals are untrue, does not mean that they cannot be scientifically significant. It merely means that counterfactuals are in themselves not useful, unless they shed light on factual history, or provide some other pragmatic advantage. Although all historical science is founded on empirical facts, this does not mean that facts is all with which historians are concerned. Elster has argued that if historiography was only empirical, it would be nothing more than an account of a series of facts, and quite boring at that. Instead, Elster believes, "We want to know not only *that* a given event had a cause, but also *which* cause".[18] When historians ask which causes were relevant for the chosen event, they construct theories. These theories necessarily build upon logical constructs, some of which may include counterfactual thought-experiments.

It is important to realise that it is not the truth value of the counterfactual assertion we want to establish, but its scientific coherence and plausibility. Counterfactual theories derive scientific coherence in about the same way as factual historical theories.

Take the understanding that Brutus' political convictions probably played a part in his decision to assassinate Caesar as an example. Alternatively, we can also reason that if Brutus had had weaker convictions, he would not have conspired with Cassius and other senators. Although counterfactual in nature, this should not be a very controversial statement. It is scientifically coherent, because it is based on the same reasoning as in the factual hypothesis, in this case that political conviction was a cause of Brutus' action. As for the plausibility of the scenario, one must also establish whether political conviction was a necessary cause of Brutus' actions. If that can be argued, then the theory must also be considered plausible.

17 See McCullagh, 2004, p. 5, see *supra* note 2; Øystein Sørensen, *Historien om det som ikke skjedde: Kontrafaktisk historie* [History That Did Not Happen], Aschehoug, Oslo, 2004, p. 168.

18 Jon Elster, *Logic and Society: Contradictions and Possible Worlds*, John Wiley, Chichester, 1978, p. 5.

2.2. Types of Counterfactuals: Causes, Effects and Histories

2.2.1. Tetlock and Belkin's Approach to Counterfactual Ideal Types

What are the types of counterfactuals? Tetlock and Belkin list five:

1. *Idiographic case-study counterfactuals*, when one attempts to prove that things were not inevitable.
2. *Nomothetic counterfactuals*, when a Hempelian law is present and one alters a decision or a policy to see what would have happened. For example: "Given the connection between money supply and inflation, what would have happened if the Russian central bank had another policy in 1992?".
3. *Idiographic-nomothetic counterfactuals*, when game theory is applied to historical cases. The entry point is a historical decision, but generalisations for maximisation of results are used to predict the outcome and to explain why the causes could have been different.
4. *Computer simulation counterfactuals/pure thought-experiments*, when such counterfactuals are designed to strengthen or weaken general theories by pointing to counterfactual historical examples: For example, if simulated history shows that Hitler or Napoleon could have conquered the world, this would weaken any theory stating that anarchic international relations make a power balance inevitable.
5. *Mental simulations of counterfactual worlds*, when such counterfactuals are designed to show psychological inconsistencies by pointing to counterfactual scenarios. Tetlock and Belkin use this example: "If Bosnians had been bottle-nosed dolphins, the slaughter would have been stopped far sooner".[19]

Tetlock and Belkin's approach has some immediate problems, as I have pointed out in the introduction. First, the approach seems not to distinguish between a type of a counterfactual and its pragmatic advantage, or "function" in their terminology. I have labelled the five points above as 'types', but Tetlock and Belkin define them through their pragmatic advantages. They seem to think that types follow from the pragmatic ad-

[19] Tetlock and Belkin (eds.), 1996, pp. 7–14, see *supra* note 7.

vantages of the counterfactual scenario, meaning that, for example, idiographic case-study counterfactuals is defined by the pragmatic advantage of showing that history was not inevitable. However, there might be many other potential pragmatic advantages of this type, and the same goes for the four other types. I list a number of such pragmatic advantages in Chapter 4, but, to prove the point, it should be suffice to say that a common pragmatic advantage of an idiographic counterfactual is to shed light on what causes should be deemed necessary or sufficient in a given historical scenario. Another potential pragmatic advantage could be to provide the basis for reasoning by analogy in other historical cases or in a present day situation where the counterfactual scenario might be similar.

Furthermore, a given pragmatic advantage can also potentially result from more than one of the five types listed above. If the aim of a counterfactual is to shed light on international relations theory, as exemplified in type 4 above, there are also possibilities for doing the same based on an idiographic case-study. Indeed, the case-study approach is a common method for doing exactly this in international relations theory. For these reasons, it is necessary to separate pragmatic advantages and types in our terminology, and the above list should be considered as 'types' of counterfactuals.

However, rather than the terminology, it is more important to know whether the categorisation above represents a fruitful approach to counterfactual theory. It should be observed that, although the aim of Tetlock and Belkin's project is to explore counterfactuals in world politics, all of their types share a common premise: they are based on a given historical situation under scrutiny. The reason is that it would be logically meaningless to speak of counterfactuals in reference to present day or future policies: there are no facts about the future, hence it is pointless to speak of a counterfactual future scenario. Therefore, all relevant counterfactual scenarios are historical, and must comply with rules of historical inquiry.

It should also be observed that out of the five types listed above, only the first one, idiographic case-studies, seems seriously to consider the historical feasibility of an altered antecedent. Two of the other four, nomothetic counterfactuals and pure thought-experiments, focus only on the feasibility of the consequent, and no effort is made to specify a plausible altered antecedent. Instead, these two invoke 'miracle causes' to alter the antecedent. Tetlock and Belkin explain that, in these cases, "[t]he goal is not historical understanding; rather it is to pursue the logical implications of a theoretical framework".[20] However, as a counterfactual has at least one altered antecedent, in addition to at least one altered consequent, is it worthwhile, in a scientific sense, to describe a scenario that only discusses the plausibility of one of these alterations?

The remaining two, idiographic-nomothetic (game theory) and computer simulation counterfactuals, do include the idea of specifying both plausible antecedents and consequents. However, the alteration of the antecedent appears mainly theory-driven, and not dictated by historical consistency. In the game theory approach, the chosen theory will dictate the possible counterfactual decisions. Thus, there is no necessary distinction between whether the historical decision-makers were consciously aware of the possible choices or not.[21] I suggest that both the idiographic-nomothetic and the computer simulation approaches, if seriously attempting to specify plausible antecedents as well as consequents, are actually no different from the idiographic type. The difference between these three variants is not in kind, but in choice of theory. Tetlock and Belkin explain that the idiographic type is distinguished by its pragmatic advantage of showing the inevitability of events. However, this can be equally shown by the use of computer simulation or game theory. Similarly, computer simulation is defined by Tetlock and Belkin, by its pragmatic advantage of weakening or strengthening general theories, but this may also be proven by an idiographic counterfactual. Therefore, to differentiate between these three types seems to needlessly complicate the theory of counterfactual history.

In regard to the last type on the list, mental simulations of counterfactual worlds, is it possible to make the statement that "had Bosnians been bottle-nosed dolphins, the slaughter would have been stopped"? Although the statement may be intuitively appealing, it is actually empirically nonsense, and cannot lead to meaningful insights. Bosnians are not, have never been, and can never be bottle-nosed dolphins. The statement is akin to saying "if this house was a planet ...". Since houses cannot be planets and Bosnians cannot be dolphins, it is impossible to draw conclusions from such a starting point, and no statement made on such a premise can produce new information. I would argue that this conclusion holds, even if one was

---

20 *Ibid.*, p. 9.

21 There is a debate about whether a counterfactual hypothesis should be based on scenarios that were actually contemplated by contemporaries ("the subjectively possible", of which the negation is "the objectively possible"), which I describe in the next chapter.

to re-formulate the hypothesis into a more realistic 'miracle cause'. One of Lebow's examples of a 'miracle cause' is postulating the population of South Sudan to be Caucasian and Christian.[22] In fact, the population of South Sudan are predominantly Christian, although with many idiosyncratic local beliefs and traditions. However, of such a thought-experiment might serve to reveal, in this case, possible moral double standards. Nevertheless, I remain doubtful whether this type of experiment can be said to serve a scholarly purpose. The thought experiment cannot prove anything *per se*. If the purpose is to show that Caucasians and Christians tend to sympathise with other Caucasians and Christians, this can be best proven with regular psychological experiments, rather than a counterfactual experiment.

Maybe the Bosnian-dolphin example is too extreme. What about the last type on the list? As mentioned, the nomothetic type of counterfactuals invokes 'miracle causes' to alter the antecedent. This conflicts with some theories on counterfactuals, most notably Elster's approach, which argues that one must rationalise both the consequent of the hypothetical antecedent, which this type does, and the plausibility of the counterfactual antecedent in the given historical context, which this type does not.[23] In this type of counterfactuals, Tetlock and Belkin argue that it is impossible to make any relevant historical arguments about what would have happened if the Russian central bank had a different policy in 1992, unless one can show that there are reasons to believe that the policy could have been different at the time. If one does not attempt to specify a plausible antecedent, the counterfactual argument relies only on the law used to explain the occurrence of the consequent. After making the historical inquiry, one would be left with only what was brought into the argument, that is, the law that was used. Not only will the counterfactual produce no new or relevant insights, there is also the inherent danger that the theory of the given law might appear to have been strengthened, when in fact nothing has been uncovered at all.

However, if one could show that a decision could have been made to alter the Russian central bank's policy in 1992, then the counterfactual consequents could potentially lead to interesting historical conclusions, particularly in regard to the degree of inevitability of events in Russia in the

---

22 Lebow (ed.), 2010, p. 45, see *supra* note 1.

23 Elster, 1978, pp. 190–192, see *supra* note 18; Tucker, 2004, p. 227, see *supra* note 6.

1990s. Still, the notion of a 'miracle cause' should be explicitly justified before being used in a counterfactual hypothesis.

Historical consistency is the key factor in regard to the permissibility of 'miracle causes'. The introduction of a cause that is not explained as a feasible antecedent must, at least, not conflict with other known facts that are significant to the counterfactual hypothesis. Consider an example from the Norwegian oil economy. If someone needs to explain how the Norwegian economy would have developed from the 1970s onward in the absence of North Sea oil revenues, then he would have to argue how this might have been possible. Out of several possible counterfactual antecedents, I find the following three to be particularly illustrating:

- *The Norwegian government had a different oil policy*. For example, if the Norwegian government had sold search and production rights to foreign oil companies cheaply, and would therefore have been unable to extract extensive revenues. Such a counterfactual antecedent is not a 'miracle cause', as it relies on choices made by individuals in government. It would be considered historically plausible if we can show that cabinet ministers contemplated this course of action, for example, before they knew about the vast oil reserves in the North Sea. The antecedent should, in this case, be considered permissible.
- *There is no oil in the North Sea*. This would be a 'miracle cause', as no further explanation is provided for how this might have been the case. However, if one can argue that the absence of oil in the North Sea would not affect other significant aspects in the counterfactual scenario, that is, the development of the Norwegian economy, then one might still be able to draw up a feasible counterfactual scenario. The antecedent could therefore be considered permissible in a counterfactual hypothesis.
- *There was no offshore drilling technology available*. This would be a 'miracle cause', as there can be no feasible explanation for the antecedent. The antecedent should also be seen as inadmissible in a counterfactual hypothesis, because it is not consistent with other significant facts. The absence of offshore drilling technology would likely also require other technologies to be absent, as it depends on the level of technology in society as a whole. Any attempt to describe the development of the Norwegian economy

with a counterfactually lower level of technology would be impossible, as it would require the theory to change too many factors for any scenario to be feasible.

The example of the oil economy indicates that miracle causes may be permissible in certain circumstances. At this point, it should also be noted that functional explanations will also, as discussed above, be permissible in counterfactual history in the cases where the 'miracle cause' in question can be deemed admissible.

However, even in the case of a permissible 'miracle cause' in a nomothetic counterfactual, the question remains as to the uncertainty of differentiating this from idiographic explanation. In both, it is necessary to consider the historical context, as the Norwegian oil example shows. Therefore, it seems difficult to defend the existence of unhistorical social science counterfactuals, and it would be more precise to speak only of counterfactual history. This change of labels is not mere rhetoric, but serves to make the area of scientific scrutiny more precise. I believe a more accurate label will also help formulate more precisely the criteria that should be drawn up for separating scientifically coherent and plausible from scientifically incoherent and/or implausible counterfactuals.

2.3. Counterfactual Categories: Causes, Effects and Alternative Histories

I have already noted the important distinction between counterfactual antecedents, which I have narrowed to causes, and consequents or effects. Another useful category is 'alternative histories', defined as n-order consequents, like 2nd order, 3rd order, and so on.[24]

2.3.1. Counterfactual Causes

2.3.1.1. Grand Causes

In relation to the possibilities, impossibilities and necessities of history, a key issue is the size of the changed antecedents. Generally, counterfactuals are more speculative if the changes are greater. Changing constant or collective historical phenomena is more difficult than changing individual actions or decisions. Tucker is among those who have commented on this,

[24] Daniel Snowman makes a similar point about the difference between counterfactual effects and alternative histories in Daniel Snowman, *If I Had Been ... Ten Historical Fantasies*, Robson, London, 1979.

referring to a theory stating that the American colonies would have remained in the British Empire if the Glorious Revolution of 1688 had not occurred. This speculation is historically inconsistent, according to Tucker, because, without the Glorious Revolution, one would have to imagine an entirely different England with a completely different history.[25]

Alexander Demandt put it this way: "There is some point in asking what would have happened without Augustus, but there is little attraction in eliminating from history the entire Roman nobility, the entire Roman army, or the entire Roman people".[26] Regrettably, Demandt does not reflect on whether eliminating Augustus from history may also qualify as a 'greater antecedent', because of this emperor's unique historical position. In any case, the latter three factors clearly demonstrate how important it is to consider the scope of counterfactual alterations of antecedents. Most would agree that reducing the scope involved in the counterfactual alteration would increase the plausibility of the inferences to be drawn.

2.3.1.2. Accidental Causes and Cleopatra's Nose

Various examples have been used in the theory of counterfactual accidental antecedents. They are accidental in the sense of being outside human influence.[27] For example, Tucker draws up a scenario where George H.W. Bush dies in 1990 and Mario Cuomo wins the presidential election in 1992.[28] However, as mentioned in the introduction, the example most referred to in counterfactual theory is probably Pascal's: "Cleopatra's nose: had it been shorter, the whole aspect of the world would have been altered".[29] Pascal's assessment was probably that if Cleopatra had been less attractive (the cause), Anthony would not have fallen in love with her (first order effect) and consequently would not have lost the power struggle with Octavian (second order effect). Furthermore, if there was no Octavian, the world would never have seen the political genius he displayed as Augustus, and perhaps no line of emperors would have ruled the Roman Empire (n-order

25 Tucker, 2004, p. 229, see *supra* note 6.

26 Alexander Demandt, *History That Never Happened: A Treatise on the Question, What Would Have Happened If…?*, McFarland, Jefferson, North Carolina, 1993, p. 116.

27 I use the term 'accidental cause' because a major part of the scholarly debate on this issue in regard to counterfactual history has revolved around E.H. Carr's discussion of what he calls "accidents in history" in E.H. Carr, *What is History?*, Penguin, London, 1990, pp. 98–106.

28 Tucker, 2004, pp. 230–231, see *supra* note 6.

29 Pascal, *Pensées*, Section II, fragment 162.

effects or alternative history). However, no serious historical account of Roman history has ever involved explanations based on the sizes and shapes of noses, no matter how attractive. Why is that? Is it not conceivable that Cleopatra could have been uglier, and that this would have profoundly influenced history?

The problem of Cleopatra's nose has been discussed, perhaps most famously, by E.H. Carr in his *What is History?*,[30] and it has since been heatedly debated in relation to counterfactual history.[31] Carr's point is that although Cleopatra's nose certainly influenced history, this does not make it historically interesting, because it fails to teach us any useful lessons: "Accidental causes cannot be generalized; and, since they are in the fullest sense of the word unique, they teach no lessons and lead to no conclusions".[32] What do we care, over 2,000 years later, what Cleopatra's nose looked like? The point should be that Anthony's infatuation with Cleopatra had significant consequences for his political ambitions and for Roman history. It seems that the lesson is that emotions can rule even the strongest leaders, and shape the course of history.[33] One can argue that this provides insight into human nature and the nature of Roman politicians, perhaps even politics in general. Carr would say that the noses of history cannot provide such insights. Speculating about such causes is uninteresting and unhistorical.

The reason for Carr's scepticism is his instrumental approach to historical science. Carr believes that the historian "distils from the experience of the past [...] and from it draws conclusions which may serve as a guide to action".[34] In other words, historian's highest duty is to present usable

30 Carr, 1990, pp. 92–93, see *supra* note 27.

31 Among those who have debated this in regard to counterfactual history are Niall Ferguson, (ed.), *Virtual History: Alternatives and Counterfactuals*, Picador, London, 1997, pp. 12–17; Sørensen, 2004, see *supra* note 17; James F. Fearon, "Counterfactuals and Hypothesis Testing in Political Science", in *World Politics*, 1991, vol. 43, no. 2, p. 191; Geoffrey Hawthorn, *Plausible Worlds: Possibility and Understanding in History and the Social Sciences*, Cambridge University Press, 1991, p. 8; Gregory Gregory Mitchell, "Case Studies, Counterfactuals, and Causal Explanations", in *University of Pennsylvania Law Review*, 2004, vol. 152, no. 5, p. 1597; and Lebow (ed.), 2010, pp. 46–48, see *supra* note 1.

32 Carr, 1990, p. 101, see *supra* note 27.

33 This is also what Pascal originally was pointing out.

34 Carr, 1990, p. 98, see *supra* note 27.

lessons from history. This is a common assertion, though not uncontroversial, as history is certainly also studied for other reasons.[35] However, Carr argues that historians are involved in a serious science, and should not be concerned with matters for the sake of entertainment. The historian must "reason to an end".[36] If we were to follow Carr's advice, Cleopatra's nose would be historically unimportant. The only usable lessons derived are rather simplistic: looks matter, and accidents can be important in history.

Similarly, many historical facts are known simply because they are funny or curious. For example, when explaining the phenomenon of McCarthyism in the United States in the 1950s, I have found it useful to draw on an anecdote from Wheeling, West Virginia, in early 1950, not in regard to the infamous speech Senator Joseph McCarthy made there, but to the so-called 'Communist candy machines' that the city authorities decided to remove. These machines distributed geography lessons along with the sweets. One of the lessons wrote: "The Soviet Union. Population 211 million. Capital Moscow. Largest Country in the World".[37] When the city administrator, Robert Plummer, found out about this, he was reported to have exclaimed, "This is a terrible thing to expose our children to!", and the machines were thereafter quickly disposed of, in order to protect the innocent from knowledge about the largeness of the Soviet Union.[38]

The Wheeling story is not particularly important in historical terms. Removing the candy machines had no noteworthy effects on history. The event can, at most, be used as an example of a mentality from a different time. However, the story is remembered not because of any profound meaning derived, nor will anyone find it particularly useful in their everyday lives. Rather, it is remembered because Robert Plummer's reaction is amusing. If historiography was to be written without such peculiarities, it might lose some of its vigour or its general appeal.

Still, it would be difficult to justify works of historiography written only for amusement. I would say without hesitation that historical science, if it is to be taken seriously as a science, must have value beyond mere entertainment. This does not prevent us from mentioning matters such as

---

35 Will be discussed in chapter 3.

36 Carr, 1986, p. 100, see *supra* note 27.

37 Douglas T. Miller and Marion Nowak, *The Fifties: The Way We Really Were*, Doubleday, Garden City, 1977, p. 21.

38 *Ibid.*, p. 21.

Cleopatra's nose, but it would be wrong if such stories were the be-all and end-all of historiography. Understanding the past is a serious matter, because it shapes the way we view ourselves and others, and how we plan the future. Historians who ignore or forget this will quickly have trouble defending their own discipline.

Accidental and seemingly insignificant causes are popular in counterfactual history, which maybe even more so than in factual history. The reason may be the attraction in exploring how even smallest events can shape the future, such as the potential changing of the winds in the English Channel in 1588 or 1944,[39] or the possible death of St. Paul when he was lowered from the walls of Damascus.[40] However, such counterfactual thought-experiments mainly show the general importance of accidental events in history or provide good entertainment to the reader. If counterfactual history is to have any pragmatic value other than proving general points, such speculations do not appear to be particularly unhelpful.

Tetlock and Belkin justify the idiographic type of counterfactual history with the idea of showing how accidental events influence history for. This will untie historiography from the dangers of hindsight, and show how many events were less inevitable than we would otherwise assume.[41] This is an important pragmatic advantage of counterfactual history. However I argue that it is mainly when historical human decisions are altered that one sees the range of possible pragmatic advantages from counterfactual inquiries.

Many have argued that historians should focus on causes that are manipulable. Although Carr is perhaps the most debated among historians in regard to counterfactual history, certainly R.G. Collingwood and William Dray occupy central stage in mainstream historiography. Collingwood argued that the object of historiography is to explain "actions of human beings that have been done in the past", and Dray argued, in a similar fashion, that the historian should "revive, re-enact, re-think, re-experience the

---

39 See Geoffrey Parker, "The Repulse of English Fireships" and Stephen E. Ambrose, "D Day Fails: Atomic Alternatives in Europe", in Robert Cowley (ed.), *What If? The World's Foremost Military Historians Imagine What Might Have Been*, Berkley Books, New York, 1999.

40 Discussed in Michael Oakeshott, *Experience and Its Modes*, Cambridge University Press, 1966, pp. 128–129.

41 Tetlock and Belkin (eds.), 1996, pp. 8 and 15, see *supra* note 7.

hopes, fears, plans, desires, views, intentions, etc., of those he seeks to understand".[42]

Regardless of what the objective of historiography should be, however, there are certainly grounds for arguing that historical explanations in practice tend to focus on voluntary actions as causes. H.L.A. Hart and Tony Honoré have argued that human agency often is in fact both a barrier and a goal when providing explanations for events: "A deliberate human act [...] is something through which we do not trace the cause of a later event and something to which we do trace the cause through intervening causes of other kinds".[43] For example, we seldom explain a fire in a private home only pointing to a short circuit, unless the resident has previously tampered with the electrical system.

There is little point in repeating the positions in the debate about what the objective of historiography should be. However, when looking on counterfactual history in particular, the potential value added must be considered. Counterfactual history can be an acceptable method of historical inquiry only if it serves purposes that other methods do not.

I have argued above that in counterfactual history, altering an accidental cause may have the pragmatic advantages of being entertaining and providing general knowledge about the level of inevitability in historical cases. This may be enough for some, but if the focus is on counterfactual decisions, it is likely that counterfactuals may be more useful and therefore more acceptable.

2.3.1.3. Conclusions on Counterfactual Causes

The scope of counterfactual inquiry is limited by the types of causes that can be altered. One category that falls outside the scope of counterfactual analysis is the type of causes that are inconsistent with other significant factors to the counterfactual hypothesis. 'Grand' causes, meaning collective, constant or semi-constant phenomena, fall into this category. Small-scale accidental causes, may be permitted in counterfactual history, but the value added in comparison with factual history may be questionable. In general, the alteration of human decisions seems to hold the most potential value for counterfactual inquiries.

---

42 Collingwood, 1961, p. 9, see *supra* note 11; Dray, 1964, p. 119, see *supra* note 11.

43 Hart and Honoré, 1985, p. 44, see *supra* note 2. See pp. 41–44 for more on voluntary actions.

2.3.2. Counterfactual Consequents (Effects)

There are two types of counterfactual hypotheses: negative and positive.[44] The negatives say what would not have happened if a specific antecedent is changed, whereas the positives say what would have happened instead of the factual effect. Negatives can be generally formulated in the following manner: "If not A, then not B".[45] Positive counterfactuals can be formulated in this manner: "If not A, then C instead of B" or "If A2 instead of A1, then C instead of B".

2.3.2.1. Negative Counterfactual Hypotheses

Negative counterfactuals are implicit in all historical explanations, according to Elster,[46] because negative counterfactuals are the only means of sorting out necessary causes. For example, to establish whether Lenin was crucial to the success of the October Revolution of 1917, one cannot avoid asking the question "would the revolution have succeeded without Lenin?".[47] If Lenin indeed was a crucial factor, one can easily formulate a plausible negative counterfactual: "If no Lenin, no October Revolution" – "If not A, then not B".

However, it is an exaggeration to say that negative counterfactuals are implied in all historical causal explanations. It is possible to account for the causes of an historical event without stating them necessary to bring about the effect. One may argue, for example, that causes should be defined as factors that increased the probability of an effect, and it is not required to define that causes are necessary for the effect to occur.[48] However, if one really attempts to explain how a cause was necessary for an event, one must engage in thought-experiments, and, at least implicitly, in counterfactual thought-experiments.

---

44 The terms are defined in Ottar Dahl, "Objektivitet i historiegranskinga" [Objectivity in Historical Inquiry], in *Syn og Segn*, 1969, vol. 10, p. 578.

45 Ottar Dahl, *Problemer i historiens teori* [Problems of Causation in Historical Research], Universitetsforlaget, Oslo, 1986, pp. 48–49.

46 Elster, 1978, p. 176, see *supra* note 18. A similar point, but without the specification of a "negative counterfactual" is made in Richard Ned Lebow and Philip E. Tetlock, "Scholars and Causation", in Lebow (ed.), 2010, p. 137, see *supra* note 1.

47 This example is used by Dahl, 1969, p. 578, see *supra* note 44.

48 McCullagh discusses this in McCullagh, 1998, chapter 7, particularly pp. 172–173, see *supra* note 2.

Historians are able to give a satisfactory explanation of the consequent only when identifying the necessary causes. Lenin's person is a necessary cause of the October Revolution only if we can plausibly say that without him, the Revolution would not have occurred. The negative counterfactual thought-experiment is thus implicit in the factual explanation.

Defenders of counterfactual history have emphasised that all historians use counterfactual thought-experiments in their own explanations. They say the only difference is whether the counterfactuals are explicit.[49] In relation to negative counterfactuals alone, this may be true, but that does not necessarily legitimise the use of counterfactual historical reasoning. As I have mentioned, a key issue of counterfactuals is the potential value added. If counterfactual arguments are used by all historians already, it makes little practical difference if they are explicit or not. David Fischer, an opponent of counterfactual history, has written in relation to this: "It is always possible, of course, to convert a historical problem into a nonhistorical [counterfactual] one, but why should a scholar go out of his way to make a difficult problem impossible?".[50] Although one can certainly argue against Fischer's labelling of counterfactuals as impossible, the main point still seems reasonable: If the conclusions are the same in both counterfactual and factual history, there is little reason to concern ourselves with the more problematic of the two.

Of course, one could point to the satisfaction of knowing how historiography is being written on a methodological level. However, this is a matter of concern only to the most theoretical historians, not to most practitioners, and certainly not to average readers. It is possible to argue that Lenin was essential to the October Revolution, without explaining the counterfactual logic behind the statement. This can be perfectly understandable on its own, thus rendering explicit counterfactuals unnecessary. Only if there is a possibility of reaching different conclusions can the systematic practice of counterfactual history be justified. This is not to say that negative counterfactuals can only reproduce factual history, but if the aim of negative counterfactuals is merely to sort out necessary causes, it must be admitted that the difference from factual history is not great. Negative

49 See, for example, Robert W. Fogel, "The New Economic History: I. Its Findings and Methods", in *The Economic History Review*, 1966, vol. 19, no. 3, p. 655.

50 David Hackett Fischer, *Historians' Fallacies: Toward a Logic of Historical Thought*, Routledge and Kegan Paul, London, 1971, p. 19.

counterfactuals most often merely reproduce the lessons already accessible from factual history, but may nonetheless help to provide a stronger foundation for the theories in question.

2.3.2.2. Positive Counterfactual Hypotheses

The difference between negative and positive counterfactuals is not absolute. Saying that an effect would not occur (negative) implies that something would happen in its place (positive). Still, positives certainly go further than negatives, since they depart further from the empirical foundation. This means it is necessarily more challenging to put forth plausible positive counterfactuals. However, if the key issue of counterfactual history is indeed its usefulness, positives may prove to have greater potential relevance.

Positive counterfactuals are often found in military and economic history. In military history, it has long been common to re-run historical battles in war games and simulations.[51] There are also a considerable literature on the 'what ifs' in military history. One example is Robert Cowley's *What If?*, which explores scenarios such as the before-mentioned "if the wind had changed on the night of August 7–8, 1588", would it have led to a Spanish victory and occupation of England?[52] Many other examples of counterfactual war history can be given. An especially popular one is what could have led to a Nazi victory in World War II.[53]

In economic history, so-called econometric history, also called cliometrics or New Economic History, has been a champion of historical counterfactuals. Robert Fogel's treatise of *Railroads and American Economic Growth*, the best known of the kind, attempted to simulate an American history without railroads.[54] One of the main conclusions is that the prairies of the United States would most likely have been settled even without the existence of railroads, which is a negative counterfactual statement: "It is very likely that even in the absence of railroads, the prairies would have been settled and exploited".[55] However, in order to make the negative counterfactual plausible, Fogel is forced to back it up with a positive, that "the

---

51 See Sørensen, 2004, p. 161 see *supra* note 17.

52 See Parker, 1999, see *supra* note 39.

53 See Sørensen, 2004, pp. 71–94, see *supra* note 17.

54 Robert W. Fogel, *Railroad and American Economic Growth: Essays in Econometric History*, Johns Hopkins Press, Baltimore, 1964.

55 *Ibid.*, p. 219.

combination of wagon and water transportation could have provided a relatively good substitute for the fabled iron horse".[56] In other words, Fogel argues that if the railroad system had not been built, then the existing means of transportation, that is, water and wagon, would have expanded to make up for some of the losses of not having railroads.

By arguing in this manner, Fogel believed he also showed the value of counterfactual history. It was commonly held among historians at the time, and still is today, that railroads were indispensable to economic growth in the United States. This is easily proven when only the factual development is considered, since the numbers clearly show growth in areas connected to the railroad. However, by arguing counterfactually, Fogel meant to show that this thesis was flawed, or at least not as solid as the level believed by contemporary historians.[57] The growth would have occurred in other areas, where water and wagon transportation would have flourished, if these means of transportation would not have had to compete with the railroad.

At face value, Fogel's argument above seems clearly historically significant. It appears to show directly and explicitly that railroads were not as necessary a component of American economic growth as previously assumed. However, Fogel has had many critics. Among them, Elster has argued that the railroad scenario is not scientifically coherent, because the altered antecedent does not take into consideration that the absence of railroads would also mean altering the level of technological development at the time, which is too all-encompassing for any feasible theories to be made.[58]

Although Elster's point is well put, I would not dismiss Fogel's theory outright. This relates directly to the discussion about 'miracle causes'. Elster may have been right in pointing out that Fogel should have made more effort to argue that the antecedent could be theoretically altered without this conflicting with other contemporary factors, such as the level of technological development. However, this is not to say that any similar argument could not have been made. For example, if one propose that the US government could have decided to restrict or at least not subsidise railroad development, then the scenario could perhaps be defensible. Only if one

---

56 *Ibid.*, p. 219.

57 *Ibid.*, p. 207.

58 Elster, 1978, pp. 190–192 and 207–208, see *supra* note 18.

concludes that the counterfactual requires theoretical changes that significantly affect the historical consistency of the hypothesis, such as the level of technology, after a discussion of the changed antecedent, can one conclude that the railroad theory should be dismissed.[59]

2.3.3. Alternative Histories

The distinction between positive counterfactuals and alternative histories, sometimes referred to as 'alternate history', may seem unnecessary. In principle, one can argue that both concern counterfactual developments, and both have the same problems with a lack of empirical evidence. To some extent, all positive counterfactuals implicitly indicate hypotheses concerning alternative histories. Nonetheless, alternative histories, being n-order effects subsequent to the first order effect, are more problematic and certainly more scientifically questionable.

Opinions about alternative histories are varied. Gavriel Rosenfeld argues that: "Alternate history is inherently presentist. It explores the past less for its own sake than to utilize it instrumentally to comment upon the present. Based as it is upon conjecture, alternate history necessarily reflects its authors' hopes and fears".[60] In line with this, Rosenfeld argues that alternative histories do not say much of value about the past, except, interestingly, that they can be used as future sources of how past events were perceived at the time when the alternative history was written.[61]

However, the potential value added of alternative histories will depend on the specific description, and how much effort is taken to keep the alternative scenario in line with what credibly might have happened. To illustrate this, I will return to Robert Fogel's railroad-less American history, where he not only made positive counterfactual statements, but went further and tried to assess precisely how American history might have developed in the absence of railroads. For example, in relation to the theory that transport by inland waterways would have expanded, Fogel constructed a map of exactly where one might have expected these canals to be built.[62]

---

[59] For Fogel's own justification of the econometric history, see Fogel, 1966, p. 644, see *supra* note 49.

[60] Gavriel Rosenfeld, "Why Do We Ask 'What If?': Reflections on the Function of Alternate History", in *History and Theory*, 2002, vol. 41, no. 4, p. 93.

[61] *Ibid.*, p. 103.

[62] Fogel, 1964, map foldout between pp. 250 and 251, see *supra* note 54.

The result is impressive, though certainly debatable. How can one plausibly argue that hypothetical canals would have been built over decades in a counterfactual past, by unidentifiable decision-makers and in a hypothetical economic context? Certainly, some factors may be counted on in the alternative history, such as the facts that some navigable rivers could have been connected by relatively cheap canals, or that other rivers could have been made navigable with little cost. According to Fogel, absence of these canals can be ascribed to the existence of the railroad. Still, since Fogel's alternative history spans over several decades when railroads were essential to transportation of goods in the United States, it goes without saying that the account is speculative. This leads David Fischer to comment that in Fogel's account, "history is run off the rails in more senses than one".[63]

In Fogel's defence, it can be said that his main aim was not to create a plausible alternative history, but to prove a factually important point, that railroads were not indispensable to economic growth in nineteenth century USA.[64] This conclusion can be seen as historically valuable, and would have been difficult to make without indicating an alternative history.

The longer the time span of an alternative history, the less historically plausible it becomes. Tucker argues that probability theory is apt to illustrate this, pointing out that the probability of the n-order effect depends on the combined product of the evidence and the probability of the prior n-order hypotheses.[65] In other words: if the causal chains are longer, the probability of the final effect will diminish. One could say that longer alternative histories become more literature-like and less scientific.[66] Some defenders of counterfactual history have tried to remedy this by constructing simple rules or heuristics for writing scientifically coherent and plausible long-term alternative histories. For example, Demandt has suggested that one should consider the tendency of history to develop as a pendulum. He believes that history most often returns to its original point, or its natural position. If it deviates, such as the break-up into the two Germanys after World War II, it will correct itself, such as the reunification in 1990.[67]

---

63 Fischer, 1971, p. 17, see *supra* note 50.

64 Fogel, 1964, p. 207, see *supra* note 54. Niall Ferguson also emphasises this as Fogel's main point, in Ferguson (ed.), 1997, p. 18, see *supra* note 31.

65 Tucker, 2004, pp. 230–231, see *supra* note 6.

66 See Sørensen, 2004, p. 181, see *supra* note 17.

67 Demandt, 1993, p. 141, see *supra* note 26.

The immediate reason for Demandt's suggestion is his criticism of Arnold Toynbee's alternative history article "If Alexander the Great Had Lived On".[68] Toynbee's mistake, according to Demandt, was allowing Alexander won a victory after another, eventually conquering the entire civilised world in 311 B.C. and dying at the age of 69 in 287 B.C., having effectively created world unity.[69] Demandt considers such an alternative history unrealistic, because it does not take into account the enormous problems in Alexander's empire in his historical lifetime. Imagining that the king solved these problems and conquered the rest of the world simply because he was a genius is not plausible. The pendulum idea, as Demandt applies it, states to the contrary that alternative histories must take into account that everyone wins sometimes and loses sometimes, but that this game of chance corrects itself over time.

Still, I do not accept Demandt's view of history. Rather than solving any problems, it seems merely echoes its author's personal view on history. The notion that the accidental events of history even each other out may be common, but there is no clear empirical foundation for it. Following Demandt's example of the break-up and reunification of Germany, one could say that Germany eventually will break up again into several hundred small states, since this was the natural position for centuries, between the Thirty Years' War and the Napoleonic Wars. Such a prediction would be far-fetched at best. Certainly, experience dictates that balances in history can and will shift over time, but not necessarily in the predictable pattern that the image of a pendulum invokes. Rather than conforming to a general theory, such as the 'pendulum', any assessment of counterfactual consequents must be founded on a thorough assessment of historical possibilities that are inherent in events. An alternative history that attempts to outline consequences of effects, based purely on accidental events, has little possibility of becoming plausible. Of course, this does not mean that one can write off the possibility that accidental events could have changed a seemingly consistent development in a counterfactual scenario.

A more restrained heuristic may lie along the lines Max Weber's suggestion: alternative history should be written as if all things developed straight from the initial counterfactual event. By this, Weber also meant that

68 Arnold J. Toynbee, *Some Problems of Greek History*, Oxford University Press, London, 1969.

69 Demandt, 1993, p. 77, see *supra* note 26.

one should not account for just one, but all of the most plausible developments. As an example, Weber used Bismarck's decision to wage war against Austria in 1866. Had Bismarck chosen otherwise, Weber imagined it might have resulted in either reaching a Prussian–Italian agreement, a peaceful transfer of Venice, a coalition between the French and the Austrians, or an alternation of the European power balance in favour of Napoleon III instead of Bismarck.[70]

It can easily be argued that none of these scenarios are particularly plausible, but that would be attacking Max Weber's specific historical explanation, and not the general theoretical argument. Max Weber's point is that alternative histories are plausible only if they are written as natural historical developments from the initial counterfactual event. Accidental events should only be included in such accounts when used to explain general uncertainties. Including specific accidental events would be closer to guesswork than research.

What about taking into account parallel factual historical developments when writing alternative histories? Certainly, factual events that occurred after the counterfactual scenario in question could in many cases significantly influence the course of the alternative history. An example is the influence of the Great Depression on the German economy of the 1930s. If one was to imagine an alternative peace at Versailles, which had given the Germans a more viable economic situation, an alternative history of the German state needs to take into consideration the impact of the Great Depression, unless, of course, one is able to conjure up an alternative history where a more productive Versailles Treaty could somehow have avoided the Depression.

Writing parallel factual events into alternative histories is no simple matter. First, it is often hard to estimate if factual events would have developed in an alternative history. Second, it is difficult to estimate how such events would impact the counterfactual situation. For example, if the leadership of Weimar Germany was counterfactually changed in relation to the Versailles scenario above, can one calculate how these alternative leaders would have acted in response to the Depression? Perhaps they would have come up with some ingenious solution that had saved Germany from both

70 Max Weber, "Objektive Möglichkeit und Adäquate Verursachung in der Historischen Kausalbetrachtung", in Max Weber, *Gesammelte Aufsätze zur Wissenschaftlehre*, J.C.B. Mohr, Tübingen, 1922, pp. 283–284.

economic ruin and fascism? Or perhaps they would only have made matters worse. Once again, researchers' answers will vary. Weber would probably say that the safest bet is to consider all things equal. The alternative leadership was likely to be no more or less capable than the factual one. Therefore, as a rule of thumb, the most plausible alternative history would be the one that places little emphasis on extremes, such as genius and idiocy or good fortune and bad luck.

With all due respect to Weber, I believe that writing anything outside the second or third order of counterfactual effects should be avoided. The probabilities will quickly drop dramatically in such high-order timelines.

2.4. The Psychology and Form of Counterfactuals: From "What If?" to "How Could?" and "How Should?"

Theory and practice often differ. In this subchapter, I attempt to look into how counterfactual hypotheses are actually arrived upon, and ask whether this has consequences for the theory formation.

Starting with a counterfactual question, it seems that, from a methodological viewpoint, counterfactual history is usually treated from the perspective of changing the antecedents and accounting for the effects. However, when writing counterfactual history, the opposite is probably more common: changing the effects (often in the n-order) and accounting for the possible counterfactual causes This means that the relevant historical question is not "what if?", but "how could?" or even "how should?". It is meaningless to ask what would have happened if the winds had changed in the English Channel on the night of 7–8 August in 1587, since it would have made no difference, but if it happened one year later, in 1588, it could have caused a successful Spanish invasion of England.[71] In this way, one could say that most counterfactual history probably starts with the effects and then reasons backward to the causes.

Actually, even most factual history seems to reason from the effect to the cause. The causes receive their respective historical value in relation to their consequences. Carr's example is when Caesar crossed the Rubicon River. Hundreds of thousands of people have crossed the same river before and since, but only Caesar's crossing is considered historically important. The reason is that Caesar's crossing represented a resolution to seize power

71 See Parker, 1999, see *supra* note 39.

in the Roman Republic. Were it not for this effect, Caesar's crossing of the Rubicon would long since have been forgotten.[72]

Therefore, in writing historiography, the difference between reasoning from the causes or the effects is negligible. In changing the effect, one must also change the causes. Thus, the difference is not so much practical as theoretical. The emphasis put on different causes will vary according to the events that are to be explained. The process of actually changing the causes will remain much the same. An example from counterfactual history: If we were to ask how Nazi expansionism could have been contained in 1936, we might respond that French military intervention in Rhineland could have done it. If we were to ask what would have happened if the French had intervened in Rhineland in 1936, we would, following the same reasoning, answer that Nazi expansionism could have been contained. The method of explanation would, in this case, be the same. The difference is the way one derives the conclusions.

Nonetheless, it is crucial to realise that scientific results can vary greatly in regard to what extent the historian emphasises that he wants to change the causes or the effects. This occurred to me when I was researching the career of Senator Joseph R. McCarthy in the United States.[73] His breakthrough in 1950 owed much to the Senate investigation of the charges he made that 205 employees in the State Department were communists.[74] I concluded that had the Senate hearings been closed to the press and general public, McCarthy would have been effectively sidelined, because he would not have received public attention for his continued charges. Furthermore, if McCarthy had been effectively sidelined in 1950, 'the McCarthy Era' (1950–1955) may have looked very different. In this manner, I have shown the importance of the Senate hearings being public. This was uncovered because the starting point was changing the effect, to asking how McCarthy's charges could have been handled early on and how McCarthyism could have been contained in 1950. Without reasoning from the effects to

---

[72] Carr, 1990, p. 10, see *supra* note 27. This point also corresponds to McCullagh's view that historical explanations often are teleological in nature, see McCullagh, 2004, p. 173, see *supra* note 2.

[73] See Stian Christensen, *McCarthyismen i USA, ca. 1950–1955* [McCarthyism in the USA] (master's thesis, University of Oslo, 2003).

[74] The figure varied. Initial accounts of McCarthy's charges say 205, McCarthy himself claimed (at different times) he had said 57 or 81.

the cause, I would likely not have uncovered the significance of the hearings' being public. I doubt that I would have considered it important to simply ask, "What if the hearings were closed instead of public?".

Now, one could say that the significance of this factor very well could have been uncovered without the use of counterfactual history. However, at least to my knowledge, it has not been so. I suspect the reason is that it is quite common for Senate hearings to be public, and that historians did not consider that the committee's chairman, Millard Tydings, could well have chosen otherwise. In this way, 'how could' history sheds light on an important factor in history, which was difficult for both 'what if' counterfactuals and factual history to uncover.

There is also a difference between counterfactually reasoning what could have happened to what should or ought to have happened. In some cases, it is necessary to invoke the latter, particularly the case with legal procedures. If an accused is to be judged guilty of a crime, it must be proven that he should both have anticipated the results of his actions and had actual alternatives *ex ante*. Consider, for example, a person who is being tried for a homicide that we know he has committed. The starting point of the trial, whether explicit or not, is to inquire whether the killing should have been stopped by the person who committed it. In answering this, one must also provide the answer to how the person should have acted otherwise. If the killing was a completely unforeseen accident, or the killer was insane at the time, he cannot be held personally responsible for his actions. The same can be said if the killing is interpreted as necessary or unavoidable, for example if committed in self-defence. In both the accidental and the necessary killing, the court cannot justly convict the accused of murder.

On the other hand, if the killing was neither accidental nor necessary, he should be found guilty. The reason is that he should have seen the consequences and taken steps to avoid them. The accused should have chosen to act otherwise. However, in order for this argument to be reasonable, it must be plausibly shown that other possible courses of action existed which would not have led to the homicide. This holds true not only in legal cases, but in all cases of passing judgment. As Demandt puts it: "The condemned person has a right to be told what he ought to have done or left undone".[75] Furthermore, it is irrelevant if the accused claims that he did not understand

75 Demandt, 1993, p. 13, see *supra* note 26.

the consequences, if it can be reasonably held that people of normal intelligence would understand them.

A parallel to the homicide example is the group of questions most frequently asked in counterfactual history: How should wars have been avoided? If waging war is judged *ex post* to have been necessary, most people would consider it 'just'. The starting point of the reasoning is posing the question of whether or not the war could have been stopped, and if so, then how? "How should…?"

One problem that occurs in relation to 'how should' counterfactuals is that of objectivity in historiography. Since counterfactual history quite often starts with the 'how should' question, this increases the risk of biased answers. This risk is further increased by the impossible falsification of the theory, since the counterfactual consequent did not happen.

This type of reasoning seems most often motivated by wishful thinking. For example, who would not want to wish away the carnage of the World Wars?[76] However, in law and politics, the counterfactual questions serve instrumental purposes: The answers provide insight into both the possibilities for convicting the war-makers in question and for shaping potential courses of action in the next similar crisis.

Do the perspectives outlined above significantly impact the theory of counterfactuals? For now, the conclusion seems to be that such significance is limited, if at all. The form of the counterfactual theory, whether it resulted from asking 'what if', 'how could' or 'how should', would probably be the same. However, there are potential psychological pitfalls in counterfactual theory-making, particularly in regard to bias, and awareness of the different approaches is likely to limit the risks of providing biased answers.

2.5. Counterfactuals and Types of Historiography

It has been argued that counterfactuals are more relevant in some forms of historiography than others. Here I discuss the views of Alexander Demandt and Niall Ferguson, respectively.

76 See Ferguson (ed.), 1997, p. 11, see *supra* note 31.

2.5.1. Alexander Demandt and Counterfactuals in Types of Historiography

Demandt listed four types of historiography in his *History That Never Happened*: processes of civilisation, cultural history, political history and religious history.[77] He estimates that accidental events will be less important, and deliberate decisions are more important. Counterfactuals are mostly used in cases where they have the greatest potential effects. As mentioned above, where the historical development is necessary, there can be no room for counterfactuals.

Demandt believes that in civilisational development, by which he means "the field of technical and cultural progress", counterfactuals are of little use.[78] The example he uses is what would have happened if Gutenberg had not invented the printing press. Demandt believes the invention was inevitable. Indeed, Gutenberg tried to keep his discovery a secret, but failed because the basic knowledge required was already widespread. The same was the case with Columbus' discovery of America and Einstein's theory of relativity. If they had not done it, someone else probably would have a little later.[79]

According to Demandt, the potential role of counterfactuals is "stronger in cultural history", "sometimes significant in politics" and "decisive in religious history".[80] In relation to cultural history, meaning art and literature, he admits that accidental events and individual deliberations could have greatly changed individual works. However, in relation to longer periods, no such single events would have mattered much, as there would have been a Gothic Period even if the Notre Dame had not been built.[81] Demandt believed counterfactuals are more important in political and religious history, because they often owe much to the characteristics of individuals. How would the childhood death of Napoleon Bonaparte, Lenin

77 Demandt, 1993, pp. 24–34, see *supra* note 26.

78 *Ibid.*, p. 30.

79 *Ibid.*, p. 30.

80 *Ibid.*, pp. 31–33.

81 *Ibid.*, p. 32. For more on the importance of individual works of art in cultural history, see the discussion on Duccio in Hawthorn, 1991, *pp.* 123–156, see *supra* note 31.

or Hitler have affected political history? Not to mention the religious implications of the non-existence of Moses, Siddhartha, Jesus or Muhammad?[82]

Demandt's specific claims can, of course, be questioned, but is there value added of asking if counterfactuals are more feasible in certain types of historiography? If such types can be identified, it might serve to increase the precision of any theory of counterfactuals. However, there are reasons to believe that such a reduction of categories might be unsuitable in regard to the applicability of counterfactual history. An example is an essay by Max Weber, in which he argues that if the battle of Marathon in 480 B.C. had resulted in an Athenian loss against the invading Persians, the entire history of European civilisation would be different. Instead of the humanistic values of the Athenians, Europeans would have the theocratic values of Central and Eastern Asia.[83] Every other state that was conquered by the Persians adopted their theocratic manner of rule, and Weber sees no reason why the Greeks would have differed. He believes that Marathon was a crucial moment and potential turning point in the process of European civilisation. Certainly, this cannot be proven empirically, but the assertion is not without appeal. However, the point is that counterfactuals can, of course, be considered important even in the processes of civilisation.

Furthermore, the history of religion might not be as clear as Demandt supposed either. Paul the Apostle's importance to Christianity is factually momentous, but one cannot accept, at face value, that Christianity would not have existed, or been significantly different, without Paul's influence. There might have been others to take his place, and to have their epistles included in the New Testament when it was canonised some centuries later. The historical drift toward monotheism in Europe and Central Asia might have occurred in the absence of some of history's most important figures. Zoroastrianism was, after all, influential in its various forms long before the birth of Jesus.

The conclusion seems to be that Demandt's search for specific types of historiography, where counterfactuals might be more feasible, seems somewhat misconceived. As I have mentioned above, it is important that both the hypothetical antecedent and the consequent have plausibility. This

---

82 Demandt, 1993, pp. 32–33, see *supra* note 26.

83 Weber, 1922, pp. 276–277, see *supra* note 70.

depends on the situation, and not necessarily, it seems, on the type of historiography. This does not mean, however, that there may not be other types of historiography than the ones mentioned by Demandt where counterfactuals may be more or less relevant.

2.5.2. 'Grand Narratives' and 'Chaostory'

Niall Ferguson, in his *Virtual History*, writes that the weakened position of the 'grand narratives' of historiography (materialism, idealism, and so on)[84] is what makes it possible to look seriously into the method of counterfactual history.[85] In the following, I ask first whether it is right to claim that the 'grand narratives' generally exclude the possibility of counterfactual history, and second, if Ferguson's alternative 'chaostory' should be considered a fruitful approach.

'Grand narratives' in various forms have been discussed extensively over hundreds of years. The tradition's 'great age' in the last century was in the 1950s and 1960s, although it was by no means limited to this period. These twenty years were a period when the materialism of the Annales school and the Marxists, respectively, were mainstream historical theory. In these decades, more than before or since, the two schools emphasised that only underlying grand factors influence history significantly. Emmanuel Le Roy Ladurie, one of the most obvious exponents of the Annales school's theories, made it a point to write "history without people", and focused instead on cycles of population growth and food prices.[86] For many Marxists, the dialectics of class struggle occupied the same place as demography for the Annales historians. Karl Marx, for example, thought accidents in history could only delay or accelerate historical processes. Furthermore, he believed that an accidental event evened another one, so accidents would not matter after a while.[87] Several other variations of 'grand narratives' could

---

84 For more on 'grand narratives', see Lyotard, 1984, see *supra* note 8.

85 Ferguson (ed.), 1997, pp. 20–43, see *supra* note 31.

86 Georg G. Iggers, *Historiography in the Twentieth Century: From Scientific Objectivity to the Postmodern Challenge*, Wesleyan University Press, London, 1997, p. 60.

87 Marx describes his view on this point in a letter, which is referred in Carr, 1986, p. 95, see *supra* note 27. Carr labels the causes accidental, which seem to include both chance events and individual choices.

be accounted for here, such as divine interventionism and Hegelianism.[88] All have in common that they regard lesser factors, meaning accidental events and individual choices, as being irrelevant in the long run.

There is little point in repeating the many criticisms of the 'grand narratives' that have been presented over the years. The point is simply that the inherent viewpoint in this tradition seems to conflict with the idea of counterfactual history, which relies on the possibility of altering small-scale accidental causes or individual decisions. 'Grand narratives' usually attempt to explain longer spans of history. The Annales school, for example, focused mainly on longer periods of medieval history; and Marxist historiography of class struggle is based on great historical eras, such as 'capitalism', 'feudalism', and so on. When dealing with long historical periods, grand factors naturally play a greater part. In this sense, it would appear that the 'grand narratives' indeed conflict with the idea of counterfactual history.

As mentioned, Ferguson has argued that it is the decline of the 'grand narratives' which makes it possible to look more seriously into counterfactual history. Concretely, he attributes this change to the increased influence of chaos theory in natural and empirical sciences.[89] This theory describes the behaviour of nonlinear dynamical systems that are highly sensitive to initial conditions. The best-known example is the so-called 'butterfly effect', where one assumes that the flapping of a butterfly's wings on one continent, an initial condition, may ultimately be a cause of a hurricane occurring in another. Chaos theory is applied to systems that appear to be random, but are actually deterministic.

Ferguson has argued that chaos theory gives legitimacy to counterfactual history, because it proves that grand factors do not determine everything of significance.[90] Furthermore, chaos theory represents an attempt to place these seemingly countless lesser factors in a pattern that can be predictable in the short term. For example, chaos theory has been applied in meteorology to improve models of weather forecasting. Ferguson has argued that the same can be done in counterfactual history. Historians can

---

88 See Ferguson, 1997 (ed.), pp. 20–43, see *supra* note 31. For more on Hegelian determinism, see Isaiah Berlin, "Historical Inevitability", in *Four Essays on Liberty*, Oxford University Press, Oxford, 1969.

89 Ferguson (ed.), 1997, p. 79, see *supra* note 31.

90 *Ibid.*, p. 79–90.

change one small factor, and scientifically track the changes in the historical pattern. In fact, he has claimed that the impact of chaos theory is important enough to make way for a new historical paradigm of (counterfactual) history, which he has labelled chaostory.[91]

However, Ferguson's assessments are questionable for two reasons. First, he does not clarify exactly how chaos theory connects to historical and mathematical sciences. In mathematics and meteorology, it is possible to make predictions by deducing from scientific laws and including probabilistic laws, but why should the same be the case with historical science? Most historians have rejected the notion that they are, or should be, dealing with laws when writing historiography.[92] Second, what exactly is new with what chaos theory can bring into historical science? Ferguson's argument is simply that the theory proves the potential significance of small-scale historical causes. However, this has long been argued by both historical theorists and practising historians.

The conclusion seems to be that Ferguson is probably right in arguing that the 'grand narratives' of historiography tend to exclude the possibility of counterfactual history. However, his proposed alternative approach, that of a chaostory, does not appear to contribute something new.

2.6. Conclusions

The crucial point in a counterfactual hypothesis is the degree of scientific coherence and plausibility. Counterfactuals, in the sense that they say nothing directly about the truth, derive value from how they may enlighten interpretations of history and human affairs.

It seems clear that counterfactuals are mostly found in causal explanations, rational explanations or in explanations by reference to laws, such

---

91 *Ibid.*, p. 90. Several have commented on Ferguson's chaostory approach, among them Elazar Weinryb, "Historiographic Counterfactuals", in Aviezer Tucker (ed.), *A Companion to the Philosophy of History and Historiography*, Blackwell, Chichester, 2009, pp. 116–117; Charles Dyke, "Strange Attraction, Curious Liaison: Clio Meets Chaos", in *The Philosophical Forum*, 1990, vol. 21, no. 4, p. 383; and Dominic Ingemark, "Kontrafaktisk historieskrivning och dess bakgrund i kaosteori och experimentell psykologi" [Counterfactual History and its Background in Chaos Theory and Experimental Psychology], in *Historisk Tidskrift* [Swedish Journal of History], 2001, no. 1, pp. 98–99.

92 For example, Karl Popper has argued this in *The Poverty of Historicism*, Routledge, London, 1994, p. 41; Tor Egil Førland also discusses this in "The Ideal Explanatory Text in History: A Plea for Ecumenism", in *History and Theory*, 2004, vol. 43, pp. 321–340.

as in econometric history. I have argued that counterfactual hypotheses should take into account the historical consistency of both the hypothetical antecedent and the consequent. In line with this, there is little purpose in differentiating between 'nomothetic' and 'idiographic' counterfactuals. It seems untenable to speak of purely nomothetic counterfactuals in social science, which is an important premise for Tetlock and Belkin's approach to counterfactuals.

It has also been argued that it may be useful to distinguish between negative and positive counterfactuals. Negative counterfactuals are often similar in form and content to causal analyses in factual history. Therefore, it is neither as controversial nor as promising in terms of providing value added as the positive variant.

Concerning the value added from counterfactuals in comparison with factual history, it seems likely that research on counterfactual decisions would be more fruitful than looking into accidental causes. Both types of causes can be scientifically coherent, but any altered cause must be on a scale that is small enough not to lose track of any potentially co-varying factors.

As far as the consequent is concerned, attempts to draw up effects in the n-order should be avoided, as the probability of any scenario is likely to drop significantly in the second, third and subsequent orders.

It appears that there is a difference between how counterfactuals are conceived methodologically, and how concrete hypotheses are actually made. This seems fairly insignificant in regard to the theory of the ideal form of counterfactual, but there seems to be a higher risk of biased theories in counterfactual history than in factual history.

There is a case for arguing that counterfactuals are of little relevance in certain traditions of historiography, most importantly the so-called 'grand narratives'.

3

Objections to Counterfactual History

Many theoretical objections can be raised against counterfactual history. I have touched upon some of these in the preceding chapter. Those that are discussed in this chapter will probably not constitute an exhaustive list, but they are the ones that I consider most important when reviewing the relevant literature:

1. Problems of determinism: Are there any alternatives to what actually happened?
2. Challenges of collectivism: To what extent does the importance of social phenomena in history diminish the possibilities of counterfactual history?
3. Limitless possibilities: Are there too many counterfactual possibilities?
4. The problem of empirical evidence: Does lack of foundation in empirical facts make counterfactuals unscientific?
5. The problems of value objectivity: How significant is the risk of bias in counterfactual history, and can this be reduced?

These problems will be discussed below. In my opinion, the most important issue on the list is the problem of empirical evidence. The final issue on the list, regarding value objectivity, is not really a problem for counterfactual theory *per se*, but the risk of subjectivity is generally considered to be greater when writing counterfactually than factually.

3.1. Problems of Determinism

The regular determinist viewpoint is that there is no room for significant historical developments from accidental events in history, and that everything in history happened out of necessity. This line of thought has its counterpart in voluntarism, that free will decides the course of events. As mentioned in Chapter 1, if a historical event is necessary, there is little point in speculating in counterfactuals.

Ferguson debates the deterministic objections to counterfactual history at length in *Virtual History*, so does Hawthorn in *Plausible Worlds* and

Demandt in *History That Never Happened*.[1] Particularly, Ferguson portrays many well-known critics of counterfactual history as determinists, including E.H. Carr. His conclusion seems to be that for counterfactual history to be interesting, there must be at least a slight possibility for alternative past decisions or events.

Dahl makes a useful distinction between two main variants of determinism. The first is the belief that the notion of cause-and-effect in the final sense means that all events are predetermined, even as far back as the Big Bang.[2] This variant, which implies an infinite regress of causes and effects, is dismissed by most philosophers of history. Carr is of the opinion that infinite regress of the causal chain is a philosopher's problem, and not of much relevance to ordinary men or, in this case, practising historians.[3] McCullagh, in a criticism directed at Lewis' theory of causation, argues from a pragmatic position. He writes that the Big Bang may be a cause of a leaf falling today, but in reality we do not use such remote events as causes.[4] The remoteness of Big Bang excludes it from a historical explanation in the world today, as much as Cleopatra's nose is not used to explain the founding of the Roman Empire. This will probably be an acceptable point of view to many historians. Taking such a viewpoint would mean that it would also be permissible to interfere in the causal chain by altering a cause without at the same time having to explain how this changes all history backward in time.

Dahl's second category of determinism is what he labels "conditional determinism", meaning the belief that if A is the causes of B, then B had to occur.[5] This category does not present major problems to the possibility of

---

1 Niall Ferguson (ed.), *Virtual History: Alternatives and Counterfactuals*, Picador, London, 1997, pp. 20–43; Geoffrey Hawthorn, *Plausible Worlds: Possibility and Understanding in History and the Social Sciences*, Cambridge University Press, Cambridge, 1991, pp. 6–9; Alexander Demandt, *History That Never Happened: A Treatise on the Question, What Would Have Happened If…?*, McFarland, Jefferson, North Carolina, 1993, pp. 43–47.

2 Ottar Dahl, *Om årsaksproblemer i historisk forskning: Forsøk på en vitenskapsteoretisk analyse* [Problems of Causation in Historical Research], Universtitetsforlaget, Oslo, 1970, p. 169.

3 Carr has been labelled 'determinist' by Niall Ferguson in Ferguson (ed.), 1997, pp. 5 and 53, see *supra* note 1, but I would argue that Ferguson has not understood Carr correctly on this point.

4 C. Behan McCullagh, *The Truth of History*, Routledge, London, 1998, p. 177.

5 Dahl, 1970, p. 169, see *supra* note 2.

counterfactual hypotheses. On the contrary, one could argue that conditional determinism implies that counterfactual analysis is possible. If there is a clear connection between the cause and effect, then the absence or alteration of the cause could produce a different effect.

Therefore, it seems, that the problem that determinism poses to counterfactual analysis is insignificant. In the case of infinite regress determinism, there seems to be consensus that this category is redundant in factual history, and should therefore not be problematic to counterfactual history. As for conditional determinism, there is no inherent conflict between this category and the possibility for drawing up counterfactual hypotheses.

3.2. Challenges of Collectivism

Related to the issue of determinism is the concept of 'collectivism' in historiography.[6] This concept has been defined in different ways. One definition is that collectivism is the belief that "society affects the individual's aims".[7] This should be seen as representing the minimum requirements of a collectivist viewpoint. Another definition is that it represents the viewpoint that "social phenomena must be explained in terms of social wholes or collectives".[8] In this line of thought, an individual decision-maker is not seen as a likely source of change, as historical processes depend mostly on collective phenomena in society. The counterpart is "methodological individualism", which Elster defines in this way: "to explain social institutions and social change is to show how they arise as the result of the action and interaction of individuals".[9]

The challenge to counterfactual history from the collectivist viewpoint is more a question of the practice of history, rather than of the theory of historiography. Collectivist viewpoint does not rule out counterfactuals.

---

6 Related terms are 'methodological collectivism' and 'methodological holism', which – depending on the definition – may be used synonymously with 'collectivism'.

7 Joseph Agassi, "Methodological Individualism", in John O'Neill (ed.), *Modes of Individualism and Collectivism*, Gregg Revivals, Aldershot, 1992, p. 186.

8 Lars Udehn, "The Ontology of the Objects of Historiography", in Aviezer Tucker (ed.), *A Companion to the Philosophy of History and Historiography*, Blackwell, Chichester, 2009, p. 210.

9 Jon Elster, *Nuts and Bolts for the Social Sciences*, Cambridge University Press, 1989, p. 13; Jon Elster, *Making Sense of Marx*, Cambridge University Press, 1985, p. 5. For more on methodological individualism, see McCullagh, 1998, pp. 290–297, see *supra* note 4; O'Neill (ed.), 1992, see *supra* note 7; Tor Egil Førland, "Mentality as a Social Emergent: Can the Zeitgeist have Explanatory Power", in *History and Theory*, 2008, vol. 47, no.1, pp. 44–56.

However, there seems to be a clear tendency among historians who favour explanations based on generalised theories to disregard counterfactual history.[10]

From a collectivist viewpoint, a counterfactual individual decision is likely, to a varying degree, to conflict with the historical context at the time of the decision, making the counterfactual antecedent historically inconsistent. This means that the altered antecedent must either be made defensible by also altering these collective phenomena, or be dismissed. As counterfactual history in many cases is based on individual choices, collectivism may thus represent a challenge.

In concrete examples of counterfactual history, the collectivist challenge is often present when a counterfactual scenario involves the removal of a specific historical character.[11] An example used by Tucker is what would have happened if Adolf Hitler had died in World War I.[12] The methodological question is whether Hitler shaped the German society or whether Germany would have taken the same path regardless. The strict collectivist might answer that Hitler would merely have been replaced by someone else, since the course of history is seldom decided by any one person. He would say that the historical role of the *Führer* could have been cast with another character, perhaps Joseph Goebbels or Hermann Göring. On the other hand, historians with an individualist inclination might suggest that history could have taken an entirely different course if Hitler had not played the role that he did. Tucker, by the way, refers to Ian Kershaw's theory that a Nazi regime would probably have been installed in Germany in the 1930s even in Hitler's absence, but it would probably have been less anti-Semitic.[13]

---

10 Lebow and Tetlock attempts to prove this in Richard Ned Lebow and Philip E. Tetlock, "Scholars and Causation", in Richard Ned Lebow (ed.), *Forbidden Fruit, Counterfactuals and International Relations*, Princeton University Press, Princeton, 2010, pp. 137–165. They use the terminology of "generalizers" and "particularizers" (p. 139), but regardless, this is applicable in the discussion here.

11 See for example Demandt, 1993, pp. 53–54, see *supra* note 1.

12 Aviezer Tucker, *Our Knowledge of the Past: A Philosophy of Historiography*, Cambridge University Press, 2004, p. 228.

13 *Ibid.*, p. 228. The reference is to Ian Kershaw, *Hitler 1899–1936: Hubris*, Norton, New York, 1998.

It seems unlikely that there can be an either-or answer to whether collective phenomena or individual decisions are the central historical actors. "Supervenience" has been suggested as a keyword for explaining the relation between collectives and individuals: Collectives can be seen as being supervening entities in relation to individuals, as the collectives can only have properties that exist in the individuals.[14] However, it is difficult to see how this can function as an applicable theory for explaining the relation between individuals and collectives in each concrete historical case.

For example, the question of how Neville Chamberlain, the then-British Prime Minister, could have avoided World War II in 1938, has been heatedly debated. The interpretation of Chamberlain's degree of freedom of choice has varied. KHONG Yuen Foong has argued that the debate can be divided in three stages: After the war, following the publication of Chamberlain's letters, and following the publication of contemporary government papers.[15]

Importantly, the interpretation of Chamberlain's room for manoeuvre was probably also one of the most important elements in American foreign policy after World War II. American politicians believed that if Chamberlain had taken a strong stance in Munich in 1938, that is, not surrendering Czechoslovak Sudetenland to the Nazis, the war might have been avoided. This is one of the main reasons for American containment policy towards the Soviet Union, producing both the Truman Doctrine (1947) and the Korean War (1950–1953). If Chamberlain had chosen otherwise, so the Americans' reasoning went along, then the war could have been avoided. The lesson was that in similar cases in the future, where the Americans considered the Soviet Union's foreign policy relatively similar to Nazi Germany's, a strong stance could prevent war.[16]

---

14 C. Behan McCullagh, *The Logic of History: Putting Postmodernism in Perspective*, Routledge, London, 2004, p. 112; Førland, 2008, p. 45, see *supra* note 9; Udehn, 2009, p. 217, see *supra* note 8.

15 KHONG Yuen Fong, "Confronting Hitler and its Consequences", in Philip E. Tetlock and Aaron Belkin (eds.), *Counterfactual Thought Experiments in World Politics: Logical, Methodological, and Psychological Perspectives*, Princeton University Press, 1996; Tucker, 2004, p. 232, see *supra* note 12.

16 Numerous books have argued in this manner, but I recommend the under-rated doctoral dissertation of Les K. Adler, *The Red Image: American Attitudes toward Communism in the Cold War Era*, Garland Publishing, New York, 1991, pp. 263–264 and 275.

One can easily object to this, and argue that the Americans' argumentation was false. One could claim that Chamberlain did not have any real choice, because he was forced into the Munich policy by the situation, particularly pressure from the Parliament, his own party, and the British media. If this was the case, it would make counterfactuals less plausible. Naturally, Chamberlain, like any other person with great responsibility, was not free to do as he pleased, but this does not mean that he had no room for manoeuvring within the limits defined by the situation. From a pragmatic position, it might be acceptable to perceive this as a question of degree of individual room for manoeuvre, which should be measured in each separate historical case.

3.3. Limitless Possibilities?

Alexander Demandt discusses this objection in his *History That Never Happened.*[17] Demandt's formulation of the objection is this: "Is the *Weltgeist*, the spirit of the world, not a thousand times more inventive than our keenest imagination?".[18] There is no way of knowing what would have happened if a historical antecedent is changed, because we can never imagine all the outcomes. The objection to counterfactual history is that there are, in theory, countless alternative histories after the changed antecedent.

Certainly, it seems true that we can never imagine all hypothetical possibilities. History often takes turns no one had expected beforehand, and this would be the same when assessing possibilities *ex post* as well as *ex ante*. However, that does not mean that history is a complete chaos. If it was, there would be no point even in writing factual history, because no events can be explained if causes could theoretically have had limitless effects. To deny cause and effect is to deny almost all historical science today, and when we accept the notion of cause and effect, we can certainly claim that, from knowing the causes, it should be possible to imagine possible effects. In counterfactual history, this can never be exact in the sense of being 'verifiable'. It stands to reason that we can imagine many effects but not all, and that our task is to choose the one(s) that are the most plausible among the many imagined. The key issue is how we can know which route is the most plausible.

---

17 Demandt, 1993, pp. 5–6, see *supra* note 1.

18 *Ibid.*, p. 5.

Part of this has been discussed in Chapter 2. To recapitulate, the longer the alternative history, the less probable it will be. Furthermore, there are some tenable criteria for selecting the most plausible counterfactual path. However, when discussing first or second order counterfactuals, it should be possible to make qualified judgements in regard to plausibility. In addition, with Weber, we can say that there can be grounds for drawing up more than one line of counterfactual effects. If many routes seem plausible, there is no reason not to consider them. In sum, the problem of indeterminism actually comes down to the degree of plausibility of the separate case.

3.4. The Problem of Empirical Evidence

It is said that counterfactuals, by definition, are not empirical. This is probably the main reason for historians' dismissal of the approach.[19] Carr is among the most referred authors to criticise in this regard, as he thought counterfactual thought-experiments had nothing to do with history.[20] Another is David Fischer: "History is tough enough, as it is – as it actually is".[21] At face value, the lack of empirical evidence seems an insurmountable obstacle. However, as hinted in the previous chapter, it is not accurate to say that counterfactuals are completely detached from empirical facts. The discussion below divides the problem in two: the issue of counterfactual antecedents (causes), and the issue of falsifiability, including the testability of the principles connecting antecedents and consequents.

3.4.1. Antecedents and Empirical Foundation

When an antecedent is altered in a counterfactual hypothesis, a historian is, in many cases, still left with a set of facts that existed at the time. If we were to consider a Roman history where Brutus had not conspired to assassinate Caesar, we would still have much the same political situation up to 15 March 44 B.C. in the counterfactual world as the factual.

All counterfactual thought-experiments must be required to be founded on the empirical evidence and facts that are likely to remain true

---

19 Briefly discussed in *ibid.*, pp. 4–5.

20 E.H. Carr, *What is History? The George Macaulay Trevelyan Lectures delivered in the University of Cambridge January–March 1961*, Macmillan, London, 1986, p. 91.

21 David Hackett Fischer, *Historians' Fallacies: Toward a Logic of Historical Thought*, Routledge and Kegan Paul, London, 1971, p. 19.

in the counterfactual scenarios. As explained in Chapter 1, this requires both logical and historical consistency, such that one cannot change phenomena that would be inconsistent with other phenomena of significance to the counterfactual.

The most widely used term for the criterion of empirical consistency is 'the minimal rewrite rule'. James Fearon's definition of this rule should be mentioned: "The fewer the changes from the actual world required by a counterfactual supposition, the easier it will be to draw and support causal inferences, and the more defensible they will be".[22] The minimal rewrite rule is also one of Tetlock and Belkin's criteria for plausible counterfactuals.[23]

Of course, it is necessary to point out that the demand for historical consistency can probably never be met completely, because causes have causes of their own, as explained above. Thus, Counterfactual causes need their own counterfactual causes, and so on. However, as was discussed in relation to determinism, the existence of choices and accidental causes also has a place in historical science. Therefore, it is reasonable to speak of levels of consistency. If these two criteria are upheld to a satisfactory degree, it means that there are certain factors in the factual scenario that would also be reliable in the counterfactual one.

3.4.2. The Subjectively Possible

The search for an empirical foundation has led some researchers to conclude that a specific criterion should always be present in alternative histories, which I will refer to here as the 'subjectively possible'.[24] This means that historians should found counterfactual research in what the contemporaries themselves saw as possible. In this case, we can find empirical basis in historical actors' own thoughts and, sometimes, intentions.[25] This would

---

22 James F. Fearon, "Counterfactuals and Hypothesis Testing in Political Science", in *World Politics*, 1991, vol. 43, no. 2, pp. 193–194.

23 Tetlock and Belkin (eds.), 1996, p. 23, see *supra* note 15. See also Demandt, 1993, p. 116, see *supra* note 1.

24 The term is taken from Ottar Dahl, "Objektivitet i historiegranskinga" [Objectivity in Historical Inquiry], in *Syn og Segn*, 1969, vol. 10, p. 578. Others have touched upon the same criterion as a part of the broader concept of 'minimal rewrite', for example, Tetlock and Belkin (eds.), 1996, p. 23, see *supra* note 15.

25 Ferguson is an exponent of this line of thought, although he does not use the term 'subjectively possible', see Ferguson (ed.), 1997, p. 86, see *supra* note 1.

be one way of increasing the level of scientific coherence and plausibility when altering counterfactual decisions. As Elster has argued, if a relevant actor believed that a different choice could have been made (*ex ante*), then it would seem historically legitimate to inquire into the realities of this counterfactual proposal (*ex post*).[26]

Some regard this criterion too restrictive to be an absolute rule.[27] The reasons for this will be discussed below. For the time being, the point is that there are ways of founding counterfactual antecedents on empirical facts. 'Subjectively possible' is a way of doing this.

3.4.3. Falsifiability

With regard to the demarcation of sciences, the general consensus in the philosophy of science seems to be, as mentioned in the introduction, that there is no such consensus.[28] However, I believe, that the Popperian critical rationalism, as it has been called, may prove useful in order to discuss the demarcation of scientifically coherent counterfactual hypotheses. The most immediate alternatives, which I consider to be the Hempelian deductive-nomological model, that is, explanation by reference to a 'covering law', Feyerabend's deconstructionism, that any methodology of science that is not historically inaccurate would be empty of normative content, and Bayesian confirmationism, which I deem less applicable. The Hempelian approach has been heatedly debated for decades, and, as mentioned above, is considered by most to be less relevant in historical science.[29] Feyerabend rightly points out that the problem of induction is, in all likelihood, unsolvable, and thus he rejects the concept of a coherent scientific method.[30] However, in doing so, he suggests no clear alternatives. I see little need to either

26 Jon Elster, *Logic and Society: Contradictions and Possible Worlds*, John Wiley, Chichester, 1978, p. 6.

27 Lebow (ed.), 2010, pp. 48–49, see *supra* note 10; Øystein Sørensen, *Historien om det som ikke skjedde: Kontrafaktisk historie* [History That Did Not Happen], Aschehoug, Oslo, 2004, pp. 170–172.

28 Wesley C. Salmon, "Scientific Explanation: How We Got from There to Here", in Wesley C. Salmon, *Causality and Explanation,* Oxford University Press, Oxford, 1998,

29 See, for example, Richard Ned Lebow and Philip E. Tetlock, "Scholars and Causation", in Lebow (ed.), 2010, p. 139, see *supra* note 10.

30 Paul Feyerabend, *Against Method: Outline of an Anarchistic Theory of Knowledge*, NLB, London, 1975, p. 175; see also Paul K. Feyerabend, "Realism, Rationalism and Scientific Method", in *Philosophical Papers*, vol. 1, Cambridge University Press, Cambridge, 1981,

refute or accept this demand for 100 percent precision of philosophy of science. Rather, I elect to follow common sense in arguing that it is possible and desirable to strive for a workable theory of science, and to accept that such a theory may never be fully comprehensive.

Tucker considers Bayesianism, as he interprets it, to be the best basis for explaining the actual practices of historians. He writes that "the Bayesian theorem purports to state formally the relation between a particular piece of evidence and a hypothesis, the degree of probability the evidence confers on the hypothesis".[31] One could perhaps criticise this view by arguing that Bayes' theorem is applicable only for phenomena that is quantifiable, whereas historiography mostly studies qualitative evidence.[32] In my opinion, this is not a decisive argument, as the exact quantification of probabilities is not necessary in order to assess the plausibility of a hypothesis. For example, if, there is much and strong evidence that strengthens a hypothesis, it should be acceptable to argue that there is a 'high probability', without this necessitating the provision of an exact figure.

However, in regard to counterfactual history, I am not convinced that Bayesianism is particularly apt to define the parameters of scientifically coherent counterfactual hypotheses. Tucker's approach takes, as its starting point, that the subject matter of historiography is evidence, and not events. However, the practice of counterfactual history begins with the counterfactual event and reasons back to the possible antecedents, as discussed in Chapter 1.[33] The common question in historiography of how the evidence can be explained, is, in this sense, not important in counterfactual history. Rather, the important question is whether there is any available evidence that can serve as basis for assessing the probability of the counterfactual antecedent and consequent. Approaching the scientific coherence of counterfactual history through a theory of falsification might thus make more sense.

---

p. 205; and Nancy Cartwright et al., "Paul Feyerabend", in Ted Honderich (ed.), *The Oxford Companion to Philosophy*, Oxford University Press, Oxford, 1995, p. 277.

31 Tucker, 2004, p. 96, see *supra* note 12. On Bayesianism in historiography, see also Mark Day and Gregory Radick, "Historiographic Evidence and Confirmation", in Tucker (ed.), 2009, pp. 89–96, see *supra* note 8.

32 Tucker mentions this criticism in Tucker, 2004, p. 99, see *supra* note 12.

33 *Ibid.*, p. 18.

Popper has argued that the most important criterion for the scientific coherence of any scientific claim is its falsifiability. He writes: "I shall certainly admit a system as empirical or scientific only if it is capable of being tested by experience".[34] With this, one can argue that hypotheses must conform to the demand for falsifiability, which, in historical science, relates to the existence of evidence. In historiography, experimentation is not possible as practised in the natural sciences. Instead, historians focus on potential evidence.

Popper's line of reasoning has been heavily criticised. One important critic is Imre Lakatos, who has argued, in essence, that real falsification only occurs when a rival theory defeats the previously dominant theory, and that Popper's model is problematic because there are no 'crucial experiments' that lead immediately to theory alteration.[35] Paul Thagard also criticises Popper, and argues that a principle of demarcation must take the community of practitioners into account, particularly its willingness to develop the theory towards solutions of unsolved problems, and to evaluate the theory in relation to others, while avoiding selectiveness in considering confirmations and disconfirmations.[36]

These are weighty arguments in a broad debate, which I will make no attempt to settle in these pages. However, there may be reasons to argue that demarcation of counterfactual history, as a scholarly exercise, poses problems of a different kind than demarcating astrology from science, as in Thagard's example. It is a main problem with counterfactual history that theories deviate from the facts, hence counterfactual, which leads to a reduction in potential evidence. Therefore, a principle of demarcation should be instrumental in differentiating between scientific inquiries on the one hand, and hypotheses that deviate so far from the facts that it becomes too difficult to assess their plausibility in a meaningful way, on the other hand. For example, a hypothesis about the social structure of Austria today given a German victory in World War I would probably be impossible, or nearly so, to strengthen or weaken by pointing to evidence. Such an account would

---

34 Karl Popper, *The Logic of Scientific Discovery*, Hutchison, London, 1975, p. 40.

35 Imre Lakatos, "Falsification and the Methodology of Scientific Research Programmes", in Imre Lakatos, *The Methodology of Scientific Research Programmes, Philosophical papers I*, Cambridge University Press, Cambridge, 1978, pp. 111–113.

36 Paul R. Thagard, "Why Astrology is a Pseudoscience", in *PSA: Proceedings of the Biennial Meeting of the Philosophy of Science Association*, vol. 1, University of Chicago Press, Chicago, 1978, pp. 227–228.

likely be closer to counterfactual fiction than to counterfactual history as a scholarly exercise. For this reason, I believe that a principle of falsification should be taken into account in the theory of counterfactual history. However, such a principle of falsifiability should not be seen as an attempt to demarcate counterfactual history exactly in comparison with fiction. Rather, the difference between the two categories should be seen as a continuum, where the degree of potential evidence determines the degree of scientific coherence. Of course, The vagueness of this approach is problematic, but I believe it may serve a useful purpose.

Are there ways of falsifying counterfactuals through empirical evidence? Plenty of empirical evidence may be available that can strengthen or weaken the given hypothesis. In many scenarios in contemporary history, the facts and sources are in abundance. An example is as follows: A counterfactual claim that French military intervention in Rhineland would have reversed the German occupation can be founded in the evidence that the occupying force was ordered to retreat at the first sight of French soldiers. However, if evidence can be found that the commander for the intervening German forces was a hard-liner who intended to ignore those orders, it would back a claim that a French intervention risked disaster if it had been half-hearted. These facts are not tests in the narrow sense, and, in fact, it is impossible to re-run this historical event and test empirically what would have happened if a factor changed.[37] However, the facts provide evidence that can strengthen or weaken a counterfactual hypothesis. Therefore, I argue that such facts show that counterfactuals are indirectly falsifiable. This is similar to what Peter Achinstein has called "potential evidence".[38] Such facts can be comparable to symptoms in medical science, where the observation of such facts could lead to a correct theoryor nothing.[39]

Tetlock and Belkin also point to a similar concept, arguing that a criterion of 'projectability' should be met in scientifically coherent counterfactuals. By projectability, they refer to the possibilities for teasing out test-

37 An attempt to re-run history has been made, however. See Lars-Erik Cederman, "Rerunning History: Counterfactual Simulation in World Politics", in Tetlock and Belkin (eds.), 1996, see *supra* note 15.

38 Peter Achinstein, *The Nature of Explanation*, Oxford University Press, Oxford, 1983, p. 323.

39 *Ibid*, p. 323.

able implications of the counterfactual and determining whether the hypotheses are consistent with additional real-world observations.[40] A problem with this concept is that it is closely tied with the idea of connecting antecedents and consequents through some form of a test, which I do not consider to be decisive. When discussing the scientific coherence and plausibility of a counterfactual antecedent, a test, even if possible, would not be useful, because what is important is that the antecedent is consistent with other phenomena of significance to the counterfactual scenario. This would be measured against the available factual evidence.

When discussing the connection between the antecedent and the consequent, any test in the strict sense is impossible. However, one may weaken or strengthen the hypothesis by pointing to the available evidence, for example, planned reactions to a counterfactual decision.

In this sense, counterfactuals can, in many cases, be indirectly falsifiable. The existence of contemporary plans, orders, assessments and the like, formulated as preparations for the counterfactual scenarios in question, can serve as empirical evidence for strengthening or weakening the hypotheses. It is also important to realise that this form of falsification is shared in counterfactuals and factuals alike, as neither employ testing as in the natural sciences.

3.5. Problems of Value Objectivity

It is notable that the main reason for Carr's scepticism towards counterfactual history was due to his belief that such hypotheses are founded in 'wish-dreams'.[41] The example he uses was from his own field of interest, the October Revolution. Carr claimed he had been attacked many times for depicting the revolution as inevitable, when, in fact, many factors could have prevented it. Examples include, according to Carr, "if Stolypin had had time to complete his agrarian reform, or that Russia had not gone to war".[42] However, these objections were always made by the opponents of the revolution, who had suffered from it, directly or indirectly.

If this was indeed the case, then Carr may be right in dismissing counterfactuals as "purely emotional" and "unhistorical".[43] Had he taken the

40 Tetlock and Belkin (eds.), 1996, p. 18, see *supra* note 15.

41 Carr, 1986, pp. 91–92, see *supra* note 20.

42 *Ibid.*, p. 91.

43 *Ibid.*, p. 92.

time to explore the matter more thoroughly, however, he would likely have seen that it is no theoretical or methodological necessity that counterfactual history should be merely wishful dreams. There are no methodological obstacles that would prevent a Communist from posing the question of how the October Revolution might have been stopped or delayed. Of course, the Anti-Communist would likely be more interested in that matter than the Communist, but the difference is one of interest, not method. In fact, dystopian alternative histories are probably just as common as utopian, as shown by the literature on a counterfactual Nazi victory in World War II.[44]

That said, it may be easier to project one's wishes onto counterfactual history than factual, especially with conflict counterfactuals, which deals with questions of how wars could have been avoided. It is natural to ask such questions, not only because we wish it had been so, but because we want to avoid any similar development in the future.

3.5.1. Risk of Bias in Counterfactual History

Carr is not alone in addressing that many counterfactual accounts are too heavily influenced by personal wishes and subjective values. Tetlock and Belkin argue that this increased risk of bias is probably due to the many possibilities in a counterfactual, which leaves the room more open for the thinker to produce theories that represent his or her own subjective perceptions.[45] If so, it seems evident that the risk of bias is a practical and not theoretical problem, in the sense that counterfactual thinking does not necessitate bias, but has fewer obstacles for doing so. This means that we do not need to alter any theory in order to deal with the problem of bias in counterfactuals, but there may be reasons to be cautious when writing or reading a counterfactual theory.

To my mind, Gregory Mitchell offers the best summary for why counterfactuals have a high risk of being biased:

1. Falsification is impossible;
2. there is no direct observation or testing;
3. the basis for the counterfactual hypothesis is often unclear of not explicitly formulated;

---

44 Sørensen presents a list and a discussion on this theme in alternative history in Sørensen, 2004, pp. 71–94, see *supra* note 27.

45 Tetlock and Belkin (eds.), 1996, p. 32, see *supra* note 15.

4. the real historical record is often also unclear; and
5. there are no normative criteria for counterfactuals' scientific coherence.[46]

All these points seem reasonable to me. As regards the concern that counterfactual history has a greater risk of being biased than factual history, however, point 4 may not be relevant. However, for the other four, it seems counterfactuals fall short of factual history. Direct falsification is indeed impossible, because there is no evidence to prove a direct causal link or other connecting principle between the antecedent and the consequent. There are no tests or direct observation. The basis for counterfactual hypotheses is very often unclear or not explicitly formulated, as is evident in, for example, the Munich analogy. Also, there are no agreed normative criteria for counterfactuals' scientific coherence.

How can these risks be minimised? The first, and most easily remedied point on the list above, is the problem of unclear counterfactual hypotheses. It is a main objective of this book, as of other works on the subject matter, to clarify when and how counterfactual hypotheses should be used. The mere knowledge of this would probably serve to minimise the risks involved in counterfactual hypotheses, and not just in regard to the risk of bias. Second, a set of criteria for judging the scientific coherence and plausibility of counterfactuals will help limit the scope of possible errors, and in a broader sense than just the risk of subjectivity. Third, for the problems of impossibility of testing and falsification, I have already suggested that the criteria of scientific coherence should include a demand for indirect falsifiability. Compliance with this criterion will not solve the problem of bias risk, but it will likely reduce it, because fewer counterfactuals would be accepted as scientifically coherent and because it would increase the awareness of the problems and potential of the hypothesis being put forward.

3.5.2. Bias when Altering a Historical Decision

I suggest that it is particularly easy to produce a biased hypothesis when the counterfactual is based on altering an individual decision. An altered decision would often involve a consideration of conflicting reasons or other personal factors. Since many factors cannot be observed in any evidence, it is easier to project one's own values onto the historical decision-maker. For

46 Paraphrase from Gregory Mitchell, "Case Studies, Counterfactuals, and Causal Explanations", in *University of Pennsylvania Law Review*, 2004, vol. 152, no. 5, p. 1564.

example, in the case of the Rwandan genocide in 1994, *The Economist* has presented counterfactual hypotheses that takes, as its starting point, that it would have been right to stop the genocide.[47] Of course, I agree personally with this starting point, but I do not believe any ethical viewpoint should be projected onto historical decision-makers without a closer consideration of the situation. The article takes the concept of universal or objective values as its starting point. Otherwise, for the counterfactual to make sense, the reasons why the relevant decision-makers should have made other decisions would have had to be presented.

One could say that it is self-evident for the decision-makers in question would want to stop the genocide. In fact, one would be hard-pressed to find a clearer example of an act that is more clearly and universally condemned than genocide. However, this is not to say that one should assume that any historical decision-maker should automatically be expected to have agreed to this or any other ethical standard, and less so that this value should have dictated a specific course of action.

Of course, there are those who have argued in favour of including the concept of universal or objective values in historiography, notably Heinrich Rickert.[48] But this is not unproblematic. First, the concept of universal or objective values cannot be applied independently from other factors to judge the actions of historical decision-makers. In general, it is not likely that any value can dictate 'right actions' in any situation, since all valuations can be overridden by some other consideration in a given situation. In the case of the Rwandan genocide, certainly the ones who were executing the mass murder did not agree to the universal value that genocide is criminal. For the Western states contemplating intervention, one must consider that the pace and extent of the murders were unclear at the time; sending in forces would be seen as supporting Paul Kagame's insurgency; that the result of deploying forces was uncertain; and that politicians probably believed they would have risked domestic unpopularity by sending forces. A thorough counterfactual analysis should take all these factors into account, before making a judgement about the possibilities for action. Otherwise,

---

47 *The Economist*, 27 March 2004, p. 11.

48 Heinrich Rickert, *Science and History: A Critique of Positivist Epistemology*, D. Van Nostrand Company, Princeton, 1962, pp. 96–97. See also McCullagh, 1998, p. 129, see *supra* note 4.

the risk of projecting one's own moral values onto history would be significant.

The conclusion seems to be that when altering a historical decision, care should be taken in investigating the personal motives, intentions and character of the decision-maker. Having a clearer picture of the dispositions of the decision-maker, counterfactual hypotheses should then not deviate too far from the factual, as is also in compliance with the 'minimal rewrite rule'.

3.5.3. Conclusions

There are certainly a number of theoretical difficulties with counterfactual history. Some of these can only be addressed if one is willing to accept that there must be a degree of pragmatism in the approach to counterfactuals. For example, one could theoretically argue that altering an antecedent in theory also requires altering an infinitely long series of preceding causes, because of the notion of cause-and-effect, but such a position would conflict with common sense and the practice of science. The 'solution' is to take logical and empirical consistency into consideration when altering an antecedent, and strive to limit the impact of the alteration, thus maintaining historical consistency.

The same pragmatic approach should be taken in meeting the challenges in the other categories listed in the beginning of the chapter. As regards both the challenges of collectivism and limitless possibilities, it seems there is little hope of establishing a general theory. Rather, one will need to scrutinise closely the concrete counterfactual case in order to make a judgment in regard to its plausibility.

The problem of empirical evidence is a crucial issue. There is neither any way to verify the counterfactual hypothesis, nor to directly falsify it. However, as is the case in factual history, it is decisive that there is a possibility of finding 'potential evidence' that may strengthen or weaken the hypothesis. I have labelled this process as indirect falsification, and argue that this is essential to the scientific coherence of counterfactuals.

Finally, there are considerable risks of bias in counterfactual history. However, this is not a theoretical but a practical problem. As such, the problem does not have any implications for theory. However, as a heuristic, the risk of bias suggests that extra care should be taken when altering a historical decision. Such decisions should not deviate far from the decision-makers' actual values.

4

Pragmatic Advantages of Counterfactual Conflict History

In the previous chapters, I argued that the pragmatic advantages of counterfactuals are vital to counterfactual historiography: Since factual history offers stronger conclusions, it is essential that counterfactual historiography offers some value added. In this chapter, I attempt to see what theoretical pragmatic advantages can be drawn from counterfactual history. However, in order to do this, one must first have a theory which pragmatic advantages can be found in factual history, because counterfactuals, as a research method, must say something about factual history. This is not an easy task, because there is no consensus on any comprehensive theory of the pragmatic advantages of historiography today. Therefore, I will mention several approaches to the pragmatic advantages of counterfactual and factual history, and attempt to draw up a list which, though neither exhaustive nor comprehensive, would at least present valuable insights into the potential value added of counterfactual history.

4.1.1. Tetlock and Belkin's 'Functions'

First, I have already argued that the list of pragmatic advantages presented by Tetlock and Belkin represents an unclear combination of "pragmatic advantages" which I would rather call 'functions' and 'types'. However, this is not to say that the various pragmatic advantages may not be relevant in themselves. The pragmatic advantages Tetlock and Belkin emphasise are these:

1. Proving that things could have been otherwise;
2. pursuing the logical implications of a theoretical framework, when applying laws in historiography;
3. strengthening or weakening general theories;
4. showing psychological inconsistencies; and

5. untying historiography from hindsight.[1]

I argue that points 2 and 4 are actually not scientifically coherent, and that points 1 and 5 are actually the same. In Chapter 2, I concluded that the case used to "show psychological inconsistencies" ("If Bosnians were dolphins") is so far removed from empirical facts that it cannot provide any reliable insights. I further argued that applying laws in a counterfactual scenario cannot shed light on the law which is applied, and is therefore not scientifically useful. As for point 1, proving that things could have been otherwise will only be a new and interesting insight, if it in fact does untie historiography from hindsight. If one does not see the course of historic events as more or less inevitable, in hindsight, then it is not new to show that things could have been otherwise.

As for point 3 above, strengthening or weakening general theories, this would probably be a useful pragmatic advantage of counterfactual history in certain cases. For example, if one could argue counterfactually that a democratic state in a certain case would have waged war on another democratic state, this would be useful in regard to the theory – or 'law' – of 'democratic peace', although I am not saying that such cases can actually be found. Thus, it seems that Tetlock and Belkin's approach leaves us with only two pragmatic advantages of counterfactual history, namely untying historiography from hindsight and strengthening or weakening general theories.

4.1.2. McCullagh's List of Pragmatic Advantages in Historiography

Practically all philosophers of history, at one point or another, attempt to state the main pragmatic advantages of historiography. *History and Theory* published a theme issue in 2004, dealing with "historians and ethics", where the subject is debated extensively.[2] Certainly, the perceived purposes of historiography have also varied over time. Among works on the subject in recent years, McCullagh's attempt to map historiography's pragmatic advantages is particularly interesting, as it is broad enough to include many alternative views. He mentions three categories of pragmatic advantages in *The Logic of History*:

---

1 Philip E. Tetlock and Aaron Belkin (eds.), *Counterfactual Thought Experiments in World Politics: Logical, Methodological, and Psychological Perspectives*, Princeton University Press, Princeton, 1996, pp. 7–15.

2 *History and Theory*, 2004, vol. 43, no. 4 (Theme Issue: Historians and Ethics).

1. Historiography may provide entertainment, which is a relevant but subordinate pragmatic advantage.
2. Historiography may provide the basis for general critical thinking, as a by-product.
3. Historiography may provide at least three social pragmatic advantages:
   a. Establishing the identity of social groups, institutions or nations;
   b. identifying trends at work which can enhance or diminish the quality of life;
   c. teaching lessons "about the value or disvalue of beliefs and practices, traditions and institutions which we have inherited, enabling us to see the value of those worth preserving and the need to change those which are not".[3]

I will base the following discussion of the pragmatic advantages of counterfactuals on McCullagh's list, but broaden the focus to include aspects not covered directly by him. For example, there are reasons to believe that historiography shapes several aspects of people's perception of their own reality, and not just their identities. Furthermore, in regard to the 'lessons' of history, McCullagh focuses mainly on the institutions, values and practices that have been inherited. I believe there are strong reasons to also argue that historiography can teach lessons in the form of more specific instructions.

However, the greatest divergence between McCullagh's list and my own approach below is that rather than discussing historiography as a basis for more critical thinking, I will discuss counterfactuals' relevance to the intrinsic value of historiography. This pragmatic advantage is based on the assumption that knowledge of history has its own value, which is not dependant on any instrumental pragmatic advantage. McCullagh writes about the overriding principles of fairness and impartiality, which may be interpreted in light of the self-value of historical knowledge.[4] Others go further and talk about historical research as being important because of the self-

---

3 C. Behan McCullagh, *The Logic of History: Putting Postmodernism in Perspective*, Routledge, London, 2004, pp. 192–193. I have abstracted the list from the book, as it is not presented in list's form by McCullagh.

4 *Ibid.*, pp. 192–193.

value of truth. Dahl labels this the "theoretical function" of historiography, which, in the following pages, I will refer to as the 'theoretical pragmatic advantage'.[5]

In regard the pragmatic advantage of stimulating general critical thinking, I assume that this would be a pragmatic advantage of counterfactual history, if such historiography is found scientifically coherent, because stimulation of generally critical thinking can be said to follow from all coherent analyses in all sciences. Therefore, I will not treat this pragmatic advantage as thoroughly as the others on McCullagh's list.

It is also important to take into consideration that the various pragmatic advantages of historiography are, of course, emphasised differently by philosophers of science or history. Some emphasise the idea that the goal of all science should be to become useful, meaning to increase man's mastery of his surroundings.[6] Others point to the fact that historiography – because by definition it only deals with the past – can have no such purpose, and must attempt only to establish the truth about the past. According to Max Weber, this has traditionally separated historians from scientists in other fields dealing with cultural and social institutions.[7] I will discuss this point below, whether there is a main pragmatic advantage of historiography.

4.2. Historiography as Entertainment

One of the central debates in the philosophy of history in the past decades concerns the relationship between historiography and facts. A particularly heated topic is the controversy which arose after the publication of Hayden White's *Metahistory* in 1973, which essentially argued that the choice between historiographic narratives is undertaken on personal and aesthetic grounds.[8] This viewpoint is part of the more general postmodern outlook

---

5 Ottar Dahl, *Grunntrekk i historieforskningens metodelære* [Fundamentals of Historical Method], Universitetsforlaget, Oslo, 1967, p. 124.

6 E.H. Carr, *What is History? The George Macaulay Trevelyan Lectures delivered in the University of Cambridge January–March 1961*, Macmillan, London, 1986, p. 80.

7 Max Weber, "Die 'Objektivität' Sozialwissenschaftlicher und Sozialpolitischer Erkenntnis", in Max Weber, *Gesammelte Aufsätze zur Wissenschaftlehre*, J.C.B. Mohr, Tübingen, 1922, p. 148.

8 Hayden White, *Metahistory: The Historical Imagination in Nineteenth-century Europe*, Johns Hopkins University Press, Baltimore, 1973, p. 433. See also Aviezer Tucker, *Our Knowledge of the Past: A Philosophy of Historiography*, Cambridge University Press, 2004, p. 44.

on the purpose of historiography, where it is deemed impossible for historiography to establish objective understanding about the past, let alone provide guidelines for the future.[9] I will not attempt to enter into the substantial debate, but I mention it here because it indicates the controversy concerning the position of aesthetics in historiography.

Few practising historians really believe that historiography should be written only, or even primarily for the sake of entertainment. On the other hand, equally few historians would say that entertainment has no place in historiography at all. Historiography's entertainment value, or aesthetic function, as Dahl labels it, is commonly regarded as inherent in historiography.[10] This pragmatic advantage is probably the most important in getting the general public to read historical science. Arthur Marwick has explained that historiography is "poetic, in the sense that there is inborn in almost any individual [...] a curiosity and sense of wonder about the past".[11] However, Marwick argues that historiography's entertainment value is but one of the important pragmatic advantages of historiography, and that other pragmatic advantages must not be forgotten.

Another, perhaps clearer exponent of the idea that historiography should be entertaining is G.R. Elton. According to him, historiography's social pragmatic advantage may indeed be primarily entertainment:

> A good many people simply want to know about the past, for emotional or intellectual satisfaction, and the professional historian fulfils a useful 'social' function when he helps them to know better. He is also, of course, satisfying his own desire for knowledge, and he also is, after all, a part of society.[12]

The 'social function' that Elton refers to is a form of intellectual entertainment. However, Elton denies that this makes historian a mere entertainer. Instead, he likens historians to poets and artists. He believes historian fulfils an important social role not only in entertaining, but also in providing

---

9 The postmodern challenge to the ethics of history is debated in Keith Jenkins, "Ethical Responsibility and the Historian: On the Possible End of a History 'Of a Certain Kind'", in *History and Theory*, 2004, vol. 43, no. 4, pp. 43–60; and Elizabeth Deeds Ermarth, "Ethics and Method", in *History and Theory*, 2004, vol. 43, no. 4, pp. 61–83.

10 McCullagh, 2004, p. 192, see *supra* note 3. Dahl, 1967, p. 122, see *supra* note 5.

11 Arthur Marwick, *The Nature of History*, Macmillan, London, 1970, p. 14.

12 G.R. Elton, *The Practice of History*, Sydney University Press and Methuen, London, 1967, p. 48.

some basis for reflection, which, however, is regarded as secondary by Elton.[13]

In any case, most historians agree that entertainment is not enough to constitute a sound basis for the importance of historical science. McCullagh and Dahl believe the aesthetics of historiography must only be emphasised when they do not conflict with the truth of historiography.[14] This seems to me a satisfactory viewpoint: Historiography should be entertaining only when it does not conflict with the more important pragmatic advantages. Still, the entertainment factor of counterfactual history should not be underestimated. Certainly, this has been a sustaining factor for counterfactual history from the outset. It can be entertaining to imagine what could have been. Most of all, this applies to historical settings where seemingly unimportant factors could have changed all-embracing historical developments. An example mentioned above is the Spanish Armada and the changing of the winds on 7–8 August 1588.

4.3. Historiography's Self-value: Knowledge About the Past

Historiography's self-value is separate from any potential instrumental pragmatic advantages historiography may have. If we can agree with McCullagh that fairness and impartiality are the overriding principles in historical inquiry, then the intrinsic value of historiography must always be the primary pragmatic advantage. If this is the view, then counterfactual conflict history can be justified if it has the potential to uncover more about the past than factual history alone. The main criterion of the usefulness of counterfactuals, in this respect, is whether they can provide any value added, either in the form of conclusions that differ from factual history, or by providing new arguments to strengthen established theories. There are at least four ways in which counterfactual history may have such a pragmatic advantage:

1. Measuring the significance of causes;
2. measuring the level of power of decision-makers;
3. avoiding the teleology inherent in historiography; and
4. strengthening creativity in historical research.

---

13 *Ibid*., p. 48.

14 McCullagh, 2004, p. 192, see *supra* note 3; Dahl, 1967, p. 124, see *supra* note 5.

4.3.1. Measuring the Significance of Causes

According to Max Weber, this pragmatic advantage of counterfactuals is "self-evident".[15] If a historian attempts to establish a hierarchy of the causes in an explanation, it will require judgments of possibilities. This means that historians are forced to make implicit arguments of what would or would not have happened if any cause had been removed from history.

There are other possibilities for explaining historical events than pointing to causal mechanisms, as Weber was doing. Still, if one believes that causal explanations are useful in historiography, there is a strong case for arguing that counterfactual history is relevant. Negative counterfactuals are, in fact, the only means of showing that a cause was necessary for an event to occur. Thus, Weber argues that in order to see the real causal connections, we construct unreal ones.[16]

It is common to argue that counterfactuals are used in all historiography.[17] I concluded, in Chapter 1, that counterfactual reasoning may be implied in most causal explanations, but explicating that it is only useful in as much as it can provide value added. If not, then there is no need to use counterfactuals. Negative counterfactuals may be used to strengthen or weaken existing theories of causal connections.

Positive counterfactuals may also provide value added in comparison with factual history. Arguably, Fogel's counterfactual railroad history showed that railroads were not necessary for the rapid economic growth experienced in the United States in the late nineteenth century. Among others, McCullagh has argued that Fogel's article effectively demonstrates a clear value of counterfactual reasoning in establishing the significance of causes.[18] He argues that "when one is measuring the importance of a cause in a system [...] one has to judge how the system would have operated in

---

15 Max Weber, "Objektive Möglichkeit und Adäquate Verursachung in der Historischen Kausalbetrachtung", in Weber, 1922, pp. 267–268, see *supra* note 7.

16 *Ibid.*, p. 287.

17 Jon Elster, *Logic and Society: Contradictions and Possible Worlds*, John Wiley, Chichester, 1978, p. 7; Tetlock and Belkin (eds.), 1996, p. 4, see *supra* note 1; Robert W. Fogel, "The New Economic History: I. Its Findings and Methods", in *The Economic History Review*, 1966, vol. 19, no. 3, p. 655.

18 C. Behan McCullagh, *Justifying Historical Descriptions*, Cambridge University Press, Cambridge, 1984, pp. 195–199.

the absence of that cause […] and compare that with the actual performance of the system".[19]

McCullagh's argument seems sound. If it is possible to describe a scientifically coherent and plausible counterfactual scenario of the kind which Fogel describes, then the significance of the removed cause can be clarified.

4.3.2. Levels of Power

According to Jon Elster, 'power' is the production of intended and desired results.[20] In measuring the power of historical decision-makers, we must uncover their desires and intentions, and compare them with the results. However, if the result differs from the desire and intention, we do not always know if it is the decision-maker being powerless, or whether his actions were merely misguided. In answering this, we can ask how he could have produced the desired and intended results. Of course, this is, a positive counterfactual. An example is the peace negotiations over Palestine in 1948 and 1949. If it can be established that the UN mediator, Ralph Bunche, desired and intended to create a foundation for lasting peace in the Middle East, and succeeded only in part in 1949, we must assess his tactics. If, say, the refugee problem in Palestine was a major obstacle to lasting peace in the region, does that mean it was a blunder not to discuss it in 1948, or was Bunche powerless in reaching an agreement on the issue? As explained above, the only means of reaching a conclusion on this point is by using positive counterfactuals.

Another example is Jeffrey Record's argument that "none of America's wars since 1945 have been wars of necessity".[21] Record's assessment was that all of America's wars since World War II were subject to choice. More specifically, he claimed that American presidents could have chosen not to get involved. If indeed all presidents after Franklin D. Roosevelt could have avoided going to war, it can only be proven by counterfactual reasoning. One is forced to ask the question: What would have happened if the choice of non-involvement had been made? For example, President Harry S. Truman believed that not going to war in Korea in 1950 might

---

19 *Ibid.*, p. 199.

20 Elster, 1978, p. 49, see *supra* note 17. Elster is partly paraphrasing Bertrand Russell.

21 Jeffrey Record, *Making War, Thinking History: Munich, Vietnam, and Presidential Uses of Force from Korea to Kosovo*, Naval Institute Press, Annapolis, 2002, p. 2.

have led to a greater war with the Soviet Union some years on, which the United States could not avoid.[22] In other words, he may have felt forced to wage war in Korea. If Truman's assumption was wrong, and he had more power of choice than he believed himself, it is historically important to uncover this.

This leads to another important pragmatic advantage of counterfactual history: Insight into the decision-maker's own perception of the situation at hand. Assessing the counterfactual possibilities, inherent in a situation involving a choice, can provide insight into the mind of the decision-maker. In many situations, a historical decision-maker will have felt that more than one option was available at the time of choice. Factual history will only consider the option that was actually chosen, or it must resort to counterfactual thought-experiments. It would do the historical actors more justice to try to understand the situation as it seemed *ex ante*. When choosing war in 1950, President Truman is likely to have considered the plausible development if the United States did not engage in Korea. Assuming that his main desires and intentions were to check Communism and to preserve non-aggression between the superpowers, how well-guided was the decision to wage war in 1950? If Truman's fears were justified, the decision would seem rational. However, if the decision was based on illusions about the possible development in international politics, the decision would seem misguided. This would increase the likelihood that the Truman administration's foreign policy was influenced by ideology or other factors besides rational analysis. In other words, positive counterfactual might shed light on the factual course of events.

Could the same insight be achieved by means of factual history? Possibly. For example, the power of ideology in the Truman administration manifested itself in many ways that can be shown in factual history.[23] Still, the counterfactual analysis provides one more tool for understanding the

---

22 Harry S. Truman, *Years of Trial And Hope, vol. 2, 1946–1953*, Hodder and Stroughton, Bungay, 1956, p. 351. Although memoirs are problematic as historical sources, I see no reason to doubt President Truman's fear of a greater war with the USSR if the USA did not take military action in Korea.

23 This is of course heatedly debated. Some of the most quoted works arguing in favour of ideological explanations of the Truman administration's policy are Athan Theoharis, *Seeds of Repression: Harry S. Truman and the Origins of McCarthyism*, Quadrangle Books, Chicago, 1971; and Richard M. Freeland, *The Truman Doctrine and the Origins of McCarthyism: Foreign Policy, Domestic Politics and Internal Security 1946–1948*, Alfred A. Knopf, New York, 1972.

decision-makers' personal perception. If, in some cases, these perceptions are hard to prove, counterfactuals may be useful.

4.3.3. Avoiding Teleology

This is another way of formulating Tetlock and Belkin's argument that counterfactuals can free historiography from hindsight. Lebow has made a similar point.[24] John Lewis Gaddis is another proponent of this view: "Our responsibilities as historians is as much to show that there were paths not taken as it is to explain the ones that were, and that too I think is an act of liberation".[25] If one accepts the view that history is not pre-determined, counterfactual history is necessarily implied in some sense, which can be underscored by actually pursuing those possibilities in historiography. At least, in order to understand how some moments in history were more crucial than others, historians may find it useful to compare the factual to the counterfactual. This has also been a main point for Niall Ferguson:

> [I]n considering only the possibility which was actually realised, he [the historian] commits the most elementary teleological error. To understand how it actually was, we therefore need to understand *how it actually wasn't* – but how, to contemporaries, it might have been.[26]

Thus, Ferguson seems to believe that counterfactuals are important in avoiding historical teleology. An example could be the negotiations on the Comprehensive Peace Agreement (CPA) of Sudan in 2004, called the 'Naivasha process'. It can hypothetically be argued that the Darfur conflict in western Sudan could have been stopped, if it had been seriously addressed in the North-South peace negotiations. At the final stages in Naivasha, the Darfur crisis exploded and became international front page news, being called 'the world's worst humanitarian crisis' and 'genocide'. Several pressure groups and think tanks argued that the negotiations in Naivasha should have included talks about the Darfur crisis, because of

---

24 Richard Ned Lebow (ed.), *Forbidden Fruit, Counterfactuals and International Relations*, Princeton University Press, 2010, pp. 38–39.

25 John Lewis Gaddis, *The Landscape of History: How Historians Map the Past*, Oxford University Press, 2002, p. 141. Demandt makes a similar point in Alexander Demandt, *History That Never Happened: A Treatise on the Question, What Would Have Happened If...?*, McFarland, Jefferson, North Carolina, 1993, p. 2.

26 Niall Ferguson, (ed.), *Virtual History: Alternatives and Counterfactuals*, Picador, London, 1997, p. 87.

suspicions that the government of Sudan used Naivasha to draw attention away from what they were doing in Darfur.[27]

In order to argue that peace was possible in Darfur in 2004, one could use a positive counterfactual to show that the Darfur crisis could have been included in the Naivasha process, and could have been resolved in 2004. If a solution would have been possible at that time, it is a historically important conclusion, because it shows that the deterioration of the Darfur conflict was not inevitable. It also provides insight into the power of the participants in the negotiations in that situation. At the same time, if the positive counterfactual would yield a negative conclusion, that the Darfur crisis was unsolvable in 2004, or that raising it would have made other issues impossible to resolve, it would also be equally historically important. In this case, we would know more about the necessity of the course of events in Naivasha and about the limitations of the power of those participating.

Could one have reached the same conclusions by means of factual history? Perhaps, although it would have been more difficult, since the Darfur issue was treated fairly superficially in Naivasha, so that no real discussion of it ever took place. Granted, the involved parties were aware of the issue, and some contemplated of raising it, but the probable effects were unknown to them, because they never occurred. By using counterfactual analysis, the effects of raising the non-issue of Darfur during the Naivasha talks can be considered.

However, counterfactual history is not a necessary means for avoiding teleology in historiography. It is perfectly possible, in factual history, to point out crucial factors and moments where history could have taken drastically different turns, without explicitly arguing counterfactually. An example of this is so-called 'contrastive explanations'. By means of comparison, one may avoid the simple teleological errors that may occur in historiography, when a series of causes is traced back from the event one is trying to explain, that is, genetic explanations.[28] Contrastive explanations may have an advantage in showing the possibilities inherent in events and

[27] The International Crisis Group made the most powerful argument in this direction, which was repeated extensively in the media around the world. International Crisis Croup, *Africa Report No. 80: Sudan: Now or Never in Darfur*, 23 May 2004.

[28] See C. Behan McCullagh, *The Truth of History*, Routledge, London, 1998, p. 173; McCullagh, 2004, p. 171, see *supra* note 3.

causes. One could also argue that a contrastive explanation would be preferable to a counterfactual theory, because it is based on factual, not counterfactual, antecedents.

To sum up, historiography can be teleological, but not necessarily. It is possible to avoid teleological explanations by means of factual historical explanations, specifically by using contrastive explanations. Still, counterfactual history can be useful for avoiding unwarranted teleology in historical explanations.

4.3.4. Creativity in Historical Research

Counterfactual history is based on creativity. A historian without imagination cannot write counterfactually. If a historian was to, say, inquire into how the Rwandan genocide in 1994 could have been stopped or avoided, there are never any clear answers. Instead, he would need to dream up many possibilities, before limiting the scope to the scientifically coherent options, and checking the plausibility of these against the evidence. An example is *The Economist's* attempt of pointing to counterfactual solutions in Rwanda: "[W]estern powers could have used force to end the killing. Romeo Dallaire, the UN's soldier on the spot, said it would have taken only 5,000 troops."[29]

How does this clarify matters in factual history? If Dallaire, along with many others at the time, strongly favoured military intervention, why did the Western powers not intervene militarily in time to stop the genocide? Surely, uncovering the reasons for the military non-intervention in the genocide's early stages is as important as uncovering the measures the Western powers actually attempted. In this way, the counterfactual scenario sets historian on the path of posing questions that are important in factual history.

Could the same have been discovered in factual history? To some extent yes, because there will be evidence of debates of intervention and of the official reasons not to intervene, but the reason for the interest in the matter is counterfactual. The non-intervention policy is only interesting if it is plausible that military intervention could have stopped the genocide. If we assume that stopping the genocide was indeed the policy aim of the involved Western powers, then the counterfactual reasoning will deem non-

[29] *The Economist*, 27 March 2004, p. 11.

intervention a failure. Furthermore, since military intervention seemed obviously appropriate to many in 1994, and certainly seems so in retrospect, we must ask why it was not implemented. *The Economist* points to the failure of the American intervention in Somalia the previous year as an important cause.[30] Perhaps this was the case, but the point is that without a plausible counterfactual scenario, the question would probably not even have been asked.

There is no necessary connection between creativity and the quality of research. Still, it is often, to the scientist's advantage, to detach oneself from the common mode of thinking. Not allowing historian to utilise counterfactual thought-experiments at all, even when they help uncover important causes in factual history, is counterproductive.

4.3.5. Necessity of Great Effects?

It has been argued that the relevance of counterfactuals depends on how much the counterfactual effects differ from the actual historical event. Sørensen illustrates this point with an example of a counterfactual assassination of Adolf Hitler. If *der Führer* had been killed in 1944, it would probably have only been slightly important for the course of World War II, but had he been killed in 1939, it may have had far-reaching consequences. Likewise, Sørensen argues that if Hitler had escaped and lived on after 1945, it would probably not have mattered much, since Nazism was already dead.[31] This would imply that the importance of the counterfactual scenario is decided by the effects of the altered event.

There are, however, problems with this view. The pragmatic advantage of a counterfactual is often to strengthen conclusions in factual history. This would mean that counterfactually altering a cause or an event would not necessarily lead to altered effects. In such cases, the value added of the counterfactual thought experiment can for example be to shed light on the level of necessity of the causes and event. If it is widely believed that the American intervention in Somalia in 1993 would have been successful if it had been more forceful, then it would certainly be valuable if this could be disproved. In this case, proving that an altered event would not have

30 *Ibid.*

31 See Øystein Sørensen, *Historien om det som ikke skjedde: Kontrafaktisk historie* [History That Did Not Happen], Aschehoug, Oslo, 2004, p. 167.

made any significant difference may be just as useful as proving the opposite. This is a common pragmatic advantage of a counterfactual, and rules out a criterion of great effects.

In summing up this section, we can make seven general statements:

1. Counterfactual history is only useful to factual history if it can provide different conclusions or strengthen or weaken existing theories.
2. Negative counterfactuals are implicitly invoked in sorting out necessary causes, but this does not necessarily require explicit counterfactual argumentation.
3. Positive counterfactuals can sometimes clarify the level of necessity in historical events.
4. Counterfactuals can be useful in measuring the level of power held by historical decision-makers.
5. Counterfactuals can give insight into the decision-makers' own perception of their power.
6. Counterfactuals can stimulate creativity which may be useful in factual history.

The conclusion is that counterfactuals seem to have their uses in providing insights into factual history.

4.4. A Main Pragmatic Advantage of Historiography?

Before going on to discuss the potential social pragmatic advantages counterfactuals may have, an important question must be addressed: Should historical science only be concerned with the past? If so, there is little point in addressing potential social pragmatic advantages of counterfactuals.

Opinions on the matter are divided. In his attempt to clarify the issue, Jonathan Gorman turned to the United Kingdom's Higher Education Quality Assurance Agency's 'benchmark' for teaching history. The benchmark stated that it is "self-evident that knowledge and understanding of the human past is of incalculable value both to the individual and to society at large, and that the first object of education in History is to enable this to be acquired".[32] The benchmark primarily stresses the intrinsic values of historiography. The social pragmatic advantages are described as important, but subordinate to the intrinsic value.

Many philosophers of history agree that historiography's intrinsic value comes first, and some argue that this, in fact, requires the historian to disregard the social pragmatic advantages. One example is G.R. Elton's notion that the "future is dark, the present burdensome; only the past, dead and finished, bears contemplation".[33] Elton further explains his view on this matter:

> [Understanding the past] involves, above all, the deliberate abandonment of the present. The historian studying the past is concerned with the latter only in so far as it throws light on the part of the past he is studying. It is the cardinal error to reverse this progress and study the past for the light it throws on the present.[34]

Elton writes that he believes his view is unpopular among historians, and the majority emphasises the uses of historiography for the present and future.[35] Others disagree about what the consensus view is, such as David Staley, who writes:

> Very few historians venture predictions about the future, and those who do are viewed with skepticism by the profession at large. On methodological grounds, most historians reject as either impractical, quixotic, hubristic, or dangerous any effort to examine the past as a way to make predictions about the future.[36]

---

32 Jonathan Gorman, "Historians and Their Duties", in *History and Theory*, 2004, vol. 43, no. 4, pp. 109–110. The benchmark was published in 2000 and was produced by the History Subject Benchmarking Group, whose members were: Dr. M. Arnot; Professor D. Bates (Glasgow); Professor C. Clark (Warwick); Professor M. Daunton (Churchill College, Cambridge); Professor H. Dickinson (Edinburgh); Dr. Susan Doran (St. Mary's College, Twickenham); Professor W. Doyle (Bristol); Professor D. Eastwood (Swansea); Professor E. Evans (Lancaster); Professor A. Fletcher (Chair); Professor A. Jones (Aberystwyth); Mr. R. Lloyd-Jones (Sheffield Hallam); Dr. E. McFarland (Glasgow Caledonian); Professor A. Porter (King's College London); Professor P. Stafford (Huddersfield); Professor J. Tosh (North London).

33 Elton, 1967, p. 1, see *supra* note 12.

34 *Ibid.*, p. 48.

35 *Ibid.*, p. 47.

36 David J. Staley, "A History of the Future", in *History and Theory*, 2002, vol. 41, no. 4, p. 72.

Granted, there is a time gap of over 30 years between the time Elton and Staley published their respective opinions. Still, it seems clear that no one knows what the majority of historians believe is the main pragmatic advantage of historiography. What is certain is that, in the past decades, opinions have remained divided, and the pragmatic advantages of history remain a topic of division among historians and philosophers of science.

From one perspective, it may seem rather obvious that a historian's task is, as Elton perceives it, to study the past in its own capacity, since the present and future, by definition, fall outside the scope of historiography. However, it seems equally true that knowledge must be usable for it to be valuable. According to Carr, "Intellectuals may sometimes reason, or think that they reason, for fun. But, broadly speaking, human beings reason to an end".[37] If so, one must consider the uses of historiography for the present and future.

However, what most historians seem to mean by saying "the truth comes first" is that putting any other values first will produce subjective and unscientific historiography. Arthur Marwick has written:

> [I]t is often true that the less overt attention the historian pays to his social role, the better in fact he fulfil[s] that role. The historian [...] is quite justified in apparently neglecting the social purposes of his work. [...] [T]he historian who is too conscious of social needs may well produce bad history.[38]

Marwick does not defend the view that knowledge about the past alone is enough. Quite the contrary, he argues that people's lives are, in fact, governed by history.[39] All the same, his point is that the value of historical science will be less, if it is guided by its potential social pragmatic advantages. However, he agrees that historiography must have purposes outside itself, either by providing grounds for comparing our and others' lives and culture, furthering people's self-perception, or enlightening future action. Gorman takes a similar view, arguing that nothing must interfere with historian's duty to tell the truth about the past, but also that "historical understanding is and has to be an essential part of present-day self-understanding, both individual and social".[40]

---

37 Carr, 1986, p. 100, see *supra* note 6.

38 Arthur Marwick, *The Nature of History*, Macmillan, London, 1970, p. 14.

39 *Ibid*., p. 240.

40 Gorman, 2004, p. 114, see *supra* note 32.

This is a paradox: admitting that historiography must have some social pragmatic advantages and, at the same time, encouraging the elimination of these pragmatic advantages from historical research. If historical science has value because of its social pragmatic advantages, how can historian know which facts are valuable if he has no notion of these pragmatic advantages? To solve this problem, one needs to believe that historical knowledge will likely be useful no matter what. However, in a society where millions of articles and books are published each year, can it really be argued that all are important? A historian who does not take this view is Howard Zinn, who points out that historiography "can bury us in mountains of trivia, which will make any action seem impossible".[41] Without knowing the social pragmatic advantages of historiography, it will be difficult to write any historiography at all. It will certainly be difficult to justify the profession. Zinn's opinion on the matter is this:

> We who think about history need to decide from the start whether history should be written and studied primarily "for the benefit and use of men," rather than primarily "for lucre and profession." Indeed, the first question to be asked by anyone philosophizing about any activity is: What is it for? Without knowing our goal, how can we judge whether one kind of historical work is preferable to another?[42]

Zinn's point is that in order to write good historiography, we should consider its social pragmatic advantages. Whichever view one chooses to take, it is evident that there are arguments suggesting that the socially instrumental value of historiography should be a part of historians' foundation for inquires. Furthermore, since many historians consciously start with these instrumental pragmatic advantages, they can hardly be ignored when discussing historical theory and method.

4.5. Social Pragmatic Advantages I: Identity and Understanding of the Present

An important pragmatic advantage of historiography is that it can enlighten the way we perceive ourselves and our own society. As many philosophers

41 Howard Zinn, *The Politics of History*, Beacon Press, Boston, 1970, p. 54.

42 *Ibid.*, p. 289.

of history and historians have pointed out, historiography is crucial in shaping people's self-image, because it deals with their own 'becoming'.[43] Our knowledge of the past shapes our understanding of the present. Certainly, historiography shapes collective identities, such as nation and class. This can mean both strengthening and destroying conceptions of identity.

The self-perceptive pragmatic advantage includes history as a grounds for comparison. Insight into historical cultures and societies can shed light on our own time. The most general lesson is that our own culture is not the only way of structuring society. Instead, history shows that there are seemingly endless cultural variations in which individuals can function. Comparison with other periods of time and other cultures can also give insight into our own values. For example, if a historical case can show that waging war has actually proven to be productive in the long run, this conclusion is important to anyone who considers himself a pacifist.

It is often difficult to separate the self-perceptive pragmatic advantage from the other social pragmatic advantage, which is history's use as a guide for the future. People's perception of themselves and the world they inhabit is often, though not always, connected with their actions. Still, many historians and theorists argue that self-knowledge is valuable in itself. The important question is if counterfactual history can provide insights into the present-day state of affairs that factual history cannot.

If one thinks of such perceptions in the most general sense, counterfactual history can have much to offer. General lessons have already been hinted at above and in Chapter 1. For example, counterfactual history may be useful in showing how contingent our own civilisation actually is. The example used by Max Weber is the mentioned battle of Marathon: Had the Athenians lost, the entire history of European civilisation would have been different.[44] Such counterfactual reasoning may lead to a questioning of the foundations of our own society. If our culture could easily have evolved into something radically different from what it actually is, then this says something about the values we hold to be important. However, such general

---

[43] McCullagh, 2004, pp. 192-193, see *supra* note 3; Joyce Appleby, "The Power of History", in *The American Historical Review*, 1998, vol. 103, no. 1; Ottar Dahl, *Problemer i historiens teori* [Problems of Causation in Historical Research], Universitetsforlaget, Oslo, 1986, pp. 99 and 105.

[44] Weber, 1922, pp. 276–277, see *supra* note 15.

lessons may often be uncovered also in factual history. Teleology in historiography can be avoided for example by using contrastive explanations.

An interesting example from the so-called econometric history is the slave economy of the American Confederate South before and during the Civil War. It was previously assumed that the slave economy of the South was vastly inferior, because it collapsed during the Civil War. However, reasoning counterfactually, Stanley L. Engerman has argued that in the absence of the war, the economy probably would have survived.[45] This conclusion implicitly shows that slave labour, immoral or not, will not necessarily be incompatible with economic growth. However, this example is problematic because it invokes a 'miracle cause' to do away the civil war. Nevertheless, if one were to find a sound theory of how the civil war could have been avoided, then the slave economy theory would be significant in shaping people's perception of society and morality. In other words, the theory illustrates that there are possibilities for counterfactuals providing social pragmatic advantages as described.

Another general lesson which can be drawn from counterfactual history is about the relationship between possibilities *ex post* and *ex ante*. According to Jon Elster: "If we feel that we have a real choice *ex ante*, it would seem legitimate to explore *ex post* what would have happened if some other option had been chosen".[46] Elster's point is an argument against historical determinism. However, if turned on its head, one may also conclude that if we can show that real choices existed in the past, this would show how real choices exist in the present. In this way, counterfactual history can have an empowering pragmatic advantage.

To some extent, the same pragmatic advantage may well be achieved in factual history. Howard Zinn has argued that factual history can be empowering. The empowering pragmatic advantage implicit in historical possibilities can be achieved in describing 'small victories'. In Zinn's words: "We [historians] can recapture those few moments in the past which show the possibility of a better way of life than that which has dominated the

45 The theory is described in Fogel, 1966, p. 647, see *supra* note 17. Stanley L. Engerman's article was forthcoming at the time and later published as "The Effects of Slavery upon the Southern Economy: A Review of the Recent Debate", in *Explorations in Entrepreneurial History*, 1967, vol. 4, pp. 71–97.

46 Elster, 1978, p. 6, see *supra* note 17. See also Tetlock and Belkin (eds.), 1996, p. 15, see *supra* note 1.

earth thus far".[47] Although 'historical possibilities' does imply some degree of counterfactual reasoning, this does not need to be made explicit. For example, I have, on occasion spoken, with anarchists who argue that the progress of anarchist groups during the Spanish Civil War shows their form of governance can function under certain circumstances. They do not invoke explicit counterfactual arguments to draw this conclusion, but nevertheless find reasons to believe in political alternatives today. The factual 'small victories' provide this empowerment.

A crucial point in regard to the social pragmatic advantages of counterfactual history is that people often do use counterfactual analogies to interpret the world. One of the best examples is the Munich analogy, which has been a dominating influence on international relations since the 1940s. It seems clear that for most American politicians in the immediate post-World War II era, 'Munich' had become the major framework in which international acts of aggression were interpreted.[48] The lesson of Munich, Truman believed, was that appeasement should be avoided and that one should not hesitate to use military force when necessary.

One could argue that Truman's line of reasoning was based on the factual assertion that appeasement policy led to continued and strengthened aggression on the part of the aggressor. This would imply that no counterfactual reasoning is necessary. However, as outlined in the introduction, it is impossible to prove or disprove that appeasement led to World War II without engaging in a counterfactual argument. To prove a causal connection between appeasement and aggression, one must point to the exact historical events in which this connection manifested itself, such as the Rhineland crisis in 1936 or, indeed, the Munich deal in 1938. Furthermore, it is necessary to prove that if Britain and/or France had taken a strong stance in these settings, it would have stopped the fascist aggression in the long run. Even if one could prove that using force or the threat of force would have made Hitler back down in 1936 or 1938, this is different from proving that World War II would not have occurred. Hitler would still be in power, and could even conceivably be strengthened, since he could now claim that the German people had hard evidence that the Western powers were conspiring against them.

---

47 Zinn, 1970, p. 47, see *supra* note 41.

48 For more on the actual uses of the Munich analogy, see Record, 2002, see *supra* note 21.

So perhaps the seemingly solid lessons of Munich are not so solid after all? We shall not know until the counterfactual case is thoroughly explored. For the time being, the point is that counterfactuals such as the Munich analogy shape people's perceptions of reality, whether historians want them to or not. And the only way to prove or disprove these analogies is to engage in a serious exploration of their scientific coherence.

We can conclude that counterfactual history seems to have only limited uses in regard to knowledge about the present, when compared to factual history. There are three categories of pragmatic advantages that seem interesting:

1. General lessons of counterfactual history, like "things could have been different", may be important, but can also be uncovered in factual history.
2. The empowering pragmatic advantage of counterfactuals can be important. Proving that individual choices could have shaped history shows us that individual choices can shape history today.
3. Proving or disproving actually used counterfactual analogies. In cases where counterfactuals actually shape people's perception of reality, only counterfactual exploration can confirm or disprove the analogies.

4.6. Social Pragmatic Advantages II: Trends and Lessons for the Future

From the very beginning, historical science was intended to be a guide for the future. It is well-known that Thucydides wrote the history of the Peloponnesian Wars so that future decision-makers could learn from it.[49]

However, this was founded in a circular understanding of history. In modern times, where most do not believe that history repeats itself, it is more difficult to believe that history is useful for guiding the future. Despite this, as will be argued below, it seems that history does influence important political choices to a great extent, regardless of professional historians' own beliefs. It is equally clear that this influence is often misguided, and has led to misconceptions and faulty actions. Therefore, it is important to ask if

49 See, for example, Richard E. Neustadt and Ernest R. May, *Thinking in Time: The Uses of History for Decision Makers*, The Free Press, New York, 1986, p. 232.

there are problems with how historiography is used, and then ask how counterfactuals may have value added either by correcting this process or providing usable lessons in other ways. However, it is necessary to first discuss whether history can and should be used to make predictions at all.

4.6.1. Possibilities for Making Predictions from Historical Cases

Having established that lessons for the future are a part of historical inquiry, the question remains: Is it possible to learn valuable lessons from history? Or rather: Can historical mechanisms be generalised?

Carr argues that "the historian is bound to generalize, and provides guidelines for the future in doing so". However, Dahl explains,that there is no clear connection between historical and future events, since "history by definition says nothing *directly* about the future".[50] For this reason, making statements about the future is an especially difficult matter in historical science. Another historian, Eric Hobsbawm, thinks that "all prediction about the real world rests to a great extent on some sort of inferences about the future from what has happened in the past, that is to say from history. The historian ought therefore to have something relevant to say about the subject".[51]

Thus, Hobsbawm thinks it is desirable, possible and necessary for the historian to forecast the future to some extent. That does not mean the future is determined or knowable, but merely means there are certain limitations on possibilities and eventualities.[52] Furthermore, Hobsbawm argues that historical explanations and political forecasting are similar in kind, because both analyse the consequences of causes and events. Moreover, both have to take into account the vastness of human relations and the matters of the real world of human affairs.[53] This indicates that historiography is as apt to make predictions as any other social science.

Certainly, there are those who would disagree with Hobsbawn's conclusions. For example, Popper is one of the most vocal critics of the view that history should be used to 'prophesise' about the future.[54] Thus, it seems

---

[50] Dahl, 1986, p. 101, see *supra* note 43.

[51] Eric Hobsbawm, "Looking Forward: History and the Future", in Eric Hobsbawm, *On History*, Weidenfeld and Nicolson, London, 1997, p. 37.

[52] *Ibid.*, p. 39.

[53] *Ibid.*, p. 43.

[54] Karl Popper has argued this in *The Poverty of Historicism*, Routledge, London, 1994, p. 43.

there is no consensus on this issue. This should be kept in mind when considering the arguments below, as a great many of them rest on the assumption that history can inform us about future developments.

4.6.1.1. Types of Predictions from History

Exactly how a historical prediction can be scientifically coherent, or how coherent it can become, will be discussed below. First, it is important to specify which type of prediction is relevant for counterfactual history. According to Dahl, there are two types of historically founded predictions: (i) direct predictions, meaning continued trends or regularities, and (ii) hypothetical predictions, meaning prognoses based on generalisations.[55] It is the second that is of interest in counterfactual history. Dahl has explained that hypothetical predictions have two steps: First, explicitly setting up general hypotheses or 'laws', on the form "if A, then B". Second, making a specific prognosis based on these generalisations.[56] The argument that historical predictions must be founded in laws is a tricky matter, since the very notion of 'historical laws' provokes objections from many philosophers of history, and practising historians as well.

However, it is important to separate between historical laws, regularities and analogies based on causal mechanisms. A 'law', in the strict sense, would mean a covering law, such as the economic law of demand. A 'regularity' describes a correlation, meaning that two phenomena correlate, but it says nothing about why they do. An example, given by Geoffrey Hawthorn, is that in the 1980s, it was a regularity that countries where people were fond of dancing had unmanageable debts. Although the taste for dancing likely preceded the taking of loans, we cannot thereby conclude that the former caused the latter.[57] A 'causal mechanism' states that event B was caused by antecedent(s) A. If such a mechanism is relevant in more than one instance, there may be a case for arguing that the mechanism can en-

---

55 Dahl, 1986, p. 101, see *supra* note 43.

56 *Ibid.*, p. 102.

57 Geoffrey Hawthorn, *Plausible Worlds: Possibility and Understanding in History and the Social Sciences*, Cambridge University Press, Cambridge, 1991, pp. 19–20.

lighten comparable situations by analogy, without requiring historian to formulate any 'covering law'.[58] All three types of generalisations, laws, regularities and comparisons (as basis for analogies), may be used in making a historical prediction, although comparisons are by far the most common. The point is that some form of generalisation must be made if one historical case is to shed light on another.

4.6.1.2. Historical Predictions

If historical science is to be useful for guiding action, it must be because a case is potentially similar to a contemporary or future case. Although no historical conflict pattern will repeat itself in the exact same manner, there should be little doubt that it is possible to find similarities between events. Otherwise, any attempt to systematise human actions at all would be futile. For example, we would have to give up any attempt at law-making, since no law can be constructed if they are only applied in one specific case. We must accept that historical generalisations can sometimes be useful. The real difficulty is establishing when and why these generalisations are scientifically coherent.

Since David Hume's *A Treatise of Human Nature*, philosophers have tried to find ways of logically connecting the 'which is' and the 'which will be'. No attempt has so far been accepted by philosophers in general. However, ways of bypassing the problem have been suggested. Nelson Goodman has argued that Hume may have made a mistake in assuming that predictions were created by observation of regularities. In this sense, it would require events to set the mind in motion in looking for generalisations. This left Hume with the problem of differentiating between scenarios that created predictions and those which did not. However, Goodman regarded the mind as being in motion from the start, "striking out with spontaneous predictions in dozens of directions, and gradually rectifying and channelling its predictive processes".[59] According to Goodman, "We ask not how predictions come to be made, but how – granting they are made – they come to be sorted out as valid and invalid".[60]

---

58 On causal mechanisms and limited generalisations, see Doug McAdam, Sidney Tarrow and Charles Tilly, *Dynamics of Contention*, Cambridge University Press, Cambridge, 2001; William Dray, *Laws and Explanation in History*, Oxford University Press, Oxford, 1964, p. 118.

59 Nelson Goodman, *Fact, Fiction and Forecast*, Bobbs-Merril, Indianapolis, 1973, p. 87.

60 *Ibid*., p. 87.

Goodman's description may give a more accurate account of how the human mind, at least the scientist's mind, really works. Seldom does the historian start off with a correct general hypothesis. Instead, one begins with one or more, checks them against the data, then discards or corrects the hypotheses, checks them again, and so on.

In counterfactual history, the only means of establishing a hypothesis of a causal connection or a law is by indirectly checking the hypothesis with evidence. However, this is often merely an idiosyncratic hypothesis, designed to fit specifically in with the historical case in question. An example is the previously mentioned *The Economist*'s claim that 5,000 Western troops in Rwanda in 1994 may have been sufficient to stop the genocide. This hypothesis can be weakened or strengthened, for example, by uncovering sources of the planned countermeasures by the Rwandan government. If the hypothesis after this check is deemed scientifically coherent and plausible, it may also be generalised. In the Rwanda case, a generalised version could be to say, "Western troops can put an end to civil wars like Rwanda in 1994 with only a small number of troops". Of course, this is not a universal generalisation in as much as it refers to a specific case, but it is a generalisation nonetheless.

Now, can this type of hypotheses be falsified? Again, the possibilities for checking the evidence are limited. Since no two conflicts are exactly the same, it is impossible to falsify the hypothesis altogether. However, if conflicts occur where most or all relevant factors can be said to be similar to the Rwanda case, comparisons may be made. Examples of such factors would be the capabilities of the armies involved, the existence of a civil war with basis in ethnicity, and the risk of large-scale atrocities if the war is not stopped. Such cases may be the recent civil wars in Côte d'Ivoire or Liberia. Therefore, the actions taken in response to the crisis in Liberia could conceivably be enlightened by way of comparison with the Rwanda hypothesis.

McCullagh argues that explaining historical events by analogy is incomplete if taken alone.[61] Of course, the weight of the argument will depend on the quality of the generalisation on which the analogy is based. McCullagh believes that the generalisation must be based on a sufficient and varied number of instances, and that there must be grounds for believing that the causes and effects are connected in accordance with some

61 McCullagh, 1984, pp. 85–90, see *supra* note 18.

known process.[62] The second criterion, regarding the connection between cause and effect, is fairly self-evident. However, the first is somewhat unclear: Clearly a generalisation will be considered stronger if based on many and varied cases, but just how many are a 'sufficient' number of such instances? There can probably be no precise answer to this question. A generalisation based on one instance can, in principle, be true, although it would be impossible to prove it. McCullagh concludes that analogies may be useful probably only as starting points for further investigations, and should not alone be taken as proof of causal connections in a given case.[63] This seems acceptable. Although analogies should not be used as the sole grounds for explanation, they can probably be used to, in Jeffrey Record's words, "clarify the circumstances confronting decision makers, shed light on the stakes involved, and point to courses of action".[64]

Nevertheless, what cannot be ignored is that analogies are used to form actions in response to crises.[65] Specifically, politicians and journalists use analogies both in order to inform actions (employment of an analogy), and to explain the decision to take a concrete action (deployment of an analogy).[66] The Rwanda hypothesis was both employed and deployed by pressure groups and press commentators when the Americans decided to intervene with a small number of troops in Liberia in 2003.[67]

According to Robert Jervis, avoiding the repetition of failures in the immediate past is one of the most common types of lessons drawn by policy-makers.[68] As an example, he refers to Henry Kissinger's description of the rule of Austrian emperor Francis II: Seeing the failure of Joseph II's reform policies, Francis tried to avoid all reform. Furthermore, since the

---

62 *Ibid.*, p. 86.

63 *Ibid.*, pp. 89–90.

64 Record, 2002, p. 3, see *supra* note 21.

65 See, for example, Robert Jervis, *Perception and Misperception in International Politics*, Princeton University Press, Princeton, 1976, p. 217.

66 Record, 2002, p. 3, see *supra* note 21.

67 See, for example, Fergal Keane, "Not since Rwanda have we so cynically abandoned a people as in Liberia", in *The Independent*, 26 July 2003; or John Sullivan, "Foreign Policy is Not About Looking Back", in *Chicago Sun-Times*, 15 July 2003. Interestingly, President George W. Bush did not use the Rwanda parallel to justify action in Liberia. One possible reason may have been that during his presidential campaign, he had claimed (counterfactually) that had he been President in 1994, he would not have intervened in Rwanda, See James Traub, "The Tug of Paternalism", in *The New York Times*, 3 August 2003.

68 Jervis, 1976, p. 275, see *supra* note 65.

attempt to rally public support for achieving Austrian victory in 1809 had failed, all reliance on public support was to be avoided, according to Kissinger.[69]

A similar common lesson of history is the repetition of a success. For example, one reason why Japanese authorities decided that limited war with the United States in 1941 was possible was the lesson from their war with Russia in 1905. In this war, the Russians had settled for a limited defeat instead of pursuing a costly war to regain its lost territory.[70] Another example is the Scandinavian countries' belief that they could stay out of World War II, just as they had stayed out of World War I.[71]

Many examples of deploying analogies can also be mentioned. One of these is US Secretary of Defence Donald Rumsfeld's attempt to justify the invasion of Iraq, by drawing on a parallel between Hitler and Saddam Hussein.[72] The reasoning in this case was much the same as the Munich analogy.

It seems obvious that decision-makers are influenced by historical examples. Therefore, one of historiography's main pragmatic advantages, regardless of what historians themselves may believe, is providing guidance for actions. In so far as historical cases do, in fact, provide guidelines for action, it can also be argued that historical science has a responsibility for providing the most meaningful lessons. This is the case with scenarios where analogies are used with an awareness of the differences and similarities between the given situations, but it is even more important for historians to make their voices heard when false analogies are utilised. If the similarities are few and the differences great, then the person most qualified to uncover these facts would be a historian with competence in the historical case used to formulate the hypothesis.

---

69 Example used by *ibid.*, pp. 275–276, taken from Henry Kissinger's *A World Restored*, Houghton Mifflin, Boston, 1957, p. 211.

70 *Ibid.*, p. 278.

71 *Ibid.*, p. 278.

72 Julian Borger and Richard Norton-Taylor, "Rumsfeld steps up Iraq war talk: US 'cannot wait for arms proof' like appeasers of Hitler did", in *The Guardian*, 21 August 2002.

4.6.2. Problems with the Lessons of Factual History

Rarely does historiography provide explicit guidance for how it can teach lessons of relevance for contemporary decision-makers, or for the limitations of such lessons. It is easy for a historically uninformed policy-maker to draw the wrong lessons or utilise a wrong or false analogy. As Ernest May has explained:

> [P]olicy-makers ordinarily use history badly. When resorting to an analogy, they tend to seize upon the first that comes to mind. They do not search more widely. Nor do they pause to analyze the case, test its fitness, or even ask in what ways it might be misleading.[73]

There are many examples of the wrong analogy being applied. According to Record, one is the Vietnam War, where the Munich analogy was wrongly applied and with disastrous consequences:

> Ho Chi Minh was a totalitarian, but his territorial ambitions were both limited and historically supportable. In any event, his North Vietnam, even when backed by the Soviet Union and China, was not capable of sustaining a program of aggression beyond the borders of Indochina.[74]

Meanwhile, the much more relevant lessons from the French experiences in Indochina were ignored.[75] However, this problem is mainly one of policy-making, which historians can hardly be blamed, although one could perhaps argue that the inclusion in historiography of explicit reflections about the possible lessons of history might reduce the possibilities for false analogies.

A related problem is that factual history provides limited possibilities for extracting more than two types of lessons from a single historical event: one has the choice of either trying to repeat a past success or avoid repetition of a past failure. It is a truism that he who does not learn from history is forced to repeat it. The other side of the coin is, as Robert Jervis puts it, that "[t]hose who remember the past are condemned to make the opposite

---

[73] Ernest R. May, *"Lessons" of the Past: The Use and Misuse of History in American Foreign Policy*, Oxford University Press, New York, 1973, p. xi.

[74] Record, 2002, pp. 17–18, see *supra* note 21.

[75] *Ibid.*, pp. 158–159.

mistakes".[76] History has many examples of choices being justified because they were opposite to previously failed policies. In this category, one finds, as mentioned above, President Truman's attempt to avoid a repetition of the Munich appeasement.

In order to establish more than two possibilities for action based on a single historical case, one is forced to apply counterfactuals. In mapping past possibilities, there are numerous potentially useful lessons. Again, drawing on the Rwanda scenario, *The Economist* proposed several counterfactual measures. One was troop deployment, another was higher pressure from the countries that donated to Rwanda, as the contemporary regime was heavily dependent on aid:

> If donors had made it clear that aid would cease for ever unless the genocide ceased immediately, the *génocidaires* would have found it much harder to persuade the rest of the Hutu elite to go along with their plan. [...] Sterner warnings might have had a calming effect.[77]

Whether or not this measure would actually have helped limiting the genocide is difficult to assess without further inquiry, but the point is that counterfactual history, in this way, can shed light on unrealised possibilities. These possibilities may have uses in other conflicts.

One could argue that it is not necessary to use counterfactual history, because there is never only one historical conflict that decision-makers can draw lessons from. However, there are not always any historical successes that can be drawn upon in a given conflict scenario. Realising this, it is difficult to deny that using counterfactual method may broaden the range of possible courses of action. In establishing which measures were factually effective in conflict management, counterfactual method can also give insight into how and why some measures should be repeated. In establishing counterfactual alternatives that might have worked better, counterfactual history could broaden the range of alternatives even more. Thus, counterfactual history seems able to provide additional useful heuristics for guiding future action.

---

76 Jervis, 1976, p. 275, see *supra* note 65. Jervis refers to George Santayana's famous maxim that "Those who cannot remember the past are condemned to repeat it".

77 "Rwanda, remembered", in The Economist, 25 March 2004, p. 11.

4.6.3. Explicit Lessons for the Future?

To what extent can and should an historian make his projections explicit? If the desired pragmatic advantage of a historical case study is to project it onto the future, must he not explicitly try to explain what lessons his research teaches? For historians, they may not necessarily have any such duties. His aim, after all, is to study the past, not the future. The point I have tried to make is that historiography that is written without any concern for the present and future can easily lead to trivial conclusions. Even if one holds that the 'self-value of truth' is important, it is difficult to deny that most people put a premium on science that may be of at least potential use. The 'potential' part is essential in historical science: Given the restrictions of the discipline for studying only the past, any historical information's relevance to the present and future is by definition potential, and does not need to be made explicit.

However, this realisation, does not lay any restrictions on a historian's attempts to project the lessons of his research. Though it may not be the historian's duty to explicitly explain the uses of his research, it can certainly still be done. Some may even argue that it is the historian's duty, as a human being and member of society, to convey the practical lessons of his knowledge. If one believes that history should, and actually is a central part of the general political discourse, it would also be natural to attempt to formulate generalised hypotheses as a basis for future analogies and/or to explain the limitations of such analogies. This goes for both factual and counterfactual history. As for counterfactual history specifically, this method of inquiry may have a potential for providing a better approach to drawing lessons from cases, because it can point to several lines of actions in a scenario similar to a current situation. In the Rwanda case, it is the counterfactual lessons which are most often used. The cases about military intervention and donor cut-off have been mentioned. This may or may not have worked in 1994, but reasoning in this way can point to many potential solutions to one problem. By consequence, it would provide a basis for analogies to similar situations in the future. Robert Jervis has argued that politicians "who are familiar with multiple possibilities will be less influenced by any single historical case".[78] Counterfactual history is well-suited to provide possibilities additional to those in factual history, because the scope of inquiry into deliberate action is broader. A pragmatic advantage of

[78] Jervis, 1976, p. 270, see *supra* note 65.

conflict counterfactuals could be to collect a pool of projectable lessons, even if one does not make the actual projection until it is desirable.

4.7. Conclusions on Historical Predictability

Since historical predictions are used politically, most often when drawing on analogies, it is reasonable to say that historiography does have a predictive pragmatic advantage. Although these analogies are sometimes false, it can also reasonably be said that historians do have a responsibility – if not in the capacity of a scholar, then at least as an informed citizen – in pointing out that the hypothesis in question has shortcomings. As for historians making general predictions themselves, there is no consensus among historians whether this should be a part of their profession or not. Such predictions can never be 100 percent precise, but there are arguments that suggest that some level of inaccuracy can be tolerated. If one does choose to include lessons in historical treatises, counterfactual analysis can provide value added because it widens the scope of inquiry.

5

Criteria for Counterfactual Conflict History

In this chapter, I aim to draw together the conclusions from the preceding chapters, in order to construct a list of criteria for the scientific coherence and plausibility of counterfactuals. I take, as a starting point, the list of criteria for plausibility as presented by Tetlock and Belkin. As mentioned, this list does not distinguish clearly between plausibility and scientific coherence.

1. Clarity: Specify and circumscribe the independent and dependent variables (the hypothesized antecedent and consequent).
2. Logical consistency or cotenability: Specify connecting principles that link the antecedent with the consequent and that are cotenable with each other and with the antecedent.
3. Historical consistency (minimal rewrite rule): Specify antecedents that require altering as few 'well-established' historical facts as possible.
4. Theoretical consistency: Articulate connecting principles that are consistent with 'well-established' theoretical generalisations relevant to the hypothesized antecedent-consequent link.
5. Statistical consistency: Articulate connecting principles that are consistent with 'well-established' statistical generalisations relevant to the antecedent-consequent link.
6. Projectability: Tease out testable implications of the connecting principles and determine whether those hypotheses are consistent with additional real-world observations.[1]

In the discussion below, I treat points 4 and 5 as one, namely reference to generalisations.

[1] Philip E. Tetlock and Aaron Belkin (eds.), *Counterfactual Thought Experiments in World Politics: Logical, Methodological, and Psychological Perspectives*, Princeton University Press, Princeton, 1996, p. 18. The criteria are further explained in on pp. 18–31.

5.1. Clarity

At first glance, this criterion may seem natural. Certainly, in order to form a hypothesis that may be scrutinised by others, it has to be as clear as possible. However, in this sense then clarity is a criterion of all science, not just of counterfactuals. Therefore, unless clarity has any specific significance to counterfactuals that is not evident in other scientific methods, it should be regarded as superfluous here for our purpose, which is setting up criteria for the scientific coherence and plausibility of counterfactuals specifically.

One could argue that since counterfactuals deviate from facts, it is more important to be clear about the antecedents and consequents than in factual history. This seems reasonable. However, in practice, I would say that it is actually only the clarity of the antecedents that is problematic. I argued in Chapter 2 that most counterfactual scenarios are constructed when starting with the question "how could…?" or "how should…?", but not "what if…?", because a counterfactual scenario is most often constructed with an eye to show significant alterations in the consequents. As a result, the consequents in a counterfactual scenario are not particularly prone to be unclear simply because they are counterfactual. Thus, there is no particular need to focus more on clarity in the consequents in counterfactual history than in factual history, and clarity is in this sense superfluous.

There are stronger reasons for arguing that a criterion of clarity of the antecedents, many counterfactuals are difficult to evaluate, as they do not include the necessary specifications of the altered antecedents. Usually, these are cases where 'miracle causes' are invoked, and as was discussed in chapter 1, there are reasons to argue that such cases should not be permitted in counterfactual history unless there is are further specifications of the causes.

It seems then, that the criterion of 'clarity' should be defined more narrowly. I suggest that a criterion of specifying the branching point should be inserted, in place of clarity. 'Branching point', a term first coined by Elster, is the point in time and place where the counterfactual hypothesis changes the antecedent(s).[2] For example, in the Munich counterfactual, the

---

2 See Jon Elster, *Logic and Society: Contradictions and Possible Worlds*, John Wiley, Chichester, 1978, p. 191.

branching point would need to be specified to when Prime Minister Chamberlain could have decided against appeasement. This would not necessarily mean the Munich negotiations, but probably an earlier date.

It is necessary for a counterfactual hypothesis to specify the branching point in order to provide a clear hypothesis. Facts that can strengthen or weaken the given hypothesis will depend on the time and place of the counterfactual cause. However, it is not always obvious what point in time can be chosen. For example, if the altered cause is somewhat vague, such as 'increased political pressure', then one will find that there may not be any specific meeting or session at which increased pressure could have been decided. There may have been many of such sessions over a certain time period. Still, a specification of the branching point is valuable for a counterfactual scenario. The more specific the hypothesis is, the more likely it is that evidence can be found to strengthen or weaken it.

5.2. Logical Consistency/Cotenability

The principle of cotenability is one of the most commonly accepted criteria of counterfactuals. The term 'cotenable' was coined by Nelson Goodman, who argued that a counterfactual is scientifically incoherent if the antecedent is incompatible with the set of conditions that are necessary for the counterfactual inference.[3] For example, we cannot accept a counterfactual that takes as its starting point "If triangles were squares ...". Such a counterfactual would be impossible to explore. It follows from this that one cannot be free to choose any antecedent for a counterfactual scenario. To do so might break with the condition of cotenability.

Tetlock and Belkin put the most emphasis on the part of Goodman's theory, dealing with the "connecting principles" of counterfactuals. However, it should be noted that the criterion of cotenability in Goodman's terminology does not necessarily require us to "specify connecting principles", as Tetlock and Belkin seem to argue. The specification of such con-

3 Nelson Goodman, *Fact, Fiction and Forecast*, Bobbs-Merril, Indianapolis, 1973, p. 15. Cotenability is a mainstream term in counterfactual theory. See also James F. Fearon, "Counterfactuals and Hypothesis Testing in Political Science", in *World Politics*, 1991, vol. 43, no. 2, p. 193. Tetlock and Belkin also emphasise the importance of cotenability, in Tetlock and Belkin (eds.), 1996, p. 18, see *supra* note 1.

necting principles is, indeed, an integral part of the theory of counterfactuals as outlined by Goodman, but integral to 'cotenability' as such.[4] The cotenability criterion relies on the observation that a hypothesis of a counterfactual antecedent leading to a counterfactual consequent is always reliant on the present conditions. For example, if we say that the match would have lighted if it had been scratched, then we must suppose that there is sufficient oxygen and friction for the match to light.

Goodman's use of the term seems to address both empirical and logical inconsistencies as grounds for dismissing a counterfactual hypothesis. The criterion of cotenability is useful in counterfactual history in order to root out the most paradoxical statements, such as "if Nazis believed that Jews were the master race ..." or "if Muslims were Buddhists ..."[5]. It is self-evident that such statements do not have a place in scientific inquiry.

Although 'cotenability' seems to be an established term in counterfactual theory, I do have some reservations about the term in regard to its accessibility. Although known to those with a particular interest in counterfactual theory, generally historians or even philosophers of history are probably unfamiliar with the term. Therefore, I propose to substitute the term 'cotenability' with 'logical consistency', which I will use throughout the rest of this book.[6] Logical consistency signifies the requirement that a hypothesis is consistent with the logical conditions on which it is based. In the following sub-chapter, I discuss the requirement of empirical, or historical, consistency.

5.3. Historical Consistency/Minimal Rewrite Rule

Many theorists have suggested a rule of this kind. James Fearon's formulation of the minimal rewrite rule is this: "The fewer the changes from the actual world required by a counterfactual supposition, the easier it will be to draw and support causal inferences, and the more defensible they will

4 For a discussion of 'cotenability', see also Fearon, 1991, p. 193, see *supra* note 3.

5 The example of "Jews as the master race" is taken from Aviezer Tucker, *Our Knowledge of the Past: A Philosophy of Historiography*, Cambridge University Press, Cambridge, 2004, p. 227.

6 Tetlock and Belkin uses this as a substitute for cotenability in Tetlock and Belkin (eds.), 1996, pp. 21–23, see *supra* note 1.

be".[7] Tetlock and Belkin's criterion is in line with Fearon's approach. They divide the rule into three, claiming that, in principle, counterfactuals should:

- Start with the real world as it was otherwise known before starting the counterfactual;
- not require us to unwind the past and rewrite long stretches of history; and
- not unduly disturb what we otherwise know about the original actors and their beliefs and goals.[8]

The more seemingly insignificant the altered antecedent– the more consistent with established historical facts the setting – the more plausible the counterfactual history will become. For example, one cannot counterfactually undo the invention of the Gutenberg printing press, because it would imply altering other facts, such as the technological level at the time.

In all counterfactual scenarios, there will be a set of historical conditionals in addition to the changed antecedent. For example, if we counterfactually change the winds of the night of 7–8 August 1588, we would still count on the other factors to be the same. The Spanish Armada would be of an equal size, as would the English fleet and the reasons for the conflict. Thus, the counterfactual factor is consistent with the set of conditionals.

The criterion of minimal rewrite is complicated to apply in practice, because no counterfactual cause will ever be completely separated from other factors. Counterfactually altering a cause will always affect the set of conditions. This was pointed out in Chapter 3, where it was argued that, in principle, changing even a small-scale accidental factor may interfere with the causal chain leading up to the situation at the time of the changed antecedent. This follows from the principle of cause and effect. However, because of the impossibility of describing complete causal chains, it must be acceptable to attempt to limit the range of relevant causes.

Still, the demand for minimal rewrite must be a matter of degree. Some cases are certainly less plausible than others. Eliminating one Frankish knight from the battle of Poitiers in 732 would be more defensible than

---

7 Fearon, 1991, pp. 193–194, see *supra* note 3. See also Alexander Demandt, *History That Never Happened: A Treatise on the Question, What Would Have Happened If…?*, McFarland, Jefferson, North Carolina, 1993, p. 116.

8 Tetlock and Belkin (eds.), 1996, p. 23, see *supra* note 1.

writing the history of France in the eighth century without the entire Frankish cavalry. The central point is that the historian must only consider changing factors that seem to conflict as little as possible with the set of conditionals.

I have argued that a counterfactual hypothesis should ideally start with altering one accidental cause or a historical decision. These would both be small-scale causes. Limiting the number, preferably to one, and scope of the altered antecedents, would increase the chances of constructing a scientifically coherent and plausible counterfactual scenario.

The distinction between logical consistency and minimal rewrite may seem redundant. If the alteration is logically inconsistent, then it would also be unhistorical. However, it would be possible to formulate scenarios that are logically consistent, but nonetheless violate the criterion of minimal rewrite. For example, the mentioned example of a history of France without a Frankish cavalry would not be logically inconsistent.

It should be noted that the criterion of minimal rewrite is connected with the criterion of specified branching point. If the branching point is specified, chances are that minimal rewrite will also be upheld, as a specific branching point will often depend on a single event that could have happened otherwise. However, this may not always be the case. For example, one may alter a single decision of historical importance at a specific time in history, which would comply with the criterion of specified branching point, but commit the error of not taking into consideration the reasons why the decision could have been changed, which could violate minimal rewrite. This has led some to argue in favour of a criterion of the 'subjectively possible'.

5.3.1. Possibility of Choice

The demand for minimal rewrite requires us to change only minor factors, in most cases meaning accidental factors or individual choices. I have previously argued that if the pragmatic advantage of the counterfactual is to provide lessons for future action, it is necessary for the hypotheses to establish how their altered factors could have been changed by an altered choice of action of a historical decision-maker. The reason is that accidental causes cannot provide guidelines for action, as they are usually unfit to enlighten human affairs.[9]

One of Carr's examples is how Trotsky, going on a duck hunt, fell ill and thus missed a meeting which was to be crucial in the ensuing power struggle between himself and Josef Stalin. Carr argued that both the duck hunt and the illness were accidental, in that they were unforeseeable and outside human control.[10] Of course, the decision to go duck hunting was an active choice on Trotsky's part, but there are no reasons for us to believe that he could have anticipated the consequences of that choice. These consequences must be seen as accidental, and thus, in Carr's words, "they do not enter into any rational interpretation of history, or into the historian's hierarchy of significant causes".[11] According to Carr, the reason is that they cannot be used to enlighten future action.[12]

The degree of anticipation is crucial in the Trotsky example. If we agree that Trotsky missing the meeting was important for Soviet history, then a counterfactual scenario in which he did not go duck hunting is only historically significant if we can show that he could have seen the disastrous consequences of his decision. If we cannot show either that Trotsky actually did anticipate this, or that he should have anticipated it, then we must regard the effects of the duck hunt as accidental, and outside human control. In other words, the degree of choice is decided by two factors: (1) How free the decision-maker was in making the choice (that is, that it was not historically necessary and that he could have chosen otherwise), and (2) that he did or should have anticipated the consequences of that choice which were relevant for the given historical scenario.

Another example of the importance of choice is Geoffrey Hawthorn's case of Korea. Hawthorn has argued that the United States could have chosen not to occupy South Korea in 1945, and that had they so chosen, the Korean War would have been avoided.[13] The basis is that influential American policy-makers argued in 1945 that a defensive line against the Soviet

---

9 E.H. Carr, *What is History? The George Macaulay Trevelyan Lectures delivered in the University of Cambridge January–March 1961*, Macmillan, London, 1986, pp. 96–97.

10 *Ibid.*, p. 92.

11 *Ibid.*, pp. 96–97.

12 *Ibid.*, p. 98.

13 Geoffrey Hawthorn, *Plausible Worlds: Possibility and Understanding in History and the Social Sciences*, Cambridge University Press, Cambridge, 1991, pp. 84 and 88–89.

Union should be drawn in the Pacific, not on the East Asian mainland. Furthermore, American intelligence reports argued up until 1950 that Korea was of little strategic importance.[14] In other words, the first criterion of a choice is fulfilled, in that the Americans could freely have chosen differently. The second criterion is fulfilled in part, because Hawthorn implies that the Americans should have anticipated the escalation of the Korean conflict as a consequence of the occupation. The Soviets saw Korea as a potential springboard for invasion, which was an important factor in the process leading up to the eventual outbreak of the Korean War.[15] Actual or plausible anticipation is crucial, because it provides the very reason why the counterfactual choice could have been made. Of course, it is impossible to plan for unforeseeable scenarios, but if a negative development can be anticipated, then it makes sense to take measures to avoid it. If American politicians had no reason to fear conflict in Korea in 1945, there would be no reason for them to choose not to occupy.

But what if there were other reasons for not occupying South Korea, such as economic factors? This would have had the same effects as if the United States had chosen not to occupy based on strategic reasons. In this counterfactual scenario, there would be no initial anticipation of armed conflict, but the effect would nevertheless be the avoidance of war. Would it be permissible to explore such a scenario? If the pragmatic advantage of the counterfactual is to provide lessons for the future, the answer is "no". The aim for such an inquiry would be to say something about how steps could have been taken to avoid conflict, but by eliminating the reasons for planning successful conflict management, there is no way of proving what the decision-makers might have done instead. The result is that one is left with the same lesson as in factual history: The occupation in 1945 was a necessary cause for the outbreak of the Korean War, and that the war would probably not have occurred if the Americans had not decided upon occupation. As explained in Chapter 2, factual history is just as capable of establishing this as counterfactual history (although counterfactuals may stimulate creativity which leads to the conclusion). Thus, anticipation is a crucial element of a personal choice, and may strengthen the usefulness of the counterfactual scenario in question.

---

14 Lewis McCarroll Purifoy, *Harry Truman's China Policy: McCarthyism and the Diplomacy of Hysteria: 1947-1951*, New Viewpoints, New York, 1976, p. 189.

15 Hawthorn, 1991, p. 119, see *supra* note 13.

5.4. Reference to Generalisations

I choose to deal with criteria 4 and 5 under the same heading, because both deal with generalisations. Tetlock and Belkin seem to formulate two separate criteria because of the distinction between general laws and statistical law. Although this distinction is certainly significant in the philosophy of science, it is not central to the theory of counterfactual history. The implication of both variants of 'laws' is that they can be applied in order to project what could have happened if an antecedent is changed.

I mentioned in Chapter 2 that many historians reject the notion that their discipline should be founded in 'laws'. I will not argue that the concept of a 'law' is useless in historiography, but it is probably true that it can never be the only means of explanation. Very few 'laws' of history, if any, are uncontroversial. For example, Dray argued that the universal generalisations of the natural sciences are "peculiarly inept" in historical science.[16] In the real world of history, the causes are so many and so particular that universal generalisations are difficult to make. Since this holds true in factual history, one could argue that the same should be the case for counterfactual history. In this sense, one cannot argue that a reference to laws can be a criterion of the scientific coherence of counterfactuals, although it would certainly increase the plausibility.

However, there is also the concept of "law-like statements" to consider. Law-like statements have been defined in many ways,[17] but in counterfactual theory, it has been treated most significantly by Nelson Goodman. He defines law-like in the following manner: "A general statement is lawlike if and only if it is acceptable prior to the determination of all instances", and "its acceptance does not depend upon the determination of any given instance".[18] Goodman admits that the term 'acceptable' is far too loose, but claims this is still a functional definition. Also, he argues that law-like statements even include some "true singular predictions".

A counterfactual claim would undoubtedly be more plausible if it could draw on a law-like sentence. In fact, any scientifically coherent generalisation that can be used to predict an instance would be useful when

16 Dray is referring to Hempel's covering law model: See William Dray, *Laws and Explanation in History*, Oxford University Press, Oxford, 1964, p. 118.

17 McCullagh discusses "law-like regularities" in C. Behan McCullagh, *The Logic of History: Putting Postmodernism in Perspective*, Routledge, London, 2004, pp. 54–59.

18 Goodman, 1973, pp. 22–23, see *supra* note 3.

writing counterfactually. The question is if such generalisations are necessary to make counterfactual history scientifically coherent. In one sense, the answer is obviously yes, because an explanation of the connection between a cause and an effect is only fully scientifically coherent if it is based on a law-like connection.[19] If one cannot point to a law-like sentence to explain this connection, then there can be no way of knowing if the explanation holds or not.

However, there are two major problems with this line of thinking. First, differentiating between true law-like sentences and generalisations that just happen to be true is a major and unsolved philosophical problem.[20] Second, even if a defensible theory of law-like statements can be found, the fact remains that most historiography would probably be written without referring to such sentences. This is not to exclude that a future theory of law-like statements may win sufficient acceptance for this to be a criterion of scientific coherence. However, as of today, strict adherence to a criterion of reference to generalisations would render not just counterfactual history, but nearly all historiography unscientific.

What seems appropriate for references to general or statistical laws in counterfactual history also seems appropriate for references to limited generalisations: It is not necessary to specifically refer to a generalisation in order to propose a scientifically coherent counterfactual hypothesis. However, if relevant generalisations can be used, they will serve to increase the plausibility of the counterfactual hypothesis. The more explicit and certain such generalisations are, the more plausible the counterfactual will be. At the same time, one must keep in mind that, in the end the historian's interpretation is nearly always crucial, because no social laws known today can predict historical events with certainty. The key issue is whether or not the explanation can be at least indirectly falsified when checked against evidence.

In the category of limited generalisations, I would also include analogies based on comparisons between seemingly similar situations. As argued in Chapter 4, such analogies should not be thought of as potential 'proof' of a hypothesis, but may serve as a starting point for enlightening

---

19 Bas van Fraassen advocates this point in Bas C. van Fraassen, *The Scientific Image*, Clarendon Press, Oxford, 1980, p. 155.

20 Wesley C. Salmon, "Scientific Explanation: How We Got from There to Here", in Wesley C. Salmon, *Causality and Explanation,* Oxford University Press, Oxford, 1998, p. 316.

inquiries. An analogy that does not have a clear basis in a credible generalisation is questionable in its scientific value, but in both historiography and in common sense in general, such use of analogies is commonplace, as it forms the very starting point of inductive reasoning. An analogy may be relevant in shedding light on what evidence may have particular explanatory potential. Taken together with such evidence, the use of an analogy can thus serve to strengthen or weaken the plausibility of a hypothesis.

5.5. Projectability and Falsifiability

There may be an unclear distinction between what Tetlock and Belkin refer to as "projectability" and what I have referred to in Chapter 3 as 'falsifiability'. Indeed, Tetlock and Belkin speak of "teasing out testable implications" as a definition of "projectability". Some important differences must be mentioned. First, the idea of projectability is closely tied with Tetlock and Belkin's emphasis on referring to generalisations. I have argued that referring to generalisations should not be seen as a criterion for the scientific coherence of counterfactuals. Second, the idea of projectability is about directly testing the relation between antecedent(s) and consequent(s). I have argued in Chapter 3 that such direct testing of a counterfactual hypothesis is impossible. Falsifiability, on the other hand, suggests indirect falsifiability, where the hypotheses are strengthened or weakened by pointing to what has been called "potential evidence". For these two reasons, I argue that falsifiability is a more appropriate criterion of scientific coherence than projectability.

A difficulty arises when considering not just counterfactual consequents in the first order, but alternative histories. As argued in Chapter 2, the more orders of consequents in a counterfactual scenario, the less potential evidence will probably be available. However, sometimes it may be interesting to pursue second, third or n-order counterfactuals. For example, the important aspect of the counterfactual scenario of France opposing the Nazi re-militarisation of Rhineland in 1936 is not, first and foremost, whether France could have given Germany a single military humiliation. The case is important, because it can shed light on the entire appeasement policy of the Western powers toward Germany in the 1930s. The reason why post-World War II politicians obsessed about Rhineland and Munich is because they believed these were points in history in which the right decisions could have been made to prevent World War II. If Rhineland had humiliated the German army, it would perhaps have weakened Hitler's ambitions and his support base in Germany.

However, this requires that historians to engage in series of counterfactuals after the initial branching point. It might be argued that French intervention could have led to a German retreat in the short term, weakening Hitler's position in German politics and the hard-liners in the army in the medium term, and finally leading to a less aggressive Germany and even perhaps even to the collapse of Nazism in Germany in the long term. However, this is quite different from checking only the initial counterfactual consequent against the evidence. One can quite easily find plans for responding to the first counterfactual event, but less often to the second or third in the series of effects. The longer the series, the less certain the conclusion. For example, Johan Galtung has claimed that military action against Germany in the period 1933–1938 would have led to an even more unified Germany, resisting any movement "back to Versailles" even more fervently. The reason is that in this phase, Nazism had not yet shown its true expansionist and repressive colours. I leave for others to say whether this is a fair point, but it certainly seems interesting. It implies that military response in Rhineland might have led to a strengthened Hitler, who could play on public support for his policies, since he could have claimed that the Western powers again showed that they were 'anti-German'.

Counterfactuals of this sort can have an effect in shaping policies in response to conflicts. It is a common assumption today that the appeasement policy of France and Britain led to a continued aggression on the part of Germany, and that this eventually was a major cause of World War II. There is a strong case for arguing that this has been significant in shaping many post-World War II military interventions. The criterion of indirect falsifiability may be useful in defining both the limitations and the potential of such thought-experiments.

I consider the criterion of falsifiability to be the most important one for the scientific coherence of a counterfactual, but also the most difficult. Since counterfactuals never happened, which makes direct testing impossible, it is thus a matter of finding other empirical evidence to establish plausibility. However, it must be understood that the difference from factual history is not great in this regard. Here, historians are also unable to test their hypotheses. There is rarely or never any room for experimentation in historical science.[21] The crucial difference in regard to counterfactual history is that factual history can point to that one factual occurrence of the effect, whereas in counterfactual history there are none.

5.5.1. The Subjectively or Objectively Possible?

The possible criterion of limiting counterfactual history to "the subjectively possible", mentioned in Chapter 3, should be seen as tied to the concept of falsifiability, as it has to do with founding counterfactuals in facts. Niall Ferguson argues that counterfactuals should only consider those options that contemporaries thought possible. By this, he means the possible courses of action of which we can show that the historical decision-makers were aware on the basis of contemporary evidence.[22] Dahl is another champion of this criterion for counterfactual research, and he argues in a similar manner.[23] The advantage of meeting the criterion is that if a decision-maker made plans that, for some reason, were not realised, then we may claim that these plans could have been carried through in the counterfactual scenario. Thus, we would be closer to founding the counterfactual scenario in facts. As an added benefit, it also demonstrates a degree of anticipation, as has been pointed out is relevant in the discussion of counterfactual decisions above.

An example is the German occupation of Rhineland in 1936. It is well-known that the German forces were under orders to retreat at the first sight of French soldiers. We also know that, had the French decided to meet the occupation with force, then the occupation would, in all likelihood, have failed, because we have evidence that the Germans laid actual plans for, and indeed ordered, a retreat in response to an event which did not occur.

21 Thor Heyerdahl's experiments are examples of how experimentation can be used in historical science. Heyerdahl's proving that something *could* be done, however, does not prove it actually was done.

22 Niall Ferguson (ed.), *Virtual History: Alternatives and Counterfactuals*, Picador, London, 1997, p. 86.

23 Ottar Dahl, "Objektivitet i historiegranskinga" [Objectivity in Historical Inquiry], in *Syn og Segn*, 1969, vol. 10, p. 578.

We can also safely assume that certain French cabinet ministers contemplated meeting the occupation with force.[24] Thus, the counterfactual scenario for both French military intervention and the counterfactual German response falls under the category of the 'subjectively possible'.

However, what if we had no evidence that the German forces were under orders to retreat if the French intervened? In this case, we cannot speak of a subjectively possible scenario, because we have no evidence to back it up. Should we then be denied the possibility of exploring the counterfactual scenario altogether? Ferguson seems to think so.[25]

In this case, we will get entangled in the 'objectively possible', since we would be forced to speak of actions that were possible or probable, but we cannot factually prove contemporaries planned for or anticipated. Then it is up to historian's judgment to consider what was probable and what was not, on the basis of other facts. If the sources of German plans for French intervention in Rhineland in 1936 were absent, I would say a German retreat can arguably be a plausible outcome. Although Hitler could be considered to be a loose cannon, the German political and military leadership knew that Germany was not ready for a war with the Western powers in 1936. Even without the actual retreat orders, other facts suggest that the Rhineland intervention was a gamble. If we agree on this, then the objectively possible scenario is, in this case, still quite plausible.

Sørensen has argued that although the criterion of the subjectively possible has advantages, it is too restrictive to limit counterfactual research *only* to the subjectively possible. Sometimes we may encounter events which contemporaries, in all likelihood, anticipated and planned for, but where they left no concrete evidence of their thinking on the matter.[26] Another relevant point is that history often takes turns which were seen by contemporaries as impossible until they actually occurred. Sørensen uses the break-up of the Swedish–Norwegian union in 1905 as an example. Few, if any, would have argued in 1904 that the Norwegian parliament would unanimously and unilaterally declare the end of the union only one year later. But it did actually occur. Likewise, we can imagine that unexpected

---

24 Robert J. Young, *In Command of France: French Foreign Policy and Military Planning 1933-1940*, Harvard University Press, Cambridge, Massachusetts, 1978, p. 121.

25 Ferguson (ed.), 1997, p. 86, see *supra* note 22.

26 Øystein Sørensen, *Historien om det som ikke skjedde: Kontrafaktisk historie* [History That Did Not Happen], Aschehoug, Oslo, 2004, pp. 170–172.

events could occur counterfactually, without that seeming plausible to contemporaries.[27]

The conclusion is that some counterfactual scenarios do not require us to found our conclusions in the subjectively possible. At the same time, it is unquestionably helpful if we *can* claim that we are researching the subjectively possible. The more facts and sources used to uphold the counterfactual hypothesis, the more acceptable this scenario will be. Both showing plans and anticipation in contemporaries will strengthen the hypothesis. That does not mean that *only* evidence of plans and anticipation will be relevant facts in counterfactual history.

5.6. Additional Criterion I: Pragmatism

In addition to the criteria proposed by Tetlock and Belkin, and the modifications of their criteria I suggested, I propose two new criteria that I believe should be added to the list. The first and most important of these is the concept of 'pragmatism'.

In order to see clearly the importance of the pragmatism of counterfactuals, one should first consider the relation between counterfactuals and truth. Counterfactuals are untrue by definition of correspondence to the real world. This means that whenever counterfactuals are to be allowed in historical science, it must be because they fulfil some purpose outside themselves. Some of the ways in which this can be accomplished have been discussed in Chapter 4. To recapitulate, the main pragmatic advantages seem to be these:

1. Measure the significance of causes;
2. measure the level of power wielded by historical actors;
3. give insight into historical decision-makers' own perception of their influence;
4. stimulate creativity in historical science;
5. provide an empowering pragmatic advantage;
6. diminish the prospect of faulty uses of counterfactual history deployed to justify policies;
7. provide creativity for future policies and minimise the restrictions of factual historical lessons; and

27 *Ibid.*, pp. 170–172.

8. provide heuristics for future policies.

It may not be necessary to state explicitly the pragmatic advantages of a counterfactual inquiry, particularly if they are intended to guide future actions. Should a historian choose to comment on the actual or potential pragmatic advantages of a counterfactual, however, it would serve to strengthen the appeal of that thought experiment. If pragmatic advantages are not mentioned, the counterfactual hypotheses run the risk of being dismissed by other scholars, because they fail to show how the research is anything but what Carr calls "a parlour game of the might-have-beens of history".[28] Implicit or explicit, if the counterfactual says little or nothing of relevance to the real world – past, present or future – there is little point in pursuing that thought experiment in the first place.

5.7. Additional Criterion II: Historical Values

As explained in the previous chapters, exploring counterfactuals will sometime imply arguing what *should* have been done. Chapter 3 makes it clear that this has some peculiar difficulties, because arguing counterfactually makes it easier to project one's own personal values onto history, which may distort the presentation of facts and theories.

I argue in Chapter 3 that, when the altered antecedent is a decision, it is necessary to consider the actual values of the historical decision-maker, as a safeguard against bias. The counterfactual should endeavour, to the extent possible, not to compromise the decision-maker's values. Specifically, personal choices can potentially be influenced by a number of factors, including habits, reasons, emotions, character traits, biological needs, personal needs, unconscious psychological dispositions, or subjectively perceived cultural norms or social norms and potential social sanctions.[29] To this list I would also add personal valuations, including perceived interests, being a probable driving force behind most significant political decisions.

An example is Colin Powell's role in shaping the American foreign policy towards Bosnia in the 1990s. Powell was a strong advocate against American troop deployment in Bosnia. This was important for the Clinton

---

28 Carr, 1986, pp. 91–92, see *supra* note 9.

29 The list of common kinds of causes of individual human actions is taken from C. Behan McCullagh, *The Truth of History*, Routledge, London, 1998, p. 214. The comprehensiveness of the list may be debatable, but the point here is merely to specify the most common kinds.

administration's decision to "lift and strike", meaning that they would support arming the Bosnians and use air power to protect them while they received weapons and training.[30] Now, if we were to counterfactually alter Powell's decisions, the alteration must be based on Powell's own valuations as much as possible. It has been argued that the most important element in Powell's dispositions was avoiding another Vietnam. As one historian puts it: "Powell made avoidance of another Vietnam his life's mission".[31] If this is correct, we would find it difficult to change Powell's carefulness in regard to American troop deployment, because it would not be in line with Powell's dispositions as manifested in his career since the 1970s. Any change in Powell's decisions should then take into account the Vietnam perspective and explain how Powell could have come to see major differences between the Bosnian Serbs and the Vietcong.

Jeffrey Record has argued that Powell actually misinterpreted the situation, and drew a false analogy between the two conflicts.[32] If this was indeed the case, then we could base Powell's counterfactual decisions on a different, but plausible, interpretation of the facts at hand. This would accomplish two things. First, it would make the counterfactual more in line with Powell's person and values. Second, it would base the counterfactual on the value of a historical decision-maker instead of the historian's value.

Two modifications must be made in regard to this. First, one must realise that it is impossible not to alter *any* of the decision-maker's valuations in counterfactual history. When changing Powell's view of the situation in Bosnia, one is bound to change some valuations, because this includes how he came to view the facts, and what weight he gave to different assessments. The point, however, is that some of these valuations are much more situational and short term than the values included in "his life's mission". When writing what should have been done, a historian must strive to rewrite such valuations as little as possible, and as plausible as possible.

Second, values can never be based entirely outside a historian's own interests. He chooses both the decision-makers and the questions he wants to explore. In this choice lies a subjective valuation. This, however, is quite

30 Steven L. Burg and Paul S. Shoup, *The War in Bosnia-Herzegovina: Ethnic Conflict and International Intervention*, M. E. Sharpe, Armonk, 1999, pp. 250–251.

31 Jeffrey Record, *Making War, Thinking History: Munich, Vietnam, and Presidential Uses of Force from Korea to Kosovo*, Naval Institute Press, Annapolis, 2002, p. 30.

32 *Ibid.*, p. 118.

unavoidable, and the problem is the same in factual as in counterfactual history. It does not mean that the answers will be as subjective as the questions.

5.8. The Rules and Heuristics

Three of the criteria that remain after the discussion above qualify as *rules of scientific coherence*, meaning that compliance is essential if the counterfactual hypotheses are to be considered scientific. Five of the criteria are *heuristics of plausibility*. These are dimensions along which counterfactual hypotheses can be measured in regard to their credibility, and the degree is decided by the analysis of the available evidence.

The purpose of the differentiation between the two categories of criteria is to clarify that the first three – the rules – represent the threshold for labelling a counterfactual hypothesis as scientific. If a hypothesis is in breach of one of these rules, it would require us to regard it as closer to counterfactual fiction than counterfactual history in a scientific sense. Non-compliance with the criteria of plausibility, however, would not necessarily require us to do the same. However, the distinction between the two categories – the rules of scientific coherence and the heuristics of plausibility – should not be regarded as definite. Typically, a hypothesis that has a high level of compliance with the rule of falsifiability would in most cases also be more plausible.

One challenge when setting up rules of scientific coherence is that many hypotheses will not be in either *full* compliance or in *full* breach. In regard to falsifiability, for example, there may be plenty of evidence for hypothesis A, and only *potential* evidence for hypothesis B. Are we then to label hypothesis B as 'scientifically incoherent'? Such an approach seems too rigid, as there would be a risk that one may abandon hypotheses that could prove fruitful in time, for example if new evidence should surface. Considering this, the rules of scientific coherence should be applied 'negatively', in the sense that a hypothesis should be labelled 'scientifically incoherent' if in direct breach of the rules. In this way, the rules will not lead to the scrapping of hypotheses with only limited or potential scientific value.

A distinction between the two types of heuristics may also be useful. The first four *heuristics* below deal mainly with the *plausibility of the antecedent*, whereas the final (reference to generalisations) deals mainly with the *plausibility of the consequent*. The division may seem somewhat artificial, because in many cases it would not be possible to separate the plausibility of the antecedent from that of the consequent. For example, the criterion of "the subjectively possible" is first and foremost important in assessing the possibility of a changed historical decision (antecedent). However, the contemporary assessment of possible decisions is inseparable from the contemporary evaluation of the possibility for the desired outcomes of such decisions, which again is likely to be based on the actual possibility for the desired outcomes (plausibility of the consequent). Still, I believe the differentiation serves a practical purpose in clarifying the heuristics' respective purposes.

5.8.1. The Rules of Scientific Coherence

A counterfactual hypothesis should be considered scientifically coherent unless in breach of these three rules:

1. Logical consistency: Counterfactual alterations must be logically consistent with the conditions on which they are based.
2. Pragmatism: A counterfactual hypothesis must be of, at least, potential significance to historiography, because otherwise the hypothesis falls outside the scope of science, as it says nothing about the real world per se.
3. Falsifiability: A counterfactual must be indirectly falsifiable. There must be at least potential empirical evidence that can be used to strengthen or weaken the hypotheses.

5.8.2. The Heuristics of Plausibility

The degree of plausibility of counterfactual hypotheses can be measured according to these heuristics:

- Minimal Rewrite Rule: Counterfactual scenarios should require altering as little as possible from history, meaning small-scale and few antecedents (preferably one accidental cause or an individual decision).
- Specified Branching Point: Counterfactual alterations of antecedents should be specified as narrowly as possible in time and place.
- The Subjectively Possible: Counterfactuals will be more plausible if they are based on alternatives which we know from evidence

that contemporaries contemplated. The alternative is to show that the hypothesis is at least *objectively possible*.

- Historical Values: When exploring counterfactual *decisions*, the alterations should take into consideration the dispositions of the historical decision-maker, in order to reduce the likelihood of biased theories.
- Reference to Generalisations or Analogous Situations: References to generalisations, whether of the limited or the general kind, will increase the plausibility of counterfactual hypotheses. This heuristic also includes analogies that are based only on comparisons between similar situations, if such comparisons help shed light on factors that may have explanatory force.

5.9. Conclusions on the Parameters of Counterfactual History

The suggested criteria for scientific coherence and plausibility attempt to provide guidelines for the evaluation of counterfactual hypotheses, in particular for whether a given hypothesis should be seen as being closer to scientific inquiry on the one hand, or to counterfactual fiction or unfounded speculation on the other. In Part III, I will attempt to apply these criteria to three specific hypotheses.

What about the relation between factual and counterfactual history? I argued in Chapter 3 that there may be cases where counterfactual history can provide value added in comparison with factual history. There is no doubt that the answers resulting from counterfactual history will necessarily be more speculative than those resulting from factual history. However, what counterfactual history lacks in precision, it may make up for in terms of *fruitfulness*. Dahl has argued that the possibility of precise answers is less important if the hypothesis is likely to produce fruitful answers, in the sense that they could inspire debate and give direction to future research.[33]

This is one reason why the criterion of pragmatism is central. I have argued that counterfactual thought-experiments are not scientific if there is no value added in regard to our understanding of history. This must be an aim in any counterfactual scientific inquiry. If a counterfactual hypothesis does not shed light on history, there is no scientific purpose in pursuing it.

---

33 Dahl, 1969, p. 122, see *supra* note 23.

Counterfactual history should be seen not as a genre or a paradigm of historiography, as Ferguson has suggested, but rather as a method of inquiry.

I have argued that counterfactual thought-experiments can lead to greater creativity in historical research. Certainly this will seem objectionable to some. But if an historian engages in counterfactual analysis and the result is more fruitful research, there is no rational reason to deny the use of this tool.

PART III

COUNTERFACTUALS IN THE HISTORIOGRAPHY OF THE ARMED CONFLICT IN BOSNIA-HERZEGOVINA IN 1993

6

Brief Historical Background and Selection of Hypotheses

6.1. Bosnia-Herzegovina in the First Half of 1993

In this chapter, I briefly describe the events immediately before the break-out of war in Bosnia-Herzegovina, the course of the war, and the international peace plans that were introduced throughout the war. I then comment on some of the counterfactual hypotheses that have been asserted in relation to this conflict, and give reasons for the selection of three of these hypotheses for further scrutiny.

By far, the most thorough description is about the events in the first half of 1993, and with emphasis on those connected with the international community's response to the crisis in general, and with the Vance–Owen plan in particular. This is because the hypotheses under discussion in the following chapters deal with the international community's response to the crisis in Bosnia-Herzegovina in the first half of 1993.

The historical description in this chapter is intended only to provide a brief background to those who may be less familiar with the course of the war. It is not intended to discuss any hypotheses, only to cover the most basic events of the war. Only those events that are clearly relevant to the discussions in the subsequent chapters will be presented here. For this reason, the chapter does not enter into the debate about the causes for the dissolution of Yugoslavia or for the origins of the war. Although there is certainly a connection between the origins of the war and the concrete war aims of the parties – which are relevant to the discussion in the following chapters – I believe it is sufficient here to describe only the latter.

This book only studies three selected hypotheses relating to the potential for conflict resolution of the war in Bosnia-Herzegovina in the first half of 1993. The narrow focus is the reason why no attempts will be made to provide an analysis of the different armed conflicts which I refer to as 'the war', its context, its ethical and moral aspects, and so on, except when this is relevant to the discussion of the hypotheses.

Critics may argue that in not providing a complete account of the origins of dissolution and war, this book may mislead readers into believing that the war criminals that were responsible for the atrocities of the war in Bosnia-Herzegovina are implicitly excused, or that the significance of their actions are depicted as less important. I would disagree with such notion. There are countless accounts of the origins of the war, and even more source material documenting these facts, including the official documents from the proceedings and rulings of the International Criminal Tribunal for the Former Yugoslavia (ICTY). My approach does not alter or downplay these facts. My interest is in narrowing the focus of this book, so that the necessary emphasis can be put on the core issues to be discussed: To show how counterfactual hypotheses are integral – consciously or not – to the historiography of the war in Bosnia-Herzegovina and to analyse how such hypotheses have both historiographical limitations and advantages that can be clarified through informed use of counterfactual theory.

6.1.1. Prologue to Bosnia-Herzegovina: The Dissolution of the Former Yugoslavia

The state of Yugoslavia broke apart, following years of dramatic changes in Yugoslavia's economy, ideology, international relations and domestic politics. On 25 June 1991, Slovenia and Croatia declared independence from Yugoslavia. This provoked a short military intervention in Slovenia by the Yugoslav People's Army (JNA), dominated and led from Belgrade.[1] The war in Slovenia quickly came to an end, however, as the JNA withdrew on 18 July 1991, when fighting in Croatia became the JNA's chief concern. 12.2 percent of the population in Croatia were Serbs.[2] This minority came to control a large part of the country, which it held until 1995. A UN-backed ceasefire was agreed on 2 January 1992, after which the UN deployed a peace-keeping force (UN Protection Force, or 'UNPROFOR') in Croatia from 8 March 1992 onward.[3]

1 ICTY, *Prosecutor v. Mladen Naletilić, aka "TUTA" and Vinko Martinović, aka "STELA"*, Judgement, 31 March 2003, IT-98-34-T, para. 13 (http://www.legal-tools.org/doc/f2cfeb/) ('TUTA and STELA Judgment').

2 Susan Woodward, *Balkan Tragedy: Chaos and Dissolution After the Cold War*, The Brookings Institution, Washington, D.C., 1995, p. 33.

3 *Ibid*., p. 188.

6.1.2. Bosnia-Herzegovina: Three Phases of War

In the same period, tensions in Bosnia-Herzegovina were growing rapidly, as the three main ethnic groups were seeking to consolidatetheir political, territorial and military bases. It is now known that the leaders of neighbouring Serbia and Croatia, Slobodan Milošević and Franjo Tuđjman, met as early as March 1991 to discuss the partitioning of Bosnia-Herzegovina between them.[4] In 1991, Bosnia-Herzegovina had a population of 4.35 million, of which 43.7 percent were Bosnian Muslims, 31.3 percent were Serbs and 17.3 percent were Croats.[5] A referendum on independence was held between 29 February and 1 March 1992. The result was overwhelmingly in favour of secession, although the process was boycotted by the Bosnian Serbs (the self-proclaimed *Assembly of the Serb Nation in Bosnia and Herzegovina* – under the leadership of Radovan Karadžić and his Serbian Democratic Party – had proclaimed the *Republic of the Serb people of Bosnia-Herzegovina* as early as 9 January 1992, as part of the federal Yugoslav state). The independent state of Bosnia-Herzegovina was proclaimed on 3 March 1992. Fighting spread, as Bosnian Serb fighters and the JNA attacked different parts of Bosnia-Herzegovina, and this soon escalated into a full-blown war.[6]

On 6 and 7 April 1992, the EC and the United States, respectively, formally recognized Bosnia-Herzegovina as an independent country. Croat nationalists in Western Herzegovina proclaimed the state of Herzeg-Bosnia on 3 July 1992.[7] It was evident that the Bosnian Croats and Bosnian Serbs were working toward the goal of joining the states of their neighbouring co-nationals.[8]

Bosnia-Herzegovina was hit the hardest by far in the wars in ex-Yugoslavia in the period 1991–1995. In the end, over 100,000 people probably lost their lives as a consequence of the war and over three million were

4 TUTA and STELA Judgment, para. 13, see *supra* note 1; International Criminal Tribunal for Yugoslavia, *Prosecutor v. Slobodan Milošević*, Amended Indictment "Bosnia and Herzegovina", 22 November 2002, IT-02-54-T, para. 57 (http://www.legal-tools.org/doc/e6c0ba/).

5 Tim Judah, *The Serbs: History, Myth and the Destruction of Yugoslavia*, Yale University Press, New Haven, 1997, p. 317.

6 TUTA and STELA Judgment, para. 14, see *supra* note 1.

7 Woodward, 1995, pp. 231 ff., see *supra* note 2.

8 *Ibid.*, p. 284.

displaced.[9] The estimates of the loss of life vary: The project "The Bosnian Book of the Dead" concluded that "at least 97,207 people were killed", but that there may have been more. The Prosecutor's Office of ICTY has put the figure at 110,000 people.[10] The CIA has estimated the death toll to be 237,500, with an additional 2.7 million as displaced or refugees, while Croatian demographer Vladimir Žerjavić has put the number of direct deaths at 215,000.[11]

During the first phase of warfare, until mid-1993, the Bosnian Serb Army (VRS, formally formed in May 1992) quickly occupied and held about 70 percent of the country's territory.[12] The Bosnian Serb Army had the advantage of having integrated significant components from the old Yugoslav People's Army, including much of its infrastructure and equipment. Serb forces in Krajina and Bosnia-Herzegovina were mainly formed from JNA units composed of residents from those areas. They were equipped with JNA equipment that was left behind after the JNA formally left Bosnia-Herzegovina in May 1992. Although it is difficult to estimate the number of fighters and equipment at the disposal of the parties – all had hidden some equipment before the war and all had some military production capacity – there is general agreement that although the VRS were fewer in numbers than the Bosnian Government forces, they were superior in weapons, and particularly in heavy weapons.[13] Most analysts also agree that the Army of the Government of Bosnia-Herzegovina (ArBiH) and Bosnian

---

9 The estimate of displaced persons and refugees is taken from Leo Tindemans *et al.*, *Unfinished Peace: Report of the International Commission on the Balkans*, Carnegie Endowment for International Peace, Washington, D.C., 1996, p. 7.

10 *BBC News*, 22 June 2007. The Bosnian Book of the Dead was a three year study carried out by the Research and Documentation Center in Sarajevo.

11 Sabrina P. Ramet, *The Three Yugoslavias: State-Building and Legitimation, 1918–2005*, Woodrow Wilson Center Press, Washington, D.C., 2006, pp. 466–467 (estimates from both the CIA and Žerjavić).

12 The figure of 70 percent is commonly accepted. See, for example, John Major, *The Autobiography*, HarperCollins Publishers, London, 1999, p. 534; and Woodward, 1995, p. 270, see *supra* note 2.

13 Barbara Ekwall-Uebelhart and Andrei Raevsky, *Managing Arms in Peace Processes: Croatia and Bosnia-Herzegovina*, United Nations Institute for Disarmament Research (UNIDIR), Disarmament and Conflict Resolution Project, Geneva, 1996, pp. 14–15. See also General Rupert Smith, *The Utility of Force: The Art of War in the Modern World*, Alfred A. Knopf, New York, 2007, p. 352.

Croat forces (HVO) suffered from less military experience, poorer organisation and less time for preparation.[14]

The second phase of the war, which lasted from mid-1993 to February 1994, was characterised by fighting between the Bosnian Croats and Bosnian Muslims. Important developments included a build-up of the capacity of the ArBiH forces and Bosnian Serb failure to win the war in Bosnia-Herzegovina outright.[15]

The third phase, from March 1994 to the end of the war, was characterised by an alliance between the Bosnian Croats and the Bosnian Government, and the successful offensives of the HV (Croatian army). Toward the end, in the summer of 1995, these forces made dramatic advances both in Croatia and Bosnia-Herzegovina, and NATO air forces and UNPROFOR ground forces carried out strikes against VRS positions. The most dramatic event in this phase was the changes in territorial control resulting particularly from Operation Flash in May and Operation Storm in August 1995.[16] The latter operation was particularly effective: In two days, the Croat forces and the ArBiH drove out the Serbs from all Serbian-held areas in Croatia except eastern Slavonia.[17] Although the operation was "strongly deplored" and partially condemned by the UN Security Council, it was a major success for the Croatian war effort.[18] Successful offensives in Bosnia-Herze-

---

14 Central Intelligence Agency (CIA), Office of Russian and European Analysis, *Balkan Battlegrounds: A Military History of the Yugoslav Conflict, 1990–1995*, vol. 1, CIA, Washington, D.C., 2002, pp. 140–144. Many estimates of the parties' strength in terms of number and equipment have been put forward. In late February 1993, the European Community Monitoring Mission put the HVO to 45,000–55,000 troops, the ArBiH to 50,000–60,000 (not including militia and paramilitary), and VRS to 70-80,000 with significantly more heavy equipment. Military historian Edgar O'Ballence, relying on German intelligence figures, has argued that in November-December 1992 there may have been some 30,000 in the HVO with an additional 40,000 mobilised policemen; 100,000 in the ArBiH, and 90,000 regulars and 200,00 paramilitaries in the Bosnian Serb ranks, see Charles R. Schrader, *The Muslim-Croat Civil War in Central Bosnia: A Military History, 1992–1994*, Texas A&M University Press, College Station, 2003, pp. 21–22.

15 CIA, 2002, vol. 1, pp. 207 and 219–220, see *supra* note 14.

16 For a brief description of the operations, see Ramet, 2006, pp. 455–456 and 463–465, see *supra* note 11.

17 CIA, 2002, vol. 1, pp. 367–377, see *supra* note 14; James Gow, *Triumph of the Lack of Will: International Diplomacy and the Yugoslav War*, Hurst, London, 1997, p. 278.

18 UN Security Council resolution 1009, S/RES/1009 (1995), 10 August 1995 (http://www.legal-tools.org/doc/abfdb0/).

govina followed the events in Croatia. By the end of August 1995, the Bosnian Serb territorial control had been reduced from about 70 percent of Bosnia-Herzegovina to about 50 percent.[19] The last major operation by ArBiH was conducted from 13 September to 12 October 1995, involving some 16,000 troops.[20]

Crimes against civilians occurred on all sides, but by far the worst was perpetrated by the Serbs, against the Bosnian Muslims. The CIA has estimated that 156,000 civilians lost their lives in the fighting, of which all but 10,000 were killed in territory held by the Bosnian Government or the HVO. Croatian demographer Vladimir Žerjavić has estimated that out of 215,000 killed, 160,000 were Bosnian Muslims, and the Serbs were responsible for 186,000 of the deaths.[21] Throughout the war, the atrocities continued and escalated, until they reached their nadir with the mass murder by the VRS led by General Ratko Mladić of between 7,000 and 8,000 Muslim men at Srebrenica on 11-15 July 1995.[22]

The Dayton peace negotiations for a final settlement of the conflict began on 1 November 1995. The parties included the United States, the European Union, the Federal Republic of Yugoslavia, Croatia, the Federation of Bosnian Muslims and Bosnian Croats, and the Bosnian Serbs, although the latter always sided with President Slobodan Milošević' ex-Yugoslavia.[23] The Dayton Peace Agreement, which ended the war in Bosnia-Herzegovina, established the Bosnian Serb *Republika Srpska* as an autonomous entity of Bosnia-Herzegovina, with control over 49 percent of the country's territory, whereas the Federation of Bosnia and Herzegovina (Muslim and Croat) received 51 percent. It was agreed that 60,000 NATO troops (Implementation Force, 'IFOR') would implement the ceasefire agreement.[24]

---

19 R.J. Crampton, *The Balkans Since The Second World War. London*: Pearson Education, 2002, p. 266.

20 Ramet, 2006, p. 465, see *supra* note 11.

21 *Ibid.*, pp. 466–467.

22 Crampton, 2002, pp. 265–266, see *supra* note 19. The ICTY has concluded that the number of individuals killed beyond reasonable doubt was at least 5,336, but that the number could well be as high as 7,826 (which was the Prosecution's estimate), see ICTY, *Prosecutor v. Vujadin Popović et al.*, Judgement, 10 June 2010, vol. II, IT-05-88-T, para. 664 (http://www.legal-tools.org/doc/1bc1cd/).

23 Crampton, 2002, p. 267, see *supra* note 19.

24 *Ibid.*, p. 268.

6.2. The International Response to the War

6.2.1. Peace-keeping and Peace Enforcement

The international response to the crises in the former Yugoslavia has been heavily criticised, particularly in regard to what has been seen by many as a lack of a forceful response in the face of ethnic cleansing and aggression. This is not to say that there was a lack of international response altogether. In the following pages, I briefly describe how the United Nations mission to Bosnia-Herzegovina evolved from being mandated for what should be seen as 'peace-keeping' tasks, to undertaking tasks more in the 'peace enforcement' category, in 1995. A differentiation between these two types of missions is important. In a similar fashion, it is also useful to distinguish intervention in the form of 'tactical air strikes' (with limited and local objectives) from 'strategic air strikes' (aimed at impacting the overall course of the war).

International peace-keeping efforts came underway early on in the conflict. UNPROFOR was deployed in Croatia from 21 February 1992. These forces were initially mandated to ensure conditions for peace talks and to maintain security in Croatia.[25] Later, the UN Security Council gradually expanded the mandate of UNPROFOR in both geographical terms and in regard to operating procedures. On 22 February 1993, the UNPROFOR mandate included a reference to Chapter VII of the UN Charter, which empowered it to use force for self-protection.[26] The operation was massive for the UN at the time, and is still one of the largest UN peace-keeping operations to date. In June 1993, UNPROFOR counted 22,749 military and 1,879 civilians in its ranks.[27] However, UNPROFOR's main task in Bosnia-Herzegovina was to secure delivery of humanitarian aid. It was not a combat force sent in to force the parties to the negotiating table. In other words, it was mainly a peace-keeping and humanitarian force, not a peace enforcement mission.

---

25 UN Security Council resolution 743, S/RES/743 (1992), 21 February 1992 (http://www.legal-tools.org/doc/e91743/).

26 UN Security Council resolution 807, S/RES/807 (1993), 19 February 1993 (http://www.legal-tools.org/doc/fee16e/).

27 Larry Minear, Jeffrey Clark, Roberta Cohen, Dennis Gallagher, Iain Guest and Thomas G. Weiss, *Humanitarian Action in the Former Yugoslavia: The U.N.'s Role 1991–1993, Occasional Paper #18*, Thomas J. Watson Jr. Institute for International Studies and Refugee Policy Group, Brown University, Providence, 1994, p. 89.

The above-statement cannot be made without certain qualifications. Unlike a classic peace-keeping mission, UNPROFOR was deployed in a conflict zone in Bosnia-Herzegovina, with no peace or cease-fire agreement in place.[28] Furthermore, the Security Council gradually approved important changes in UNPROFOR throughout the war, in the direction of asking the mission to take on a role more like peace enforcement. Significantly, the Security Council approved the creation of a UN Rapid Reaction Force in June 1995, which became operational in August, and was used in co-ordination with NATO air strikes shortly after.[29]

Throughout the war, the international community's use of force in Bosnia-Herzegovina gradually increased in means and scope. However, not until August 1995 did the international community attempt to *enforce* peace. Until then, the use of force had been restricted to tactical purposes, such as air strikes intended to draw Serb artillery away from Sarajevo, enforce the no-fly zone or protect UNPROFOR troops.[30]

NATO launched an air campaign, Operation Deliberate Force, after a mortar attack on Sarajevo on 28 August 1995. The stated objectives of the operation were limited: Reducing the threat of attacks on the Sarajevo safe area and deterring attacks there and on other declared UN safe areas; attaining Bosnian Serb compliance to cease attacks on Sarajevo and other safe areas, to withdraw VRS heavy artillery from around Sarajevo, and to the complete freedom of movement of UNPROFOR and NGOs and unrestricted use of the Sarajevo airport.[31] It was not a stated objective that the operation should coerce the Bosnian Serbs into accepting a peace settlement, but NATO planners were hoping for such an effect as well.[32] The operation differed from previous operations in the wide scope of the area of operations, the number of sorties flown and the damage inflicted. Together with the reinforcement of UNPROFOR, with its newly deployed Rapid Reaction Force, Operation Deliberate Force signalled a change in the willingness of the Western states to use military force to coerce the Bosnian Serbs. Only at this late stage in the conflict did the international community

---

28 CIA, 2002, vol. 2, p. 563, see *supra* note 14.

29 UN Security Council resolution 998, S/RES/998 (1995), 16 June 1995 (http://www.legal-tools.org/doc/408c24/); CIA, 2002, vol. 2, pp. 567–568, see *supra* note 14.

30 CIA, 2002, vol. 2, p. 563, see *supra* note 14.

31 *Ibid.*, vol. 1, p. 395.

32 *Ibid.*, vol. 1, pp. 395–396.

definitively change its *modus operandi* from peace-keeping and tactical use of air power towards peace enforcement and extensive use of air power.

It is debatable whether Operation Deliberate Force should be labelled a strategic air strikes campaign. The explicitly stated mission objectives were limited, and did not include forcing the Bosnian Serbs to agree to a peace settlement. For this reason, both Ramet and Gow has argued that the air strikes should be seen as limited and tactical, not strategic.[33] Ramet argues that the Operation Deliberate Force represented a step up from "punitive" to "tactical" air strikes, that is, the difference between pinpointed local attacks to strikes with more general, but still limited, objectives. However, I would argue that the strikes should be seen as strategic, because they signalled a clear intention on part of NATO to take part in the military conflict against the Bosnian Serbs. Furthermore, the area of operations was countrywide, not limited to local targets. Finally, one may prudently ask if the extensive use of air strikes would not have continued if a peace deal had not materialised so soon after the operation. If it would have continued, there should be little doubt that NATOs aerial intervention had strategic characteristics.

6.2.2. The International Diplomatic Response

The international diplomatic response to the conflict was multifaceted, and its main features included recognition of the breakaway republics from Yugoslavia, imposition of economic sanctions on Yugoslavia, an arms embargo and a no-fly-zone, and a series of international peace initiatives designed to get the parties to agree to compromise and end hostilities.

Germany recognised Croatia and Slovenia on 23 December 1991, and Bosnia-Herzegovina was recognised by the EC and the United States on 6 and 7 April 1992, respectively. In legal terms, these actions had the effect of changing the conflicts from a Yugoslav civil war into international conflicts. There was at the time – and has been since – criticism that the state recognition was premature, and that by holding out on recognition, the chances of containing the conflict would have been greater. EC negotiator Peter Carrington was among those who voiced this criticism, arguing against recognition of Slovenia and Croatia in December 1991, because he

33 Sabrina Petra Ramet, *Balkan Babel: The Disintegration of Yugoslavia from the Death of Tito to the fall of Milošević*, Westview Press, Boulder, 2002, pp. 233–234; James Gow: *The Serbian Project and its Adversaries: A Strategy of War Crimes*, Hurst, London, 2003, p. 194.

believed this could spark war in Bosnia-Herzegovina.[34] Cyrus Vance, the UN Secretary-General's Special Representative, presented similar arguments.[35] The British Prime Minister, John Major, partially agrees in his autobiography that recognition could have been used by the international community as a negotiation card, although he does not believe that recognition was a decisive factor leading to war.[36] It could also be argued that recognition of Bosnia-Herzegovina raised the threshold to use violence as the conflict would no longer be an internal or domestic affair.

On 25 September 1991, the UN Security Council passed resolution 713 under Chapter VII of the UN Charter, imposing an immediate, general and complete arms embargo on ex-Yugoslavia. This was the first of a total of 67 Security Council resolutions passed on ex-Yugoslavia in the following 40 months.[37] The embargo formally stayed in effect throughout the war, although the implementation of the embargo was far from complete.[38] Several unsuccessful efforts were made inside and outside the Security Council to lift the embargo for the Bosnian Government after its recognition as a sovereign state.

A ban on military flights over Bosnia-Herzegovina was introduced by Security Council resolution 781 on 9 October 1992, and expanded to include all fixed-wing and rotary-wing aircraft in resolution 816 on 31 March 1993. Economic sanctions on the Federal Republic of Yugoslavia were adopted by the Security Council in its resolution 757 on 30 May 1992, which also singled out the Federal Republic of Yugoslavia as the aggressor in Bosnia-Herzegovina. The sanctions were tightened through resolution 820 on 17 April 1993. Security Council resolutions 942 and 943 on 23 September 1994 tightened the sanctions for the Bosnian Serbs and eased the sanctions on the Federal Republic of Yugoslavia. Sanctions were suspended indefinitely by resolution 1022 on 22 November 1995.

The first among a number of international and high-level peace initiatives was the so-called 'Carrington conference', which was held in The

---

34 Woodward, 1995, p. 184, see *supra* note 2; Douglas Hurd, *Memoirs*, Little, Brown, London, 2003, p. 451.

35 Woodward, 1995, pp. 187–188, see *supra* note 2.

36 Major, 1999, p. 534, see *supra* note 12.

37 Woodward, 1995, p. 180, see *supra* note 2.

38 For a description of the clandestine arms trade during the war, see Peter Andreas, "The Clandestine Political Economy of War and Peace in Bosnia", in *International Studies Quarterly*, 2004, vol. 48, no. 1, pp. 29–51.

Hague, opening on 7 September 1991. The aim was to arrive at an agreement to restructure Yugoslavia and thereby reduce tensions. Between 7 September and 15 December 1991, this conference was at the centre of the international diplomatic effort on Yugoslavia, although other channels were also used by the UN, France, Germany, and other actors.

After the breakup of Yugoslavia was a *fait accompli*, the first international peace conference focusing on Bosnia-Herzegovina opened in Lisbon in early 1992. The central topic was the peace plan presented by Carrington and Portuguese diplomat José Cutileiro. This plan envisaged restructuring Bosnia-Herzegovina into three largely autonomous regions, each with a majority of one of the three ethnic groups, and each having a co-equal role in the government of Bosnia-Herzegovina.[39] The basis would be the 1981 census. There was, however, no agreement on the boundaries of the regions, which meant that even though all parties did sign the Plan on 18 March 1992, there was no real solution. The Serbs demanded 65 percent of the territory of Bosnia-Herzegovina and the Croats 35 percent. Therefore, the Bosnian president Alija Izetbegović rejected the plan after returning to Sarajevo, and with encouragement from the United States.[40]

Following the failure of the Lisbon Agreement, another major international initiative to deal with the war in Bosnia-Herzegovina was launched at the so-called “London Conference” on 26–27 August 1992. The Conference condemned the military aggression that had occurred, and established an indefinite peace conference in Geneva, which convened for the first time on 2 September 1992. This organisation, the International Conference on the Former Yugoslavia (ICFY), was to have a joint chairmanship between Lord David Owen, who represented the European Community (from November 1993, The European Union), and Cyrus Vance, Special Representative of the United Nations Secretary-General. Both were esteemed and experienced statesmen: Lord Owen was former British Foreign Secretary under James Callaghan, and Vance had been US Secretary of State under President Jimmy Carter. ICFY would lead the ensuing peace mediation in the ex-Yugoslav wars, in which Bosnia-Herzegovina by now held centre stage.

---

39 Laura Silber and Allan Little, *The Death of Yugoslavia*, Penguin, London, 1995, p. 219.

40 Reneo Lukic and Allen Lynch, *Europe from the Balkans to the Urals: The Disintegration of Yugoslavia and the Soviet Union*, Oxford University Press, Solna, 1996, pp. 281–282.

6.2.3. The Vance–Owen Peace Plan

The Vance–Owen Peace Plan, named after the two co-chairmen, was the ICFY's first comprehensive plan for a settlement. It became the major focal point of international mediation from its presentation on 2 January 1993, until May 1993, when it was finally dropped. The Vance–Owen plan proposed to divide Bosnia-Herzegovina into ten relatively autonomous *cantons*. The three major ethnic groups would have interim majority control in three cantons each. The tenth, Sarajevo, was to have shared rule.

Province	Capital	Governor	Vice-Governor	IPG
1	Bihać	Muslim	Serb	Muslims 7 Serbs 2 Croats 1
2	Banja Luka	Serb	Muslim	Serbs 7 Muslim 2 Croats 1
3	Bosanski Brod	Croat	Serb	Croats 5 Serbs 3 Muslims 2
4	Bijeljina	Serb	Muslim	Serbs 5 Muslims 4 Croats 1
5	Tuzla	Muslim	Serb	Muslims 5 Serbs 3 Croats 2
6	Nevesinje	Serb	Muslim	Serbs 7 Muslim 2 Croats 1
7	Sarajevo	Special status	Special status	Muslims 3 Serbs 3 Croats 3
8	Mostar	Croat	Muslim	Croats 6 Muslims 3 Serbs 1
9	Zenica	Mualim	Croat	Muslims 6 Croats 2 Serbs 2
10	Travnik	Croat	Muslim	Muslims 5 Croats 4 Serbs 1

Table 1: Interrim ethnic representation in Vance–Owen cantons.[41]

The Vance–Owen plan was a relatively intricate plan intended to preserve the sovereignty and multi-ethnicity of Bosnia-Herzegovina. This represented a departure from the presumption of ethnic partition that was central to the Lisbon Agreement. Woodward refers to the Vance–Owen plan as a "heroic effort" in this regard.[42] The plan's proponents have argued that it would have denied the Serbs two of their cardinal war aims: ethnically pure territories and, more importantly, contiguous territories.[43] At the time, however, the Vance–Owen plan was criticised in the West, and dismissed by some as appeasing the Serbs. These critics argued for the need to annul the gains of aggression, meaning the Serb gains, and believed that the plan offered the Bosnian Serbs too much.[44]

In fact, the Vance–Owen plan would have rolled the Bosnian Serbs back from a part of the territory they had occupied since the beginning of the war – 24 percent of Bosnia-Herzegovina's total territory, according to an observer.[45]

In defence of the plan, Lord Owen argued that the Bosnian Serbs were usually more rural than their Muslim counterparts, and consequently were in possession of more territory per capita before the war than the Muslims. He argued that "rural Bosnian Serbs sat on over 60 percent of the country before the war, and we are offering them three provinces covering 43 percent".[46] However, this notion is problematic due to the fact that more

---

41 Table of the interim ethnic representation in the 10 cantons, from Gow, 1997, p. 238, see *supra* note 17.

42 Woodward, 1995, p. 304, see *supra* note 2.

43 Gow, 1997, p. 241, see *supra* note 17. Laura Silber and Allan Little also comment that contiguous territory was a crucial war objective and a major concern for the Bosnian Serbs in regard to the Vance–Owen plan, in Laura Silber and Allan Little, *Yugoslavia: Death of a Nation*, Penguin, New York, 1997, pp. 220 and 276. See also Lenard Cohen, *Broken Bonds: Yugoslavia's Disintegration and Balkan Politics in Transition*, 2nd ed., Westview Press, Boulder, 1995, p. 244.

44 See, for example, Jeane Kirkpatrick, "Vance/Owen plan not good enough", in *Patriot-News*, 7 February 1993.

45 Graham Messervy-Whiting, *Peace Conference on Former Yugoslavia The Politico-Military Interface*, in series *London Defence Studies*, vol. 21, Brassey's, London, 1994, 18/41 (endnote 39). Silber and Little put the figure at one-third of Serb-occupied Bosnia-Herzegovina, in Silber and Little, 1995, p. 278, see *supra* note 39.

46 David Owen, "Interview with David Owen on the Balkans", in *Foreign Affairs*, Spring 1993, vol. 72, no. 2, p. 3.

than half of the land in Bosnia-Herzegovina was in communal ownership before 1992, making it difficult to argue that one ethnic group held a specific percentage of the territory.[47] The origin of the figure of 60 percent is unclear, but this notion was nonetheless repeated in many corners throughout the war. Former US ambassador to Yugoslavia, Warren Zimmermann, refers to a claim made by Milošević that Serbs lived on – and therefore possessed, and had a right to possess – 64 percent of the territory of Bosnia-Herzegovina, adding that he has never seen any evidence of this figure.[48]

The most important argument that contradicts the argument that the Vance–Owen plan was appeasing the Serbs was the suggested solution for the Northern Corridor. This runs through the northernmost part of Bosnia-Herzegovina and connected the Serb-held territories in the west with those in the east and with Serbia proper. For this reason, possession of the Northern Corridor was among the most important territorial war aims of the Bosnian Serb Army (VRS) from the very beginning of the war.[49] The importance of the corridor to the Bosnian Serbs is well-known. After the Lisbon Agreement was signed, for example, Croats and Serbs met to discuss internal borders in Bosnia-Herzegovina. Bosnian Serb leader Radovan Karadžić then told Josip Manolić – one of Croatian President Franjo Tuđjman's most trusted advisers, who was representing the Bosnian Croats – that the Serbs must have a land corridor across northern Bosnia: "Without the corridor, any solution is out of the question", Karadžić reportedly said.[50] Before the war, the Serbs were in a minority in this area, and the Vance–Owen plan designated it part of a Croat majority canton (Bosanski Brod). However, when the Vance–Owen plan was launched on 2 January 1993, the VRS was in control of the corridor. To meet the Serbs half way, the Vance–Owen plan suggested a "UN throughway", which was to be five kilometres wide and demilitarised on either side.[51] The Bosnian Serbs were sceptical

---

47 Carole Hodge, *The Serb Lobby in the United Kingdom*, in *The Donald W. Treadgold Papers in Russian, East European, and Central Asian Studies*, The Henry M. Jackson School of International Studies, University of Washington, 2003, p. 13.

48 Warren Zimmermann, *Origins of a Catastrophe: Yugoslavia and Its Destroyers – America's Last Ambassador Tells What Happened and Why*, Random House, New York, 1996, p. 180.

49 CIA, 2002, vol. 1, p. 141, see *supra* note 14.

50 Silber and Little, 1997, p. 220, see *supra* note 43.

51 Gow, 1997, p. 240, see *supra* note 17. For more on Bosnian Serb objections, see Cohen, 1995, p. 247, see *supra* note 43.

of the long-term reliability of this "throughway", especially since they already controlled the region themselves. Serbian President Milošević, however, accepted the Vance–Owen plan after Owen secured a Russian promise that Russian troops would patrol the corridor after the plan came into effect.[52]

6.2.4. Negotiations on the Vance–Owen Peace Plan

The Croats stood to gain the most from the Vance–Owen plan's division of Bosnia-Herzegovina. They would be given majority rule in three cantons that bordered on Croatia proper and shared control over Sarajevo, even though they constituted only 17 percent of the population before the war. One contemporary observer commented: "In essence, the Vance–Owen plan gives the Croats everything they asked for in early 1992 except for the island of territory north of Sarajevo, and with the addition of land in the Trebinje district that they had not even requested".[53] The Croats loved the plan; it gave them exactly what they wanted.[54] They accepted all three parts of the Vance–Owen plan. The Bosnian Croat leader Mate Boban signed the plan in Geneva on 4 January 1993.

The Bosnian Government was more hesitant. Their predicament was that although they felt they deserved a greater part of the land, they were at a military disadvantage, and were depending on foreign goodwill and support in order to achieve their goals. The Bosnian President, Alija Izetbegović, accepted the Vance–Owen plan after American diplomatic pressure. On 25 March 1993, he agreed to the third and final of the three parts of the Vance–Owen plan.

There has been debate about Izetbegović's acceptance in regard to both reasons and timing. Silber and Little argue that Izetbegović accepted

---

52 Silber and Little, 1997, p. 278, see *supra* note 43.

53 Robert M. Hayden, "The Partition of Bosnia and Herzegovina, 1990–1993", in *RFE/RL* [Radio Free Europe/Radio Liberty, Inc.], *Research Report: Weekly Analyses from the RFE/RL Research Institute*, Issue 22, 28 May 1993, pp. 10–11. The article was written on 13 May 1993, that is, before the official Bosnian Serb rejection. Hayden has been criticised for having an anti-Croat bias, see, for example, Thomas Cushman, "Response to Hayden and Denich", in *Anthropological Theory*, 2005, vol. 5, no. 4, p. 559. Since the Croat positive response to the Vance–Owen plan is in line with other scholars' views on the matter, however, I believe this particular comment can stand without further comment. Sabrina Ramet, for example, writes that the Croats accepted the Vance–Owen plan immediately because it granted them the territory they wanted, in Ramet, 2006, p. 441, see *supra* note 11.

54 Silber and Little, 1997, p. 307, see *supra* note 43.

the Vance–Owen Plan partly because he courted international approval and partly because he felt sure that the Serbs would never accept it.[55] Zimmermann, however, writes that the Bosnian Government's perception of the Vance–Owen plan was not as negative as others have argued. He writes that he was present at a meeting with Cyrus Vance in Geneva, when the Bosnian Government gave its first reaction to the Vance–Owen Plan: "[i]t was not only positive, but enthusiastic", and they and wanted to sign it immediately, but Vance urged them to wait, in order to not appear too eager in front of the Bosnian Serbs, according to Zimmermann.[56] Due to the US response to the plan, however, the Muslims were further encouraged to hold out for more.[57]

After Izetbegović' acceptance, all that remained was to get the Bosnian Serbs to agree to the Vance–Owen plan map, since the Bosnian Serbs had already agreed to two of the three parts of the Vance–Owen plan (the military and constitutional provisions). President Bill Clinton soon declared that the "full-court press" of international diplomacy would bear down on the Serbian side of the conflict, to get them to endorse the Vance–Owen plan.[58] On 17 April 1993, the UN Security Council passed resolution 820, which called on the Serbs to support the plan and threatened with new sanctions after a delay of nine days if no support had come.[59]

The Bosnian Serbs, however, were still reluctant to accept the map. Meanwhile, the diplomatic pressure mounted and reached its zenith at the Athens Conference on 1–2 May 1993. At this time, Milošević had accepted the plan and worked to convince the Bosnian Serb that they should do the same. The Americans implicitly threatened with air strikes against Serb targets in both Bosnia-Herzegovina and Serbia. Vance did the same in meetings with the Bosnian Serb leaders Karadžić, Krajišnik and Koljević, who

---

55 *Ibid.*, p. 277.

56 Zimmermann, 1996, p. 222, see *supra* note 48.

57 *Ibid.*, p. 222. Thorvald Stoltenberg makes a similar point, arguing that the US position encouraged the Bosnian Government to hold out for more, in Thorvald Stoltenberg and Kai Eide, *De tusen dagene: Fredsmeklere på Balkan* [The One Thousand Days: Peace Negotiators in the Balkans], Gyldendal, Oslo, 1996, p. 55.

58 John M. Goshko and Daniel Williams, "U.S. to Urge Serbs to Sign Bosnia Pact: Clinton Promises 'Full-Court Press'", in *The Washington Post*, 27 March 1993; Nita Lelyveld, "Clinton Promises 'Full Court Press' To Soften Serbs", in *The Associated Press*, 26 March 1993.

59 Gow, 1997, p. 245, see *supra* note 17.

concluded that they would not be free to leave Athens without a signature.[60] Under immense pressure, Karadžić signed the Vance–Owen plan in Athens on 2 May 1993. He made it clear, however, that his signature would still need ratification by the Assembly of the Serb Nation in Bosnia-Herzegovina (the 'Bosnian Serb Assembly').

Karadžić's signature reassured ICFY and the rest of the world that peace was within reach, and even more so when Slobodan Milošević, Greek Prime Minister Constantine Mitsotakis and Montenegrin President Momir Bulatović all agreed to go to Pale and address the Bosnian Serb Assembly with the intention of attaining its ratification of the Vance–Owen plan.[61] However, the optimism of Athens soon turned to disappointment, as the Assembly decided on 6 May 1993 to put the Vance–Owen plan to a referendum. The decision was, and is, widely perceived to have been devised to give a *de facto* rejection a veneer of legitimacy.[62] In any case, the decision of the Bosnian Serb Assembly was clear: 51 voted against ratification and for holding a referendum, two voted for the plan and there were 12 abstentions.[63]

The referendum was held on 15–16 May 1993. On 16 May, Karadžić declared the Vance–Owen plan dead, after the announcement of the preliminary results. Radio Serbia reported on 17 May that the referendum in Serbian Bosnia ended with a 90 percent turnout and over 90 percent of the votes rejecting Vance–Owen.[64]

6.2.5. Peace Plans, Continued

Although there was some talk of enforcing the Vance–Owen plan after the referendum – on basis of an argument that Karadžić' signature at Athens was legally binding – these plans were soon dropped and ICFY accepted diplomatic defeat. The mediators went back to the map room and devised new suggestions for settling the war in Bosnia-Herzegovina. The next major peace plan was the Owen–Stoltenberg Plan (Thorvald Stoltenberg, a former Norwegian Foreign Minister, took over Vance's position as joint

60 Silber and Little, 1997, p. 282, see *supra* note 43.

61 David Owen, *Balkan Odyssey*, Harcourt Brace, London, 1995, p. 159.

62 Gow, 1997, p. 246, see *supra* note 17.

63 A reason for the clear vote may have been that the vote was open, and that voting *for* ratification thus could have shamed individual assembly members.

64 RFE/RL News Briefs, 14–21 May 1993, pp. 9 and 13.

chairman and UN representative on 1 May 1993). This plan suggested that Bosnia-Herzegovina be split into three highly autonomous republics, basically a confederation of ethnic states, with Sarajevo as joint territory. The plan was discarded after the Bosnian Government rejected it on 30 August 1993.[65]

After Owen–Stoltenberg, the next major outline for a settlement was the Contact Group Plan, announced by the United States, Russia, the United Kingdom, France and Germany on 5 July 1994. The suggested solution to the map problem was to create two entities, where the Serbian part would receive 49 percent of the territory and the Croat–Muslim republic would get 51 percent. Again, Sarajevo was to have a special status. Again, the plan failed.[66]

It was not until November 1995 that a lasting settlement was reached. The Dayton Peace Agreement was signed by the involved parties on 21 November 1995 and came into effect on 14 December the same year. Bosnia-Herzegovina was to be a single state, but with two autonomous entities: the Federation of Bosnia-Herzegovina (Bosnian Muslim and Croat) and *Republika Srpska* (Serb). The agreement built on the Contact Group Plan, in the sense that it granted 49 percent of Bosnia-Herzegovina to the Serb entity. Sarajevo was to be under Croat–Muslim control.[67]

It was agreed at Dayton that control over the Northern Corridor was to be settled a year after the Agreement. Deciding the final status of the corridor (specifically the city of Brčko) became a lasting source of antagonism between *Republika Srpska* and the Federation, and it was decided in 1999 that Brčko was to be under the exclusive control of neither entity.[68]

---

65 Woodward, 1995, pp. 310–311, see *supra* note 2; Gow, 1997, pp. 253–259, see *supra* note 17; CIA, 2002, vol. 1, p. 183, see *supra* note 14; Ramet, 2006, p. 442, see *supra* note 11.

66 Gow, 1997, pp. 260–265, see *supra* note 17; CIA, 2002, vol. 1, pp. 219–222, see *supra* note 14; Woodward, 1995, p. 316, see *supra* note 2.; Ramet, 2006, pp. 449–450, see *supra* note 11.

67 Gow, 1997, pp. 279–297, see *supra* note 17; Ramet, 2006, p. 466, see *supra* note 11.

68 Michael G. Karnavas, "Creating the Legal Framework of the Brčko District of Bosnia", in *American Journal of International Law*, vol. 97, no. 1, 2003, pp. 113–114. Karnavas concludes that the Final Award for Brčko is so good that it can probably serve as a blueprint for other post-conflict situations.

6.3. Counterfactuals in the Historiography of the War in Bosnia-Herzegovina and the Selection of Hypotheses

As with any other recent international conflict, a wide range of counterfactual hypotheses has been suggested in regard to the war in Bosnia-Herzegovina. Many of these hypotheses have been formulated by the politicians and diplomats who were involved in the international response to the war. Some of the hypotheses serve the purpose of legitimising their proponents' own favoured policy options during the crisis. It is not always clear if the hypotheses have been formulated with an awareness of the fact that they represent attempts at counterfactual analysis.

6.3.1. Counterfactuals

One of the most common counterfactual hypotheses is the claim that the war could have been avoided by delaying the state recognition of Slovenia and Croatia (and in some versions of Bosnia-Herzegovina). One of the co-chairmen of ICFY, Thorvald Stoltenberg, adheres to this view. In his book on the war in Bosnia-Herzegovina, he mentions this hypothesis, but also moderates his view by stating that "no one can say for certain if the war could have been avoided if the great powers had delayed the recognition of Slovenia, Croatia and Bosnia".[69] As mentioned, John Major has written in his autobiography that the international community might have surrendered a negotiating card or two when recognising Slovenia and Croatia, but concludes that withholding recognition would not have prevented the wars.[70]

There have also been suggestions for preventive measures that could have been implemented in the years before the violent conflicts erupted, based on early warning and early response. Susan Woodward has proposed some "missed opportunities" to prevent conflict escalation in the period from 1985 to March 1991, by the use of such means as diplomatic engagement and financial support from the United States and the European Community.[71] Theories based on the concept of early warning and early response are interesting because they often imply that great effects could have

69 Stoltenberg and Eide, 1996, p. 49, see *supra* note 57.

70 Major, 1999, p. 534, see *supra* note 12; and Woodward, 1995, p. 534, see *supra* note 2. Douglas Hurd does not believe delayed recognition would have mattered, Hurd, 2003, p. 451, see *supra* note 34.

71 Susan L. Woodward, "Costly Disinterest: Missed Opportunities for Preventive Diplomacy in Croatia, Bosnia and Herzegovina, 1985–1991", in Bruce W. Jentleson (ed.), *Opportunities*

been achieved with fairly small means. Such theories may also lead to suggestions for changes in how the institutions of the international community are set up to respond to large-scale conflicts.

Another popular counterfactual hypothesis is that the early peace plans represented "missed opportunities" that could have prevented the wars or stopped them earlier. Warren Zimmermann has commented on this line of reasoning:

> In the hindsight of history, Cutileiro's plan, although it introduced for the first time the concept of Bosnia's division, would probably have worked out better for the Muslims than any subsequent plan, including the Dayton formula, since the divisions would have closely followed the actual ethnic percentages of the population.[72]

Zimmermann, however, also expresses doubts, because he believes that Karadžić would not have agreed to any specific boundaries at that time.[73] Silber and Little argue that the Lisbon Agreement was not close to peace because there was no agreement on the internal boundaries.[74] The interesting part of Zimmermann's comment is that it includes a basic assessment of how the plan would have left the Bosnian Government better off than other agreements. This is certainly a counterfactual statement, as is his assessment that Karadžić was unlikely to have been convinced to accept a peace deal at this time.

Other possible peace agreements have their own proponents, with adhering counterfactual hypotheses. James Gow has argued that the Vance-Owen plan represented a missed opportunity for peace – an argument that is closely linked with Lord Owen's account of the war.[75] Silber and Little also deal with the Vance–Owen plan in a chapter of their book entitled *Last-Chance Café: The Rise and Fall of the Vance–Owen Plan, January–May 1993*.[76] The authors point out several deficiencies with the plan, and ques-

Missed, Opportunities Seized: Preventive Diplomacy in the Post-Cold War World, Rowman and Littlefield, Lanham, 2000, pp. 133–172.

72 Zimmermann, 1996, p. 190, see *supra* note 48.

73 *Ibid.*, p. 190.

74 Silber and Little, 1995, p. 219, see *supra* note 39.

75 Gow, 1997, see *supra* note 17; Owen, 1995, see *supra* note 61.

76 Silber and Little, 1997, pp. 276–290, see *supra* note 43.

tion the commitment of Milošević to actually implement the plan, but nevertheless describe it in the following manner: "There was never a more comprehensive plan than Vance-Owen, which, despite criticism to the contrary, did preserve a multi-ethnic Bosnia within its internationally recognized borders".[77] They do not attempt to draw any clear conclusions in regard to what could have happened if the Vance–Owen plan had been accepted, but they leave an impression that it could be seen as a potentially lost opportunity for peace.

There are also a considerable number of publications that claim that a more forceful international military intervention – peace enforcement – would have ended the war earlier. Arguments in this category include such measures as strategic air strikes against the JNA, against the Bosnian Serbs, and arming the Bosnian Government. One hypothesis is that Western governments should have acted forcefully in response to the JNA's shelling of the cities Vukovar and Dubrovnik in 1991. One scholar argues that the Western inaction at this time gave Milošević a green light to pursue his ambition of creating an ethnically pure Greater Serbia.[78] Another example is Warren Zimmermann's hypothesis regarding the use of early air strikes: "Had the North Atlantic Treaty Organisation (NATO) met that [Serb] aggression with air strikes in the summer of 1992, I believe that a negotiated result would soon have followed".[79] This is a textbook example of a conflict counterfactual: If A (air strikes), then B (peace). In a seemingly similar fashion, Brendan Simms argues that the US policy of lifting the arms embargo for the Bosnian Government and using air strikes against the Bosnian Serbs "should have been tried earlier".[80]

6.3.2. Selection of Hypotheses

All the hypotheses mentioned above warrant further investigation, in my opinion. For the purposes of this book, however, there is a need to select a few. In the following pages, I will primarily deal with those hypotheses that

---

77 *Ibid.*, pp. 282 and 287.

78 Jane M. O. Sharp, "Dayton Report Card", in *International Security*, 1998, vol. 22, no. 3, p. 101. Susan Woodward discusses the hypothesis in Woodward, 2000, pp. 169–171, see *supra* note 71.

79 Zimmermann, 1996, pp. xi-xii, see *supra* note 48.

80 Brendan Simms, *Unfinest Hour: Britain and the Destruction of Bosnia*, Penguin, London, 2002, p. 342.

have been put forward by Gow/Owen and Zimmermann/Simms. The reason for this is a consideration of the timing of the branching point for these counterfactual hypotheses.

I consider the first half of 1993 to be a good starting point.[81] I arrive at this conclusion on the basis of two assumptions. The first assumption is that when the state of war is a *fait accompli*, the options of confronting the decision-makers are clearer. Before the state of war, there are always warnings and opinions regarding the impending crisis, but there is also lack of focus and/or knowledge and insight among high-level international decision-makers. Only after the crisis is a fact will the diplomats and politicians acquire the focus and detailed information about the situation that is required to make informed decisions and back up these decisions with sufficient means. I consider this to be an assumption, not a certainty, but in the case of Bosnia-Herzegovina, there is also statistical material that can be presented in its defence.[82] There are also statements by contemporary decision-makers that indicate this pattern. John Major writes in his autobiography that Bosnia "crept up on us" while the attention was on the turmoil of the Soviet Union.[83] As I am interested in investigating counterfactual hypotheses that may have the pragmatic advantage of providing lessons for the future, it seems that choosing a branching point where the decision-makers are more focused on the options at hand, and better informed about the situation, may be more fruitful. This does not mean, however, that I consider counterfactual hypotheses regarding events before the outbreak of war to be historically irrelevant or uninteresting.

The second assumption is that hypotheses that are set in the later stages of the war may also be less interesting, because the effects of the counterfactual (in terms of reduced human suffering) are likely to be less. As argued in the theory section, however, 'great effects' are not a necessary criterion of a useful or interesting counterfactual hypothesis. However, with

---

81 I return to the issue of the branching point for the hypothesis of 'early air strikes' under the discussion of this hypothesis, which is somewhat problematic and therefore warrants a more detailed discussion than can be provided here.

82 See, for example, Jon Western, "Sources of Humanitarian Intervention: Beliefs, Information, and Advocacy in the U.S. Decisions on Somalia and Bosnia", in *International Security*, 2002, vol. 26, no. 4, p. 119. Western refers to *Times Mirror Center for the People and the Press*, News Interest Indexes, December 1991, when arguing that "[p]rior to the outbreak of war in 1992, few Americans or foreign policy elites had focused on Bosnia".

83 Major, 1999, p. 532, see *supra* note 12.

an eye to those hypotheses that may provide potential lessons for the future, I am inclined to believe that the potential for great effects from the counterfactual hypothesis will make it more interesting to study the first half of 1993 than, say the first half of 1995.

I have chosen the following hypotheses as a basis for discussion in each in the three ensuing chapters:

1. 'Increased US Diplomatic Pressure': Gow and Owen have argued that stronger support from the United States for the Vance–Owen plan from January to May 1993 would have led to acceptance of the plan.
2. Progressive Implementation: Gow and Owen have claimed that American commitment to implement the Vance–Owen plan in May 1993 – in spite of its rejection by the Bosnian Serb Assembly – would have ended the war and forced the Bosnian Serbs to accept the peace plan.
3. Early Air Strikes: Zimmermann and Simms have argued that a more forceful approach to the conflict would have increased the chances of an earlier peace settlement. (In the analysis, I will comment on the partially connected policy of lifting the arms embargo for the Bosnian Government, but focus on the hypothesis of early air strikes.)

Each hypothesis will be presented and evaluated in the following manner: First, I will explain the hypothesis. Second, I will evaluate the hypothesis' scientific coherence based on the criteria discussed in Part II. Third and finally, I will discuss the plausibility of the hypothesis, first in regard to the antecedent, then in regard to the consequent.

7

Increased United States Diplomatic Pressure

One can easily see the following counterfactual hypothesis in the accounts of the war in Bosnia-Herzegovina of both Gow and Owen: Had the American support for the Vance–Owen plan been stronger, or at least clearer, it would have led to acceptance of the plan by all parties.[1] In *Balkan Odyssey*, Owen laments the lack of resolve on the part of the Americans: "The two US administrations neither pressurized nor even cajoled the parties [in the war in Bosnia-Herzegovina] to accept, let alone threatened to impose, any of the four successive peace proposals [before Dayton]".[2] Moreover, Owen argues that "[f]rom the spring of 1993 to the summer of 1995, in my judgment, the effect of the US policy […] was to prolong the war of the Bosnian Serbs in Bosnia-Herzegovina".[3]

James Gow is equally explicit, but also more precise in his accusations: "[T]he Vance–Owen plan was effectively killed off by Washington, which appeared not to understand key parts of it".[4] And further, Gow writes, "Washington's clear lack of support for it [the Vance–Owen plan] could only encourage them [Izetbegović and Karadžić], for different reasons, to think that they would have better options than to sign the agreement".[5]

The point Gow is making is actually twofold. The first element of criticism is that the Americans were unable to contain their doubts about the Vance–Owen plan right from the start, and that this made the Bosnian Serbs confident that they could get away with a rejection. The President and his spokespersons expressed doubts and criticism on several occasions, both explicitly and indirectly, according to Gow. The second element is that

---

1 James Gow, *Triumph of the Lack of Will: International Diplomacy and the Yugoslav War*, Hurst, London, 1997, p. 218; David Owen, *Balkan Odyssey*, Harcourt Brace, London, 1995, p. 399.

2 Owen, 1995, p. 399, see *supra* note 1.

3 *Ibid.*, pp. 400–401.

4 Gow, 1997, p. 9, see *supra* note 1.

5 *Ibid.*, p. 242.

the United States made it only too obvious that it was not prepared to deploy its military to enforce a settlement. This had the same effect as the first point, making the Bosnian Serbs more confident that a rejection of the Vance–Owen plan would not be met with any decisive reprisals. The end result of the American lack of will, according to Gow, was this:

> Washington's […] lack of commitment to the Vance–Owen Plan and its promotion of the 'lift and strike' option created an environment in which the Bosnian Serbs could safely fail to 'ratify' the signature of their leader Radovan Karadžić, free from the international pressure which had persuaded him to sign at the beginning of May.[6]

In other words, had the Americans given more clear-cut support for the Vance–Owen plan, peace could have been achieved in Pale on 5–6 May 1993. In this analysis, Gow suggests that the mixed signals from the United States were more important in May than earlier. However, he also makes a point of the fact that the Americans had not been able to conceal their scepticism throughout the entire Vance–Owen process. The Bush administration had not been willing to take the leadership in handling the war in Bosnia-Herzegovina.[7] The Clinton administration accepted that Bosnia-Herzegovina had to be dealt with, but clearly preferred the 'lift and strike' option to the Vance–Owen plan (lifting the arms embargo for the Bosnian Government and using air strikes against the Bosnian Serbs – I return to this in greater detail below). In Gow's interpretation, when the Bosnian Serbs picked up on the lukewarm American support for the Vance–Owen plan, they became confident enough to reject it.

The view presented by Gow and Owen has stirred much debate. Ramet includes this issue on her list of the eight most contentious issues in the scholarly debate about the wars in Former Yugoslavia 1991-1995.[8] Gow's and Owen's view is not without supporters. Carole Rogel claims that the Vance–Owen plan was "turned down by the Americans" because it granted too much to the Serb aggressor and by the Serbs because they

---

6 *Ibid.*, p. 218.

7 *Ibid.*, p. 206; Richard Holbrooke, *To End a War*, Random House, New York, 1998, pp. 27–28.

8 Sabrina P. Ramet, *Thinking about Yugoslavia: Scholarly Debates about the Yugoslav Break-up and the Wars in Bosnia and Kosovo*, Cambridge University Press, Cambridge, 2005, pp. 3–4.

wanted more.[9] By this perception, it seems the blame for the failure of the Vance–Owen plan must be shared by the Clinton administration and the Bosnian Serbs. Warren Zimmermann criticises the Clinton administration for giving backing to the Vance–Owen plan too late, thereby delaying the Bosnian Government's acceptance and losing momentum in the negotiation process.[10] Mike Bowker has written that the generally accepted view on the fate of the Vance–Owen plan is that the United States undermined it by labelling it as appeasing to the Serbs, by sanctioning ethnic cleansing, while offering no long-term solution that would be acceptable to the Bosnian Muslims. He writes that "the unwillingness of the USA to back the VOPP [Vance–Owen plan] and offer American ground troops was generally perceived to have led to its failure".[11] He refers to Owen's *Balkan Odyssey* in the footnote attached to the statement. A final example is the Carnegie Commission on the Balkans, which in its report from 1996, *Unfinished Peace*, regrets that the Americans did not respond more rapidly and forcefully to the crisis in Bosnia-Herzegovina. The report's main conclusion is that the war could have been stopped if the superpower had made a clear policy choice and put its force behind it.[12] According to the commission, it was the negative presentation of the Vance–Owen plan in the American press that prevented the Clinton administration from supporting the plan more enthusiastically. And the only alternative the administration could conceive of was 'lift and strike'. But since this was strongly opposed by the European allies, the United States was left without any clear line of action, and thus paralysed.[13]

Certainly, one may question the thoroughness of some of the treatment of the Vance–Owen plan in the examples above. Bowker does not enter deeply into the argument regarding the failure of the Vance–Owen plan. Zimmermann's book and the Carnegie Commission report are influenced by the political aims of the authors, and are not examples of detached

9 Carole Rogel, *The Breakup of Yugoslavia and its Aftermath*, Greenwood Press, Westport, 2004, p. 61.

10 Warren Zimmermann, *Origins of a Catastrophe: Yugoslavia and Its Destroyers – America's Last Ambassador Tells What Happened and Why*, Random House, New York, 1996, p. 222.

11 Mike Bowker, "The Wars in Yugoslavia: Russia and the International Community", in *Europe-Asia Studies*, 1998, vol. 50, no. 7, p. 1250.

12 Leo Tindemans *et al.*, *Unfinished Peace: Report of the International Commission on the Balkans*, Carnegie Endowment for International Peace, Washington, D.C., 1996, p. 75.

13 *Ibid.*, p. 63.

historical research. However, the examples show that the hypothesis presented by Owen and elaborated by Gow is supported in other publications. This gives reason to believe that the hypothesis is still adhered to by a significant number of people.

The hypothesis is also a clear example of a counterfactual line of reasoning. This makes it a good example and a reasonable starting point for discussing counterfactual hypotheses that have been used in the historiography of the war in Bosnia-Herzegovina. And there should be no doubt that both Gow's and Owen's line of reasoning is counterfactual. They argue that the failure of the Vance–Owen plan was a decisive moment in the war in Bosnia-Herzegovina, where the West scuttled its best chance to end the war at a relatively early stage. Instead, the war worsened and, consequently, the war crimes and atrocities continued. In this sense, they both reason that the Vance–Owen plan represents a missed opportunity for creating peace.

Gow and Owen both claim that they are justified in lamenting this missed opportunity specifically because they believe that the Vance–Owen plan could have given the West much more of what they wanted than the Dayton Peace Agreement actually provided. Gow argues that the reason why Dayton succeeded where the Vance–Owen plan did not was that the Americans were willing to enforce a settlement in 1995, but not in 1993. According to Gow, "[t]he conditions for implementing both plans were the same: Dayton worked where Vance–Owen failed because there was a willingness to use force and, crucially, because the United States was behind the plan, rather than opposing it".[14] In content, Gow and Owen believe that Dayton represented many compromises which the Vance–Owen plan did not, especially the acceptance of ethnic cleansing.[15]

7.1.1. Gow's Explanation of the American Failure

Despite the many similar hypotheses that place the responsibility for the failure of the Vance–Owen plan on the Clinton administration, Gow's work is perhaps the most elaborate in its counterfactual deliberations. According to Gow, there were three reasons for the sceptical American view of the Vance–Owen plan. First, there were *moral issues*. The Americans' aim was to reject aggression and take a stand against ethnic cleaning. To the Clinton administration, the Vance–Owen plan appeared (wrongly, according to

---

14 Gow, 1997, p. 299, see *supra* note 1.

15 *Ibid.*, p. 1.

Gow) to be a device for both making the Bosnian Government surrender and rewarding the Serbian camp.[16] Owen makes a similar point in *Balkan Odyssey*, where he accuses the Clinton administration of indulging in "a compulsive urge to moralize from the high ground while their military stayed in the air".[17]

Second, there were several and diverse *political considerations*: the activities of the growing anti-Serb Bosnian lobby in the United States, the debate on Bosnia-Herzegovina in the considerable and increasing informed public, and the writings in the press, especially the liberal press, such as *The New York Times* and its reporter John Burns.[18]

Third, the Clinton administration considered the Vance–Owen plan too *unpredictable*. Both the United States and NATO assessed that the plan could never be fully implemented. The number of internal borders that the plan created was regarded as unenforceable.[19]

7.2. The Scientific Coherence of Increased US Diplomatic Pressure

How does the hypothesis measure up to the rules of scientifically coherent counterfactual research, outlined in the theory section?

7.2.1. Logical Consistency

'Increased US Diplomatic Pressure' is a logically consistent hypothesis. It should be self-evident that the Clinton administration could have given stronger support for the Vance–Owen plan, without this breaking with any logical factors.

---

16 *Ibid.*, pp. 214–215.

17 Owen, 1995, p. 401, see *supra* note 1. Another interesting lament of the moralisation of the Bosnian Peace process is the article: "Human Rights in Peace Negotiations", in *Human Rights Quarterly*, 1996, vol. 18, no. 2, pp. 249–258. The article was published anonymously, but it is widely held that the author is Bertrand Ramcharan, who was the Director of the International Conference on the Former Yugoslavia and Political Advisor to the peace negotiators in the ex-Yugoslav conflict for four years.

18 Gow, 1997, pp. 214–216, see *supra* note 1. Burns received a Pulitzer Prize for his work in Bosnia in 1993.

19 *Ibid.*, pp. 216–217.

7.2.2. Pragmatism

Gow is not explicit as to what he believes his account can provide of use to future researchers, diplomats or politicians. Still, some pragmatic advantages are certainly implied. In Gow's account, the undercurrent is a lament of the lack of will on the part of the West, and the United States in particular – as is clearly indicated by the title of his book, *The Triumph of the Lack of Will*. The book's most immediate lesson is that ending conflicts such as the one in Bosnia-Herzegovina requires that future action be more resolute than it was in the 1990s. Although this lesson is not explicit, it is strongly implied in Gow's account.

Lord Owen has included a chapter in *Balkan Odyssey* that is entitled "Lessons for the Future". The content of this chapter, however, is more in the form of conclusions than recommendations or "lessons". Lord Owen does draw up some lessons for the European Union's handling of crises in the future, but in regard to the United States, he is not explicit.

Regardless of Gow's and Owen's lack of explicitness, however, the pragmatism of 'increased US diplomatic pressure' should be obvious. If it was indeed the case that the Clinton administration missed an opportunity to make peace in Bosnia-Herzegovina in 1993, and the causes of this miscalculation can be identified, then the hypothesis is undoubtedly useful. To historians, it would clarify to what extent the US diplomatic position on the Vance–Owen plan should be regarded as a decisive factor in the history of the war, and whether the Pale meeting represented a potential turning point in the course of the war. To diplomats and politicians, it would likely teach lessons for how to handle similar conflicts in the future.

7.2.3. Falsifiability

'Increased US diplomatic pressure' does have potential scientific coherence deficiencies because it does not precisely define the specifics of the counterfactual scenario. Gow does not elaborate on what evidence would be needed to sustain the hypothesis that the Vance–Owen plan would have created peace if the Clinton administration had given it more support. It is thus difficult to falsify many of the underlying assertions of 'increased US diplomatic pressure'. Strong falsifiability requires precise arguments. In this sense, it may be fair to argue that a clearer foundation in counterfactual theory may have improved the hypothesis.

However, even if the authors of a counterfactual argument do not specify the evidence needed to prove their own hypothesis, this does not necessarily mean that there can be no such evidence. There is indeed possible empirical evidence that shed light on 'increased US diplomatic pressure'. One would need to find material that documents how the US policy was perceived by the Bosnian Serb decision-makers. Statements by politicians could be useful evidence, but with appropriate qualifications due to the possibility of concealed motives. Serb and Bosnian Serb reactions to US pressure in similar situations throughout the war in Bosnia-Herzegovina could also provide guidance.

At the core, one must ask these two questions: First, is there evidence that the Clinton administration could have given stronger and clearer support for the Vance–Owen plan (plausibility of the antecedent)? Second, is there evidence that the Vance–Owen plan was sufficiently acceptable to the Bosnian Serbs that increased US pressure could have won them over to acceptance of the plan (plausibility of the consequent)?

Finding reliable evidence to strengthen the hypothesis is a difficult task, and it is unlikely that one will be able to conclude strongly, but there is relevant evidence available for at least making valuations. It can therefore be argued that the counterfactual hypothesis is not in breach of the criterion of falsifiability, as the term is defined here, and should be considered scientifically coherent.

7.3. The Plausibility of Increased US Diplomatic Pressure

7.3.1. Plausibility of the Antecedent

In order for the antecedent to be plausible, it is necessary to provide evidence that the Clinton administration had sufficient room for manoeuvre to decide on and carry out a different policy than the one it actually chose, that is, to provide stronger and clearer support for the Vance–Owen plan. As explained in the theory section, the plausibility of the antecedent is likely to increase if these criteria are met: (1) Evidence that a counterfactual policy was *subjectively possible*, (2) specification of a *branching point*, (3) little or no deviation from *historical values*, and (4) adherence to the *minimal rewrite rule*. Generalisations and analogies will be discussed under the sub-chapter dealing with the plausibility of the consequent. Of these four heuristics, I concentrate on the minimal rewrite rule. The reason is that in measuring the room for manoeuvre for the Clinton administration, it is crucial to examine whether it could have changed its policy through an internal decision, or whether its line was more or less dictated by public opinion, advice from the military, the political situation, and so on.

7.3.1.1. The Subjectively Possible

'Increased US Diplomatic Pressure' complies with this heuristic. Many contemporary voices called on the United States to give more support for the Vance–Owen plan. Among these voices were the co-chairmen of ICFY, Vance and Owen, who not only believed strong American support could come, but counted on it to bring the negotiations to a successful conclusion. But most importantly, the Clinton administration itself deliberated on the level of support for the Vance–Owen plan, as is shown by the fact that the level of support varied during the peace process.

7.3.1.2. Specified Branching Point

Neither Gow nor Owen explain exactly when and where the American position on the Vance–Owen plan could have changed. Gow, however, does point to some of the occasions when the American lack of support was especially important. An example is when the United States rejected a British draft of a UN Security Council resolution giving full support to the Vance–Owen plan on 30 March 1993, officially because they believed it to be unfair to the Bosnian Government and rewarded ethnic cleaning.[20] Because Gow also argues that the American lack of support was consistent over time, however, altering the position on this specific Security Council resolution would likely require a change of policy in general, and Gow does not provide evidence that this was likely at the end of March.

This represents a problem for the possibility of finding evidence relevant to the scenario, because all other historical events spring from the branching point. The fact that this is virtually absent from Gow's and Owen's accounts is testimony to the fact that their counterfactual hypotheses were developed without a clear foundation in counterfactual theory. As their hypotheses stand, it is difficult to establish plausibility for their arguments. This means that in order to evaluate the plausibility, one is forced to consider potential branching points throughout the entire Vance–Owen process, from January to May 1993.

---

[20] *Ibid.*, p. 245; Graham Messervy-Whiting, *Peace Conference on Former Yugoslavia: The Politico-Military Interface*, in series *London Defence Studies*, vol. 21, Brassey's, London, 1994, p. 18.

In this period, the US position on the Vance–Owen plan varied. Louis Sell refers to the US policy as "on-again, off-again support".[21] This is not an inaccurate description, but it would be more precise to say that the US support varied, but that the US gave stronger support later in the Vance–Owen process than in the beginning. When the process was launched in January, the US expressed doubts and even opposition in the talks with its allies. According to John Major, the Americans disliked the idea of cantonisation, which they saw that as a concession to the Serbs.[22] The Clinton administration shared this scepticism, by the way, with the outgoing Bush administration, where Secretary of State Lawrence Eagleburger had declared US opposition to cantonisation of Bosnia.[23]

The Clinton administration came into office with the policy of 'lift and strike'.[24] In early February, the Clinton administration announced that it was working on its own peace plan, which was interpreted by many as an alternative to the Vance–Owen plan.[25] Importantly, however, when the Clinton administration revealed its plan to the press on 11 February 1993, it appeared clear that the United States would support the Vance–Owen process.[26] One of Clinton's biographers, Elisabeth Drew, confirms that the Clinton administration decided at this time to engage in the Vance–Owen process, despite its reservations, by both supporting the peace plan and

21 Louis Sell, *Slobodan Milošević and the Destruction of Yugoslavia*, Duke University Press, Durham, 2002, p. 208.

22 John Major, *The Autobiography*, HarperCollins Publishers, London, 1999, p. 540.

23 Reneo Lukic and Allen Lynch, *Europe from the Balkans to the Urals: The Disintegration of Yugoslavia and the Soviet Union*, Oxford University Press, Solna, 1996, p. 319. Reference to Eagleburger's intervention at the London conference in August 1992.

24 Sell, 2002, p. 205, see *supra* note 21.

25 See, for example, Jeremy Campbell, "Clinton works on a new peace plan for Bosnia", in *The Evening Standard*, 5 February 1993; "Clinton cool on plan for Bosnia", in *The Independent*, 6 February 1993; Alan Ferguson, "U.S. sees Bosnia plan as flawed, diplomats say", in *The Toronto Star*, 9 February 1993; Thomas L. Friedman, "U.S. Will Not Push Muslims to Accept Bosnia Peace Plan", in *The New York Times*, 4 February 1993.

26 Doyle McManus, "U.S. Launches Its Own Plan for Peace in Bosnia Balkans: Like Vance–Owen proposal, strategy would not force Serbs to give up all territory they have seized", in the *Los Angeles Times*, 11 February 1993; "U.S. Offers Six-Point Plan To End the War in Bosnia – Military Forces Are Pledged In Any Multilateral Action; Envoy to Aid Vance, Owen", in *Wall Street Journal Europe*, 11 February 1993; "US muscle for the mediator", in *Financial Times*, 12 February 1993; Simon Tisdall and David Gow, "US swings to Bosnia plan", in *The Guardian*, 8 February 1993.

working to get more favourable conditions for the Bosnian Government.[27] On 9 February 1993, Clinton appointed Reginald Bartholomew as his special envoy to the peace process for this purpose.[28] On 11 March 1993, the United States urged NATO to plan for 50,000 troops in Bosnia should the Vance–Owen Plan be accepted by all sides. However, on 30 March 1993, the US rejected the French and UK draft UN Security Council resolution giving full support for the Vance–Owen Plan.[29]

Still, there was a clear shift in the administration's policy toward more support of the Vance–Owen plan. Even Gow admits that the American pressure was instrumental in getting the signatures of presidents Izetbegović (on 3 and 25 March 1993) and Karadžić (on 2 May 1993), respectively.[30]

Between mid-April and 1 May 1993, an agreement among the Clinton administration officials emerged in favour of the 'lift and strike'-option. Secretary of State, Warren Christopher, was dispatched on a trip to Europe in order to convince NATO allies to accept this policy.[31] At this stage, however, there was no practical difference between providing strong support for the Vance–Owen plan and suggesting the use of air strikes and arming the Bosnian Government. The threat of air strikes was instrumental in getting the Bosnian Serbs to sign the agreement in Athens and it was also a weighty argument under discussion in the Pale Assembly on 5–6 May 1993.[32] In fact, Gow also argues that a major reason why Karadžić signed the Vance–Owen plan map at Athens was because of implicit American threats of air strikes.[33]

---

27 Elisabeth Drew, *On the Edge: The Clinton Presidency*, Simon and Schuster, New York, 1994, p. 147.

28 Lukic and Lynch, 1996, pp. 320–321, see *supra* note 23.

29 *Ibid.*, p. 321.

30 Gow, 1997, p. 245, see *supra* note 1.

31 Wayne Bert, *The Reluctant Superpower: United States' Policy in Bosnia, 1991–95*, Houndsmills, Basingstroke, 1997, pp. 200–201; Drew, 1994, pp. 151–155, see *supra* note 27.

32 Laura Silber, "Bosnian Serbs Delay Peace Vote, Draft Conditions Balkans: Rebel chief warns of fierce attack by NATO if Vance–Owen plan is not accepted. Any changes in pact are seen as unacceptable to world community", in the *Los Angeles Times*, 6 May 1993. Also referred to in Owen, 1995, p. 163, see *supra* note 1.

33 Gow, 1997, p. 246, see *supra* note 1.

Most importantly, the Bosnian Serb President, Radovan Karadžić, was very clear on the threat of air strikes when he addressed the Bosnian Serb Assembly in Pale on 5 May 1993. In reference to the consequences of not ratifying the Vance–Owen plan, he said:

> They are threatening the total destruction of the Serbian people on these territories, the unilateral armament of our enemies, the destruction of the Serbs, Serbian military, strategic and defence targets, and also supply routes – bridges and communication routes – in which we must naturally anticipate the suffering of numerous civilians. These threats are explicit, clear and very realistic.[34]

Karadžić was justifying his own signature of the Vance–Owen plan at Athens when making this statement, and asked – albeit reluctantly – for the Bosnian Serb Assembly's ratification. His stated reason was the threat of air strikes, which he called "very realistic". In addition, Serb President Slobodan Milošević, Montenegrin President Momir Bulatović, ex-Yugoslav President Dobrica Cosic and Greek Prime Minister Constantine Mitsotakis had all urged the Assembly to ratify the plan. The Assembly, however, overwhelmingly rejected the plan.[35]

The conclusion from all this is that it seems unlikely that the US could have provided significantly stronger and clearer support for the Vance–Owen plan in the later stages of the process, as the threat of air strikes seems to have worked in pressuring the Bosnian Serbs to accept the Vance–Owen plan at Athens, although not at Pale. The conclusion is that the potential branching point for the hypothesis should be set to an earlier stage, at the very beginning of the process, in January 1993.

7.3.1.3. Historical Values

As mentioned, Gow lists three main reasons for the Clinton administration's lack of support for the Vance–Owen plan. The first on this list is *moral issues*, that the Americans perceived the Vance–Owen plan as rewarding Serb aggression. In regard to the counterfactual theory as outlined in Part II of this book, it should be assessed whether these moral issues were an expression of deep-seated historical values (which would be difficult to

34 "Karadžić Says Vance–Owen Plan 'Catastrophic', But Urges Acceptance By Assembly", *BBC Monitoring Service*, 7 May 1993.

35 Jovan Kovacic, "Bosnian Serbs reject Vance–Owen peace plan", in *Reuters News*, 6 May 1993.

counterfactually alter) or – as Gow argues – simply wrongful and based on faulty understanding of the conflict. In Gow's opinion, the Vance–Owen plan took its starting point in the ethnic composition of Bosnia-Herzegovina according to the 1991 census, that is, before the war and before ethnic cleansing had begun.[36] This is to say that the moral criticism of the Vance–Owen plan was at least partially unfounded. Another factor that confirms this, according to Gow, was the fact that the Vance–Owen plan denied the Bosnian Serbs contiguous territory from Croatian Krajina, through Northern Bosnia and to Serbia proper.[37]

Gow suggests that a possible reason for what he considers a misconception on part of the Clinton administration – that the Vance–Owen plan rewarded ethnic cleansing – may be that the idea of cantonisation was first put forth by the Serbs. In fact, Serbia had advocated the idea of ethnic territories/cantons since 1991. This had served as a charter for ethnic cleansing. The constitutional plan devised by the ICFY, however, was a major improvement of the early cantonisation proposals, Gow claims.[38]

If the Clinton administration was partly uninformed of the realities, as Gow suggests, it is likely that more reliable information could have altered their view. Gow's argumentation on this point, however, is speculative. Rather than a matter of the *degree of knowledge*, the issue of whether the Vance–Owen plan rewarded the Bosnian Serbs and sanctioned ethnic cleansing was a matter of *differing opinions*. Certainly, rewarding the Serbs cannot be said to have been the intention of the co-chairmen of ICFY.[39] Owen, for example. on certain occasions argued that air power should be used against the Serbs to get them to accept a negotiated peace.[40] However, others see it differently. Lukic and Lynch have argued that the Vance–Owen plan was tantamount to partition, as it was difficult to imagine that the Croat and Serb cantons would not merge with their neighbouring states after the

36 Gow, 1997, p. 239, see *supra* note 1.

37 *Ibid.*, p. 241.

38 *Ibid.*, p. 235.

39 Thorvald Stoltenberg writes that claims of appeasement were incorrect in Thorvald Stoltenberg and Kai Eide, *De tusen dagene: Fredsmeklere på Balkan* [The One Thousand Days: Peace Negotiators in the Balkans], Gyldendal, Oslo, 1996, p. 54.

40 See, for example, "Interview with David Owen on the Balkans", in *Foreign Affairs*, 1995, vol. 72, no. 2, p. 5 ('Interview with Owen').

plan was signed. In this regard, they question the US policy shift toward support of the Vance–Owen plan as "morally dubious".[41]

In the hindsight of history, however, one would be right in arguing that a flawed peace deal in 1993 would be preferable to the Dayton agreement, when considering the human tragedies that occurred in Bosnia-Herzegovina in the meantime. Still, in January 1993 it was much more difficult to see that this would be the case, or whether there might not be other approaches to conflict resolution in Bosnia-Herzegovina that might provide a more just solution to the war.

At any rate, one cannot argue that the moral issues related to the Vance–Owen plan *compelled* the Clinton administration not to support it from the beginning. Evidence to this is the fact that many other actors provided support – such as the Security Council Presidency in its statement of 8 January 1993 – and, more importantly, that the Clinton administration did provide support for the Vance–Owen plan at a later stage.[42] For these reasons, it would be difficult to argue that the moral convictions in January 1993 made a counterfactually stronger American support for the plan impossible.

7.3.1.4. Minimal Rewrite Rule and Political Consideration

The second reason Gow gives for the lukewarm American support of the Vance–Owen plan is the *political considerations*. Gow believes that American informed opinion was too negative to the Vance–Owen plan for the Clinton administration to support it wholeheartedly. Gow points to the influence of the liberal press and *The New York Times* in particular.[43] This echoes the views of Owen, who said on 16 February 1993 that "[t]he problem appears to have been in part that *The New York Times* editorially took a very emotive position on the issue right from the start and its assumptions spread through to other newspapers".[44]

---

41 Lukic and Lynch, 1996, pp. 320–321, see *supra* note 23.

42 Statement of the Presidency of the Security Council S/25080, printed in Daniel Bethelehem and Marc Weller (eds.), *The 'Yugoslav' Crisis in international Law: General Issues, Part I*, in series *Cambridge International Documents Series*, vol. 5, Cambridge University Press, Cambridge, 1997, p. 26.

43 Gow, 1997, pp. 214–216, see *supra* note 1.

44 Interview with Owen, p. 3, see *supra* note 40.

The reference to political considerations is relevant to the heuristic of minimal rewrite. Any assessment of whether the Clinton administration had the room for manoeuvre necessary to make a different choice on support for the Vance–Owen plan must begin with an assessment of the political situation in which the decision-makers operated. Did the political considerations dictate a certain line by the Clinton administration, or could it have chosen an alternative policy?

There is no consensus on the part played by the US media in portraying the Vance–Owen plan, or the war in Bosnia-Herzegovina in general. James Sadkovich, for example, lists a number of articles where he argues that the Serbs were portrayed as the victims of the war, and which legitimised Serb territorial claims.[45] In general, however, there are grounds for accepting Gow's view that much of American informed opinion *did* take a negative stance towards the Vance–Owen plan. It also seems right that *The New York Times* was, at times, very critical of the Vance–Owen plan, and published significant articles documenting the terrible situation of the Bosnian Muslims, as inflicted by the Bosnian Serbs.[46]

However, the crucial issue is whether the Clinton administration could have given the plan more support *in spite* of the press. If it can be held that the American opinion was so negative that the administration would face a serious credibility problem at home over its foreign policy, then it would weaken the plausibility of 'increased US diplomatic pressure'. In this case the varyingly lukewarm support must not be perceived as something for which the Clinton administration can be blamed.

Warming up to the Vance–Owen plan might have been perceived by the public as an act of appeasement, because the plan seemed to legitimise ethnic cleansing and reward Serb aggression, as explained above. This sentiment certainly had a following in the United States. One of the most active critics of the Vance–Owen plan was Democratic Senator Joe Biden, who

---

45 James J. Sadkovich, *The U.S. Media and Yugoslavia, 1991–1995*, Praeger, Westport, Connecticut, 1998, pp. 152–159.

46 See, for example, "Lord Owen's Googly", in *The New York Times*, 4 February 1993; or Leslie Gelb, "Making Peace", in *The New York Times*, 9 April 1993. For a general study of the coverage of the war in Bosnia-Herzegovina in *The Washington Post* and *The New York Times*, see Yehudith Auerbach and Yaeli Bloch-Elkon, "Media Framing and Foreign Policy: The Elite Press vis-à-vis US Policy in Bosnia, 1992-95", in *Journal of Peace Research*, 2005, vol. 42, no. 1, pp. 83–99.

argued to the public and to the President that the plan was "premised on dismemberment", and called for new negotiations.[47]

Regardless, the final choice was that of the administration. US foreign policy is not dictated by *The New York Times* or the by press in general, or even "informed opinion". The President had the power to choose either way, no matter the general opinion of the day. Through competent handling of public relations, the administration would probably also have had a good chance to display their (counterfactually) stronger support for the Vance–Owen plan to the American public as evidence of pragmatism, strong leadership and responsibility. In this case, the altered antecedent of 'Increased US Diplomatic Pressure' can be perceived as plausible also in regard to the political considerations.

Gow's third reason for the American mistrust of the Vance–Owen plan is that the Clinton administration deemed the plan too unpredictable. Particularly worrying were the many internal borders that would have to be protected by NATO peace-keepers. The question is therefore whether the Vance–Owen plan map actually was a solid plan in the military sense. Gow praises the plan and the map and believes that the plan was indeed enforceable. The judgment of military advisors in the United States and in NATO contradicted this.[48]

For the military advisors in the Clinton administration, the issue boiled down to whether one could believe that the warring parties really wanted to make and keep the peace as outlined in the plan. Just by looking at the Vance–Owen plan map, it becomes immediately apparent that the plan would be difficult to enforce if one of the warring sides would have decideed to violate the agreement and attack. The intricate system of throughways and cantons could be difficult to defend in the event of a well co-ordinated offensive. Even if the politicians who accepted the Vance–Owen plan stood by it, it could not guarantee that hard-line politicians and officers would not seek to reverse that decision later. This was war, after all, and the Bosnian Serb opposition to the Vance–Owen plan was considerable, as later demonstrated by the clear result of the Bosnian Serb referendum in mid-May 1993.

47 "Clinton to upstage Vance–Owen talks", in *The Independent*, 10 February 1993.

48 Gow, 1997, pp. 216–217, see *supra* note 1; Drew, 1994, p. 146, see *supra* note 27.

There were many who warned about the unenforceability of the Vance–Owen plan borders. Former US Ambassador to the UN, Jeane Kirkpatrick, wrote a widely circulated article in the beginning of May 1993, stating clearly that "[t]his agreement would last only as long as the balance of power among the three ethnic groups lasts. That may not be long".[49] Such concerns were also found inside the Clinton administration. There is no doubt that the US Defence Department and the Joint Chiefs of Staff were uneasy about the prospect of a situation where the United States had to implement an unwanted peace agreement. Defence Secretary Les Aspin commented on this to *Meet The Press* on 17 March 1993:

> If they [the three warring parties in Bosnia-Herzegovina] are only willing to sign the paper for a tactical reason but they want to continue the struggle [...] it is going to be a much more dangerous mission. You could have a situation where people are getting killed in small numbers but regularly. Now I don't think the American public would want that.[50]

What would the options be if American troops had been deployed and one of the sides broke with the Vance–Owen plan? In this case, the United States would have had thousands of troops inside a war zone, possibly in a potentially chaotic situation because of the intricate Vance–Owen plan map. The one alternative was that the Clinton administration would be forced to withdraw American troops, leaving Bosnia-Herzegovina in a possibly even worse state than before, and also having lost credibility both internationally and domestically. Just some months after the American military failure in Somalia, a military catastrophe in Bosnia-Herzegovina would strengthen Republicans' opposition to Clinton's domestic reforms and could even have cost the President re-election in 1996.

The second alternative would be to leave the troops inside Bosnia-Herzegovina and fight it out. Although the American public is usually supportive of military action once it actually occurs ("support our troops"), this could have a long-term negative effect on public confidence. Especially since large-scale American military warfare in Bosnia-Herzegovina would have unpredictable responses from Milošević' Serbia, as well as from

---

[49] Jeane Kirkpatrick, "Vance/Owen plan not good enough", in *Patriot-News*, 7 February 1993.

[50] Jim Hoagland, "The Pentagon's Reluctance on Bosnia", in *The Washington Post*, 17 March 1993.

newly democratic states in the former Soviet Union and Russia itself. Furthermore, even if the US military won the initial battles, it would have risked prolonged guerrilla warfare in Bosnia-Herzegovina, a country that prided itself with its guerrilla heritage (both the Partisan and the Chetnik resistance during World War II).

Both scenarios were, of course, unacceptable to the Clinton administration. In other words, if there was no real will to make peace in Bosnia-Herzegovina in 1993, the Vance–Owen plan might have brought disaster for the Clinton administration. Even if the Vance–Owen plan map won acceptance, the situation might change after implementation so as to trap both American troops and American policy.

The military factors seem to be the most compelling ground for caution for the Clinton administration – as compared with the moral and political reasons – but should nonetheless not be seen as decisive to any one policy. It is testimony to this that already in February 1993, Clinton agreed to send American peace-keepers to Bosnia in the event of an agreement on the Vance–Owen plan.[51] In early May 1993, concrete plans were made to send a significant American troop contingent (around 20,000) to function as peace-keepers, if the Bosnian Serbs accepted the plan.[52] This happened in spite of strong reasons for scepticism.

It follows from the above discussion that all the reasons on Gow's list for the Clinton administration's lukewarm support for the Vance–Owen plan explain why some caution on part of the administration was inevitable. None of the reasons, however, seem to bind the administration to the policy line that was chosen. The Clinton administration did have reasons to regard the Vance–Owen plan with some scepticism – on moral, political and military grounds – but was fully able to have supported it from the beginning, if it had been willing.

As a conclusion in regard to the plausibility of a counterfactually stronger support from the Clinton administration to the Vance–Owen plan, it seems that this should be seen as a plausible antecedent. It appears to meet all the heuristics that have been presented in the theory section: It was

51 Martin Walker, "Clinton prepared to send peace force to Bosnia", in *The Guardian*, 11 February 1993.

52 Ian Black, David Fairhall and Martin Walker, "Clinton Sceptical on Bosnia Peace", in *The Guardian*, 4 May 1993.

subjectively possible, adheres to the minimal rewrite rule, and does not appear to deviate far from the historical values of the decision-makers. The lack of a specified branching point is a weakness in the hypotheses. Still, it can be reasoned that a plausible branching point can be specified, even though the originators of the hypothesis have not explicitly done this.

7.3.2. Plausibility of the Consequent: The Bosnian Serbs' Will to Make Peace

Having established that the Clinton administration could have pursued a counterfactual policy, what remains is the assessment of whether this policy would have made a difference in terms of getting the Vance–Owen plan approved by the Bosnian Serbs. The answer to this question must be founded on an assessment of whether the Vance–Owen plan would have appeared acceptable to the Bosnian Serbs if the US had given it stronger support. In the following pages, I discuss first the criticism that has been raised against the hypothesis, and then turn to the generalisations used by Gow in support of his hypothesis.

7.3.3. Critique by Other Researchers

One criticism of 'Increased US Diplomatic Pressure' has been put forward in Steven L. Burg and Paul S. Shoup's *The War in Bosnia-Herzegovina* from 1999. The book addresses Gow's arguments directly. The authors agree with Gow when it comes to the problems Vance and Owen faced with not having Western military force to use as leverage against the Bosnian Serbs: "Their task, in the words of the deputy co-chairman of the ICFY, Ambassador Herbert S. Okun, was like 'playing baseball without a bat'".[53] Certainly, they argue, having real force to put pressure on the Bosnian Serbs could have changed matters. Still, Burg and Shoup claim that it is a misunderstanding of the Serb and Bosnian Serb decision-makers to believe that clear American pressure would have led them to accept the Vance–Owen plan:

> [H]erein lies the dilemma surrounding the Vance–Owen plan; if it had been clear in advance that the West would implement the plan with force – an approach that might be characterized

[53] Steven L. Burg and Paul S. Shoup, *The War in Bosnia-Herzegovina: Ethnic Conflict and International Intervention*, M.E. Sharpe, Armonk, 1999, p. 405. Originally quoted from the *New York Times*, 11 July 1993.

> as imposing a settlement – the Serbs would likely have rejected it outright.[54]

Burg and Shoup thus argue that the missing – and crucially important – element that could have created an early settlement in Bosnia-Herzegovina was not Western force, but rather the will to create peace on the part of the Serbs and Bosnian Serbs. Burg and Shoup argue further:

> The Serbs had fought too hard to take control of eastern Bosnia and the northern corridor – and committed too many atrocities in the effort of to do so – simply to hand this territory back to the Muslims. It seems clear, therefore, that it was the probability that the Vance–Owen plan would *not* be enforced that first led Milošević to support it in January 1993, and to urge the Bosnian Serbs to do likewise. By the same token, it was the prospect of a U.S.-led intervention to implement the plan that led Milošević to dissociate himself from the plan in February–March 1993.[55]

In this line of thought, Milošević' agenda was to gain international credibility by accepting the plan, but then frustrate its implementation.[56] Burg and Shoup particularly argue that the Northern Corridor was a piece of territory that the Bosnian Serbs could never surrender, whether the Vance–Owen plan was formally agreed to or not. On this basis, they question whether the Vance–Owen plan can be seen as a missed opportunity for peace.

Burg and Shoup's argument does not necessarily contradict that a more forceful approach from the Americans might have enforced an earlier settlement in Bosnia-Herzegovina. What they contest, however, is that stronger diplomatic commitment would have led to the acceptance of the Vance–Owen plan specifically. On the contrary, they believe stronger pressure may have made the Serbs boycott or abandon the diplomatic channel altogether, because their main objective for pursuing negotiations was not reaching a settlement, but consolidating their territorial occupation on the ground.

---

54 Burg and Shoup, 1999, p. 405, see *supra* note 53.

55 *Ibid*., p. 405.

56 Silber and Little voice the same opinion in Laura Silber and Allan Little, *Yugoslavia: Death of a Nation*, Penguin, New York, 1997, p. 279.

The differing opinions of Burg/Shoup and Gow, respectively, illustrate a common trait in debates dealing with a counterfactual subject matter: Counterfactual arguments are used in order to clarify the factual causes. Both Gow and Burg/Shoup deal with the counterfactual problem of what would have happened if the Clinton administration had been more committed to the Vance–Owen plan and to using force to settle the war in Bosnia-Herzegovina. Gow starts with the fact that the Vance–Owen plan seems to have come very close to being formally accepted, as it was officially signed by all three party-leaders, but seemingly failed on the finishing line. The statements of American officials at various times in the peace process lead him to conclude that the lack of international will was the major reason why the war in Bosnia-Herzegovina did not stop until late 1995. Burg and Shoup, on the other hand, examine the reactions of Milošević at the times when the Americans did seem to become deeply committed to the Vance–Owen plan, and they argue that in those times he dissociated himself from the process. This is a line of reasoning where repeated behaviour is used to support the hypothesis of counterfactual behaviour, in this case that of Milošević. Greater diplomatic pressure from the international community would in this line of reasoning *not* have led to a successful conclusion of the Vance–Owen plan and peace in Bosnia-Herzegovina in May 1993, because not all three parties were yet willing to make the compromises that would have been necessary to attain peace.

Another contribution to the debate on the Vance–Owen plan is Brendan Simms' *Unfinest Hour*.[57] Simms dismisses the hypothesis of 'Increased US Diplomatic Pressure' as a mere excuse to blame the Americans for why success was not achieved earlier.[58] His argument is that the Americans cannot be blamed for the failure of the Vance–Owen plan, because the most important reason why peace was not attained was that the Bosnian Serbs pursued a maximalist programme of expansion. Simms writes about this in the following manner:

> Owen, in fact, had forgotten that the Bosnian Serb war aim was not to secure a reasonable territorial settlement and constitutional arrangements, but a maximalist programme designed to create an ethnically pure 'Greater Serbia'. The VOPP [Vance Owen Peace Plan] – for all its inherent flaws

[57] Brendan Simms, *Unfinest Hour: Britain and the Destruction of Bosnia*, Penguin, London, 2002, pp. 142–157.

[58] *Ibid.*, p. 335.

> and last-minute concessions to the Serbs – was fundamentally incompatible with this project; and the Serbs never did relinquish any of their lands until they had been militarily defeated.[59]

Simms' viewpoint is thus that it is very unlikely that the Vance–Owen plan could have led to peace in 1993, regardless of diplomatic pressure from the Clinton administration. As long as the plan denied the Bosnian Serbs their principal aims, it would not be accepted voluntarily. The view that maximalist political visions were the real obstacle to peace is echoed by John Major, who writes: "How were negotiators supposed to negotiate when the twisted logic and self-interest of Yugoslav leaders was in favour of bloodshed?".[60] Simms concludes that more forceful measures would have been required, which I will return in Chapter 9.

7.3.4. The Bosnian Serb Perception of the Vance–Owen Plan

It is clear that the Bosnian Serbs saw the Vance–Owen plan as a defeating peace proposal. This was seemingly the case for all Bosnian Serb elites, including the media, the politicians and the military. One telling story from the media side is conveyed in Laura Silber and Allan Little's *The Death of Yugoslavia*:

> On the eve of the Pale session, Risto Djogo, the best-known Bosnian Serb journalist, appeared to read the TV news. He looked at a blank piece of paper, signed it, pulled out a pistol and shot himself. Wiping the stage-blood off his forehead, Djogo said that the Serbian people would not commit suicide. The message was clear.[61]

Đogo's news drama is but one example of the negative perception of the Vance–Owen plan among the Bosnian Serbs. In President Karadžić' speech to the Pale Assembly, aimed at assuring ratification of the plan, he also called the plan "catastrophic":

> The plan, as you know very well, is, basically, catastrophic for us. This plan denies our right to self-determination, to the state which we have created and have been defending by relying on

59 *Ibid.*, p. 150.

60 Major connects this statement with the fact that Tuđjman and Milošević met in a series of meeting from early 1991 to discuss dividing Bosnia between them. Major, 1999, p. 546, see *supra* note 22.

61 Laura Silber and Allan Little, *The Death of Yugoslavia*, Penguin, London, 1995, p. 315.

> our own forces. The plan demands that we return to Bosnia-Hercegovina, and it gives us, the majority people, three provinces amounting to 43% of the territory although we, as the majority people, live on 64% of Bosnia-Hercegovina's territory. These are all well-known facts.[62]

Karadžić's negative perception of the plan was not confined to him personally, nor to the time of the Pale meeting specifically. Many of the politicians in the Bosnian Serb Assembly seemed convinced that their constituencies would not approve of the Vance–Owen plan. According to one source, this seems especially to have been the case with the delegates from Western Bosnia-Herzegovina, who feared the Vance–Owen plan would cut them off completely from their allies.[63] The fact that the Vance–Owen plan would deny the Bosnian Serbs possession of the Northern Corridor and the establishment of an ethnically pure and unified Serb state would make it seem that the war had been in vain. It is clear from what we know from the Pale meeting that the President of the Assembly, Momčilo Krajišnik, and the supreme military commander, General Mladić, both fiercely opposed the plan.

What if stronger pressure has been applied to the Bosnian Serbs at an earlier stage? Of course, the Pale meeting was not the first time that the Bosnian Serb Assembly met to discuss the Vance–Owen plan. The plan was discussed in the Assembly in sessions on 5 and 26 April. Both times, the Assembly voted with crushing majorities to reject the plan.[64] In the meeting on 26 April, according to *Agence-France Presse*, 40 of the 41 MPs who spoke on the matter rejected it. Some of the speakers said that they were ready to face foreign intervention and even war with the United States.[65] This indicates a strong and clear-cut opposition to the plan on part of the Bosnian Serbs. Furthermore, the negative perception of the Vance–Owen plan in the Bosnian Serb Assembly seems to have been consistent.

---

62 "Karadžić Says Vance–Owen Plan 'Catastrophic', But Urges Acceptance By Assembly", BBC Monitoring Service, 7 May 1993.

63 Norwegian Embassy in Athens (Terje Hauge), *Fredsplanen for Bosnia-Herzegovina. Gresk engasjement* ["The Peace Plan for Bosnia-Herzegovina. Greek involvement"], 11 May 1993, p. 2 ('Norwegian Embassy Peace Plan').

64 "Serbs Reject Vance–Owen Peace Plan", Agence Europe, 6 April 1993; "Bosnian Serb MPs oppose Vance–Owen peace map", Agence France-Presse, 26 April 1993.

65 "Bosnian Serb MPs oppose Vance–Owen peace map", Agence France-Presse, 26 April 1993.

It could be argued that the Vance–Owen plan simply did not give enough to the Serb side, either in terms of territorial control or in economic conditions, to be acceptable at this stage in the war. The VRS were in control of its occupied territories and would be so for a significant period of time, unless the international community dramatically altered its policy of intervention.

In conclusion, it seems one will have a hard time arguing that all three warring parties in Bosnia-Herzegovina would indeed have been ready to make and keep the peace around the parameters of the Vance–Owen plan in 1993. It seems possible to argue plausibly that the Clinton administration could have given clearer and stronger support for the Vance–Owen plan at an earlier stage in the process. However, there is little that indicates that this alteration would have led to acceptance of the Vance–Owen plan by the Bosnian Serbs. It may just as well have been the case, as Burg and Shoup speculates, that if the Americans had pressured more strongly from the start, it may have led to a break in the negotiations.

7.3.5. Reference to Generalisations or Analogous Situations

'Increased US Diplomatic Pressure' attempts to draw plausibility from a reference to a 'limited generalisation' (by analogy). As mentioned, it is a central argument in the hypothesis that a crucial reason for why the Dayton agreement succeeded and the Vance–Owen process failed was that the United States was behind the former and not the latter.[66] According to Gow, this made the Dayton Peace Agreement possible.

However, one can certainly question the grounds for drawing this analogy. Many factors that were relevant for the successful completion of the Dayton process had changed between 1993 and 1995. To mention a few, there had been changes in the military balance on the ground in Bosnia-Herzegovina and NATO had carried out considerable air strikes against Bosnian Serb positions. I will return to the comparison between 1993 and 1995 in more detail in Chapter 9.

Gow also includes a limited generalisation in his discussion, specifically in the category of what Dahl labels "continued trends".[67] He lists

66 Gow, 1997, pp. 299 and 307, see *supra* note 1.

67 Ottar Dahl, *Problemer i historiens teori* [Problems of Causation in Historical Research], Universitetsforlaget, Oslo, 1986, p. 101. The term is roughly similar to what Eric Hobsbawn

many occasions on which the sides in Bosnia-Herzegovina responded positively or negatively to the Vance–Owen plan in response to varying signals from the United States. The Muslims, for example, signed the provisions of the Vance–Owen plan on 3 and 25 March 1993, both times after American pressure.[68] Gow also points to the momentum at Athens, where Karadžić was pressured into signing the Vance–Owen plan.

Such inductions may be misleading, however. The Vance–Owen plan was to be implemented as a whole, meaning that the entire plan would be useless unless all three parties signed all three provisions. Before the final ratification, which Karadžić all along made clear needed to be done by the Bosnian Serb Assembly, each signature had little value. Why then, should we believe that pressure really worked? Instead one could argue that the American threats only worked in bringing insignificant signatures onto the plans. When it actually mattered, it did not have a decisive effect.

Another possibility that should be taken into account, is that increased pressure may have hardened the stance of the Bosnian Serb politicians and military, by creating a "rally-round-the-flag" effect. There is some evidence that indicates that the assembly in Pale was significantly influenced by nationalist emotions, in addition to realist political considerations. A Greek participant in the Pale meeting, Charalambos Christopoulos, described the mood as highly emotional, where the representatives appeared to be unreceptive to rational arguments. This was particularly the case with the President of the Assembly, Momčilo Krajišnik, who, according to Christopoulos, was "clearly influenced" by the recent death of his wife in the war. Christopoulos summed up the mood as being characterised by the notion that "it was better to die quickly with a gun in their hands than the slow suffocation as a consequence of the peace plan".[69]

If indeed the Assembly was gripped by such an emotional mood, is it thinkable that more pressure would have made them give in? Could not stronger pressure at an earlier stage simply have roused the same emotions and led to an earlier demise of the peace plan? Naturally, one must be critical of the source of the description of the mood in the Assembly. The Greek delegation had to explain why it had failed to achieve a positive result in

refers to as a 'path analysis' as basis for historical predictions, see Eric Hobsbawm, "Looking Forward: History and the Future", in *New Left Review*, 1981, vol. 1, no. 125, p. 44.

68 Gow, 1997, p. 245, see *supra* note 1.

69 Norwegian Embassy Peace Plan, p. 1, see *supra* note 63.

the meeting, despite Prime Minister Mitsotakis' strong appeal in favour of the plan. There were certainly also plenty of rational arguments in the debates in Pale. It is a common perception that General Ratko Mladić "swung the meeting by showing a detailed map of Serb-held areas and towns which would be 'lost' under the [Vance–Owen] plan".[70] Still, it seems evident that an emotional sentiment also influenced the Pale proceedings. Mladić himself boasted that he and his men were not afraid of Western military intervention.[71]

It is difficult to see how more threats and stronger pressure would have made the Assembly accept the plan. Rather, it seems that the Vance–Owen plan was unacceptable to the Bosnian Serbs because it appeared to them both humiliating and defeating. In light of the analysis of the plausibility of the consequent, the conclusion must be that 'increased US diplomatic pressure', suggesting that the Clinton administration could have brought Bosnia-Herzegovina to peace in 1993 by supporting the Vance–Owen plan stronger and clearer, is not plausible.

---

70 Quoted from Owen, 1995, p. 164, see *supra* note 1. The view is also supported by Silber and Little, 1995, p. 316, see *supra* note 61. See also Stoltenberg and Eide, 1996, p. 64, see *supra* note 39.

71 Silber and Little, 1995, p. 316, see *supra* note 61.

8

Progressive Implementation

Contrary to 'Increased US Diplomatic Pressure', the hypothesis of 'Progressive Implementation' deals with the course of events *after* the Bosnian Serb rejection of the Vance–Owen plan. On 16 May 1993, Russian Foreign Minister Andrei Kozyrev issued a joint statement with Lord Owen, calling for 'progressive implementation' of the Vance–Owen plan, meaning deployment of new troops in Bosnia-Herzegovina.[1] Four days before, the French Foreign Minister Alain Juppé had agreed to progressive implementation, according to Stoltenberg.[2] The plan for implementation was based on the notion that Karadžić's signing of the Vance–Owen plan in Athens could be considered legally binding by the international community. Owen had argued for such a course of action since 6 May 1993, when it was clear that Karadžić's signature would not be ratified.[3] Serb opposition leader Vuk Drašković also supported this idea.[4]

The idea was to get the international community to commit troops to implementation, which was to commence in only a few of the ten cantons of the Vance–Owen plan map at first, starting in the provinces with Croat and Muslim majorities. By being 'progressive', however, the idea was to expand the presence of the international troops until they could enforce a peaceful settlement of the war in Bosnia-Herzegovina along the lines of what the Vance–Owen plan suggested. The plan gained support on 18 May, when Franjo Tuđjman and Alija Izetbegović reached an agreement to begin

---

1 James Gow, *Triumph of the Lack of Will: International Diplomacy and the Yugoslav War*, Hurst, London, 1997, p. 248. See also Christian Burckhardt, "Russia says Vance–Owen must go ahead", in *Reuters*, 16 May 1993; "Vance–Owen plan for Bosnia is still alive, says Kozyrev", *Agence France-Presse*, 19 May 1993; and Thorvald Stoltenberg and Kai Eide, *De tusen dagene: Fredsmeklere på Balkan* [The One Thousand Days: Peace Negotiators in the Balkans], Gyldendal, Oslo, 1996, p. 69.

2 Stoltenberg and Eide, 1996, p. 66, see *supra* note 1.

3 Jovan Kovacic, "Bosnian Serbs reject Vance–Owen peace plan", in *Reuters News*, 6 May 1993.

4 Gow, 1997, p. 248, see *supra* note 1.

implementing the Vance–Owen plan in the areas under their control.[5] A cease-fire was agreed to begin on 19 May, the day after the agreement, but it was never implemented.[6]

Gow has strongly supported this idea: "There should be no doubt that a programme geared to progressive implementation would have made sense".[7] According to Gow, it is important that the implementation would have concentrated the international forces and thereby made the implementation more credible. Since the foreign governments involved in Bosnia-Herzegovina were reluctant to risk fighting a war with the Bosnian Serbs, an implementation would have to have begun in Croatian and Muslim provinces.[8] Gow believes it should have started in provinces 8 (Mostar, Croat) and 10 (Travnik, Croat), and soon after that in 9 (Zenica, Muslim) and possibly 5 (Tuzla, Muslim). Of these, deployment in province 5, Tuzla, would have been the most difficult. The Serbs were unlikely to withdraw, and if they did, the Muslim forces were sure to move in. It would have required a substantial international commitment by the United States and NATO.[9] This would, according to Gow, have left the Serbs free to consolidate power in their other occupied territories and left them free to wage war other places. However, given that the implementation had been progressive, it would have to be gradually expanded to other areas, and meanwhile it would have restrained the fighting and saved lives. More importantly, in Gow's opinion, it would have left the ArBiH and HVO free to leave the safe areas and concentrate their forces in other regions. It would have enabled them to strike at the Bosnian Serbs' most important area, according to Gow, the "all-important Posavina [Northern] Corridor in northern Bosnia".[10]

The most ambitious element of the plan, at least in Gow's version of it, would have been direct implementation in this Northern Corridor – or province 3, Bosanski Brod (Croat), in the Vance–Owen map. Gow argues that "[i]mplementation in Province 3, had it been carried out, would have

5 RFE/RL News Briefs, 15 May 1993.

6 Stoltenberg and Eide, 1996, pp. 70 and 72, see *supra* note 1.

7 Gow, 1997, p. 250, see *supra* note 1.

8 *Ibid.*, p. 250.

9 *Ibid.*, p. 260.

10 *Ibid.*, p. 251.

broken the back of the Serbian military campaign".[11] He backs up this claim with a well-known quotation from Karadžić, who in 1995 said that the Bosnian Serb judgment at the time had been that their cause would have collapsed if no more than 5,000 NATO troops had been deployed in province 3.[12] Meanwhile, the media suggested that the Americans already in March 1993 had asked NATO to make plans for deploying 50-70,000 troops, while NATO planners were preparing for as much as 150,000 troops, depending on the level of local resistance.[13]

More than having a potentially crucial value of slowing down the war in Bosnia-Herzegovina, Gow believes progressive implementation would have had other significant side effects. One of these would have been to prevent the Muslim–Croat war in Bosnia-Herzegovina:

> International action [that is, progressive implementation] would have helped avert the coming war, both by building on the peace in the large areas in Bosnia which at this stage were not yet ravaged by war, as well as creating the sense in Croatian minds particularly, that the international community was prepared to do something in which it was worth having a stake.[14]

Avoiding the Muslim–Croat war was only one important side effect, according to Gow. Another would have been to improve the relationship between the United States and Russia, he argues. The debate on Yugoslavia in Moscow reflected the debate on Russia itself. The most important parties, according to Gow, were the "romantic nationalists" – or the "ideological and imperial" – on one side and the "pragmatists" or "Atlanticists" on the other. The former faction contained a small but loud group of pan-Slavists, who regarded the Serbs as "brothers".[15]

In cooperating with Kozyrev and agreeing with his plans for progressive implementation, Gow believes the United States would have improved

---

11 *Ibid.*, p. 252.

12 *Ibid.*, p. 252. Silber and Little refer to Karadžić as having said that 10,000 troops in Zvornik and the Posavina corridor was all it would take to neutralise the Serbs, in Laura Silber and Allan Little, *Yugoslavia: Death of a Nation*, Penguin, New York, 1997, p. 278.

13 Gow, 1997, p. 257, see *supra* note 1. Gow's source is *The New York Times*, 11 March 1993, p. A1.

14 Gow, 1997, p. 250, see *supra* note 1.

15 *Ibid.*, pp. 190–191.

their relationship with Russia and boosted the "Atlanticist" faction in Russian politics. The deathblow to this potential future was dealt when Kozyrev wanted to summon the P5 countries in the Security Council (the United States, Russia, the United Kingdom, China and France) to get them to support a draft resolution allowing progressive implementation, and the United States declined, saying it needed "reasonable borders".[16] Gow writes about the consequences for Russia's foreign policy:

> Although opinion was swelling in support of a Russia-first policy before May 1993 it was Washington's rejection of its proposals on implementation of the Vance–Owen Plan [that is, progressive implementation] that confirmed for Russia that it would have to reconsider its approach and ensure its equal status on the international diplomatic cast-list. The end of the Vance–Owen Plan was thus also the end of Moscow's unadulterated cooperation with the West.[17]

With this, Gow suggests that if the United States had agreed to progressive implementation, it would also have served to improve, or at least sustain, good relations with Russian foreign policy-makers.

Summing up, Gow argues that progressive implementation would have been possible, and that had it been implemented, it would have had three positive effects: (1) Quelling the fighting between the ArBiH and HVO (thereby saving lives and shortening the war), (2) coercing the Bosnian Serbs to accept the Vance–Owen plan by forcing them to relinquish control over the Northern corridor, and (3) provide basis for improved relations between the Russia and the United States.

8.1. The Scientific Coherence of Progressive Implementation

8.1.1. Logical Consistency

The hypothesis should be considered logically consistent. The counterfactual proposal that the Western states, the United States in particular, could have decided to implement the Vance–Owen plan after its rejection, does not entail any logical inconsistency.

16 *Ibid.*, p. 252.

17 *Ibid.*, p. 193.

8.1.2. Pragmatism

Gow does not draw up any explicit pragmatic advantages. Still, it seems obvious that the scenario does have considerable pragmatism. For example, it has bearing on the issue of whether, and how, peace can be enforced by an outside power. The counterfactual scenario of NATO's progressive implementation provides lessons for similar military interventions. If the conclusions indicate that the decision not to deploy troops was a responsible one, this would suggest greater caution when contemplating enforcement of peace settlements than Gow argues.

8.1.3. Falsifiability

There seems to be plenty of evidence that sheds light on the possibility of a decision to deploy NATO troops in Bosnia-Herzegovina. There are sources from NATO, the Clinton administration and others that show the thinking of the important decision-makers in the Western states at the time. The antecedent (decision on deployment) thus seems to be falsifiable.

In regard to the falsifiability of the consequents of this decision, there is also available evidence. The impact that progressive implementation would have had on the Muslim–Croat war and on the Bosnian Serb war effort can be evaluated on the basis of those statements that were made by Mladić, Karadžić and others at the time, and on what is known about the Muslim–Croat war. As for the statements, however, there is reason to be cautious about drawing strong conclusions, considering the probability of concealed planning and motives.

Even with a basis in this evidence, however, a major problem would remain in drawing up consequents in the n-order degree. The hypothesis suggested by Gow regarding the effect on the Bosnian Serb war effort involves a multi-staged operation – deploying first troops in certain sectors, and then expanding. Possible countermeasures and events in all counterfactual stages might have upset the original planning. As has been argued in the theory section of this book, setting up such an n-order counterfactual analysis would reduce the overall plausibility.

There are many conceivable factors that may have influenced the process after the initial branching point. The Bosnian Serb reactions to troop deployment, and the subsequent Croat and Bosnian Government responses to the Bosnian Serbs, are difficult to map out in all these various stages. In order to argue convincingly for the hypothesis, it therefore seems necessary to provide evidence that it was possible to commit NATO forces of such strength that it would have been unlikely that the Bosnian Serbs would be able or willing to persist in their opposition to the Vance–Owen plan. This is a difficult case to argue, but perhaps not impossible.

8.1.4. Conclusions on Scientific Coherence

The hypothesis should be considered to be scientifically coherent, despite some limitations in regard to the criterion of falsifiability.

8.2. The Plausibility of Progressive Implementation

8.2.1. Plausibility of the Antecedent: Could a Decision on Progressive Implementation Have Been Taken?

First, it should immediately be clear that the hypothesis is in compliance with the heuristic of the 'subjectively possible'. The co-chairmen, Owen and Stoltenberg, actively worked for getting sufficient acceptance and backing to implement the plan. Second, the hypothesis is also clearly in compliance with the heuristic of a specified branching point. The counterfactual decision to support the plan would have had to be made around the 20 May 1993 at the latest. The argument presented by Owen, Gow, and Stoltenberg, is that the United States killed the plan for progressive implementation on the 22 May 1993, when a resolution in the United Nations Security Council was pushed through (the Joint Action Programme, involving the establishing of safe areas). [18]

The remaining heuristics present more substantial challenges. I first discuss the issue of historical values, then the minimal rewrite rule. First, however, some specifications to the hypothesis are necessary, regarding the level and nature of the international commitment. Few would dispute that NATO forces – in a theoretical scenario – could have driven back any party to the war in Bosnia-Herzegovina. But it would have depended on the level of commitment. Since the Bosnian Serbs had not accepted the Vance–Owen plan, any implementation that represented a threat to Bosnian Serb military positions would have required a force that was mandated to, and capable of, enforcing the peace. This entails a different kind of military engagement than peace-keeping. In the areas controlled by the HVO and the ArBiH, the international force would in practice also have had to be credible enough

[18] *Ibid.*, p. 248; David Owen, *Balkan Odyssey*, Harcourt Brace, London, 1995, p. 194; Stoltenberg and Eide, 1996, pp. 73–74, see *supra* note 1.

for a peace enforcement mission. First, because there was already fighting between HVO and ArBiH. Second, because in order for the Bosnian Government and the Bosnian Croat forces to leave those areas, they would have to be reassured that the international presence would have been strong enough to protect the territories from Serb actions.

Russia and France gave the co-chairmen promises of committing troops to progressive implementation. In Gow's scenario, however, a peace enforcement mission would have required commitment also from the United States and preferably the United Kingdom. At the time, in May 1993, however, many of the decision-makers in the Clinton administration – especially in the military leadership – and in the British government, had serious problems with dispatching a peace enforcement mission to Bosnia-Herzegovina. The perceptions of the level of commitment that would have been needed to enforce peace, and the perceptions of the risks involved in such a commitment, are important reasons for why 'progressive implementation' never come to pass.

8.2.1.1. Historical Values

There is evidence that the US scepticism about engaging in a peace enforcement mission was rooted deeper than the dispassionate arguments regarding the Vance–Owen plan. Samantha Power claims that "[t]he one-word bogey 'Vietnam' became shorthand for all that could go wrong in the Balkans if the United States became militarily engaged".[19] John Major makes the same point in regard to the American opposition to ground troops for peace enforcement in his memoirs.[20] Zimmermann has also claimed that the Vietnam analogy led the American decision-makers to disfavour a more forceful military intervention.[21] The Vietnam experience thus seems to have influenced the Americans to be on the side of caution in regard to a peace enforcement intervention.[22]

---

19 Samantha Power, *A Problem from Hell: American and the Age of Genocide*, Basic Books, New York, 2002, p. 284.

20 John Major, *The Autobiography*, HarperCollins Publishers, London, 1999, p. 540.

21 Warren Zimmermann, *Origins of a Catastrophe: Yugoslavia and Its Destroyers – America's Last Ambassador Tells What Happened and Why*, Random House, New York, 1996, p. 214 (regarding Eagleburger in 1992) and p. 216 (in general).

22 See also Warren H. Switzer, "International Military Responses to the Balkan Wars: Crises in analysis", in Branka Magas and Ivo Zanic (eds.) *The War in Bosnia-Herzegovina 1991–1995*, Frank Cass, London, 2001, p. 284.

In regard to the British position, Brendan Simms has argued that the conservative ideology among the political elite in government, particularly Foreign Secretary Douglas Hurd and Defence Secretary Malcolm Rifkind, was a main obstacle to a more forceful military approach to Bosnia. Simms presents this argument when explaining why the British Government opposed the American 'lift and strike' option, but it is relevant in this regard as well, as it is a statement about the historical values of the decision-makers.[23] This ideology implied, according to Simms, that Britain's foreign policy should primarily promote its own interests (not universal values), and that Britain – as a middle-sized world power – should not use military force to police the world.[24]

However, these factors – the Vietnam memories and the potential influence of British conservative ideology – should not be taken to mean that the hypothesis in question is necessarily implausible. John Major confirms that there was division in the leadership of the British Conservative party over the use of both air strikes and ground troops to enforce peace. [25] This is not to say, of course, that this government was close to committing ground troops to enforce peace, but it does indicate that there was at least some room for manoeuvre. The Clinton administration, on the other hand, does not appear seriously to have considered sending in ground forces to enforce peace at the time. The Vietnam factor may have had some bearing on this, but it should be seen as one factor among several. It is difficult to argue that historical values alone ruled out an American counterfactual decision to commit ground troops for peace enforcement, but historical values do seem to reduce the plausibility of the changed antecedent.

8.2.1.2. Minimal Rewrite Rule

In spite of differing opinions in the United Kingdom and the United States over the use of military means to enforce peace in Bosnia, the major debate was regarding the use of air strikes, not peace enforcing ground troops. At no point in 1993 were any of the two governments close to deciding to commit ground troops for this purpose in Bosnia-Herzegovina. The question in regard to the plausibility of the antecedent that thus remains is how

---

23 Brendan Simms, *Unfinest Hour: Britain and the Destruction of Bosnia*, Penguin, London, 2002, pp. 7–8.

24 *Ibid.*, pp. 7–8.

25 Major, 1999, p. 536, see *supra* note 20.

great the alterations would have to be in order for a counterfactual decision to support progressive implementation to be made?

There is little or no evidence that indicates that the Clinton administration seriously contemplated any commitment of ground forces in mid-May 1993. Secretary of State Warren Christopher told the press at this time 1993: "I do not think that it's appropriate for the United States to try to implement a plan which has been so firmly rejected by one of the parties, because to do so you could only implement it through the use of overwhelming force".[26] The message from US officials at the time was fairly consistent: "only air power is contemplated".[27]

As with 'Increased US Diplomatic Pressure', Burg and Shoup have also criticised Gow's second hypothesis. In essence, what they argue is that although *capable* of implementing a peace plan with the force of arms, this was never actually seriously contemplated in the minds of Western policy-makers:

> From a Serb perspective, there is no doubt that a NATO military presence in Bosnia-Herzegovina would have seriously undermined Serb military superiority. Karadžić is said to have remarked that one NATO unit used as a blocking force in the corridor around Brčko would have been sufficient to undermine the Serb war effort. Yet it appears that such limited use of ground troops while fighting was still in progress was not considered by Western policy makers wary of an open-ended commitment.[28]

In one sense, this goes to the centre of Gow's account of the conflict in Bosnia-Herzegovina as a whole: The prolongation of the war was caused by a form of omission, in the sense that the West in general and the United States, in particular, did not have the will to enforce a just peace.

But while both accounts may agree that the missing element was will-power, only one (Gow) claims that the will-power *should* have been present. The other account (Burg/Shoup) argues that the deployment scenario

---

26 "United States giving up on Vance–Owen plan", Agence France-Presse, 19 May 1993.

27 James Flannery, "Confusion on Vance–Owen Bosnia plan – dead or just waiting?", in *Reuters*, 24 May 1993.

28 Steven L. Burg and Paul S. Shoup, *The War in Bosnia-Herzegovina: Ethnic Conflict and International Intervention*, M.E. Sharpe, Armonk, 1999, pp. 402–403. Brčko was not in Province 3, but the military strategic issue is the same, that is, to cut Serb territory in western Bosnia and Croatia from having continuous territory with eastern Bosnia and Serbia proper.

is so far-fetched that it is not really worth getting into: Western policy-makers wanted above all to avoid getting dragged into open war, which seemed a significant risk of deploying troops anywhere in Northern Bosnia-Herzegovina if this threatened the key Bosnian Serb war aims.

The United Kingdom was very reluctant to commit any ground troops to enforce a settlement in Bosnia-Herzegovina, as opposed to committing peace-keeping troops. Douglas Hurd clearly dismisses that an enforced implementation of the Vance–Owen plan was an option for the British government after the Bosnian Serb rejection.[29] Simms argues that this line was consistent throughout the Vance–Owen process.[30] Hurd also claims in his memoirs that a decision to commit British troops to fight a war in Bosnia would have been "deeply unpopular at all times".[31]

The British, in fact, had a quite precise policy in regard to the circumstances in which they would deploy troops with a mandate opening for peace enforcement in Bosnia-Herzegovina. In a closed session in NATO HQ on 7 April 1993, the British delegate put forth six specific criteria for their participation:

1. Commitment of all parties to the agreement and a reasonable probability of a final political settlement;
2. effective command and control by the local political and military leadership;
3. willingness of the local parties to give the force all the military information it needs;
4. an effective freeze of all significant movements of armed troops and equipment: acceptance that the military force is the authority for approving movements that are necessary;
5. an end to the fighting and a declared willingness by all parties to place all heavy weapons under the force's control with no right of access; and
6. appropriate legal underpinning and rules of engagement.[32]

---

29 Douglas Hurd, *Memoirs*, Little, Brown, London, 2003, p. 462.

30 See, for example, Simms, 2002, p. 154, see *supra* note 23.

31 Hurd, 2003, p. 446, see *supra* note 29.

32 Norwegian NATO delegation in Brussels, *Britiske 'kriterier' for å sette inn en større militær styrke for å håndheve en fredsplan for Bosnia* ["British 'Criteria' for Deploying a Greater Military Force in Order to Implement a Peace Plan for Bosnia"], 7 April 1993.

With the possible exception of point 2, none of these would be met, should the Vance–Owen plan be implemented without ratification of all parties in the conflict. There would not be commitment of all parties (point 1); there would not be willingness of all sides to give information (point 3); the freeze of movements of armed troops and equipment would likely have to be enforced with arms (point 4); the end to the fighting would also have to be coerced (point 5); and there would not be a clear legal underpinning, perhaps not even clear rules of engagement, because all of NATO's and the UN's planning was based on ratification of the Vance–Owen plan (point 6). In addition, the fact that fighting had already broken out between the Bosnian Croats and the Bosnian Government gave further evidence to the fact that deployment of peace enforcers would not be timely. Tensions between the two parties had begun to rise to a serious level in the last quarter of 1992, open conflict from 14 January 1993 and significant military operations in Central Bosnia from mid-April 1993.[33] By mid-May, Croat forces had launched an assault on Muslim positions in the south-western city of Mostar, which is in one of Gow's two suggested provinces for the initial implementation phase.[34]

In any case, there would be no British deployment without the United States. Meanwhile, no other power outside the US, including Kozyrev's Russia, was able and willing to handle the situation alone. The US position was vital to any enforcement of the plans for progressive implementation.

What were US decision-makers thinking at the time? Samantha Power has argued that there were three reasons for the Clinton administration's reluctance to commit military force in Bosnia (air strikes or ground troops): (1) The European scepticism (as has been described above), (2) the military advice was cautious or sceptical (Powell's advice was especially important), and (3) that Clinton was worried about public opinion in the US.[35]

As mentioned, many of the top military staff, including the Chairman of the Joint Chiefs of Staff at this time, General Powell, did not favour any kind of military commitment in Bosnia-Herzegovina, and for the most time,

33 Charles R. Schrader, *The Muslim-Croat Civil War in Central Bosnia: A Military History, 1992–1994*, Texas A&M University Press, College Station, 2003, pp. 4, 65 and 83.

34 Christian Burckhardt, "Russia says Vance–Owen must go ahead", in *Reuters*, 16 May 1993.

35 Power, 2002, p. 304, see *supra* note 19. The military advise in regard to air strikes was more divided than it would appear in Power's list of arguments, to which I return in chapter 9.

this included the use of air power.[36] Among the main reasons for this scepticism, as has been explained above, were doubts about the enforceability of the plan. These doubts were significant in regard to a potential *peace-keeping* operation. A peace *enforcement* operation would meet even stronger such doubts.

There were also political problems associated with sending ground forces. On 3 May 1993, a *Newsweek* poll found that there was a 60 percent opposition to sending US ground forces to Bosnia, compared with 27 percent in favour.[37] Because this poll was conducted before the rejection at the Pale meeting, and the relevant scenario was peace-keeping, it is likely that peace enforcement would have been met with even less sympathy in the US public opinion. This must have been taken into consideration when the Clinton administration formed its mind about the policy options after the Pale rejection.

However, Power also points out that Americans tend to support military operations *after* they have been put into action. Examples are the intervention in Panama against President Noriega (26 percent supported action before, 80 percent after) and Iraq/Kuwait in 1991 (a majority against intervention before the war – even against air strikes – but 80 percent support after the fact).[38] Simms has argued that Clinton's chief pollster, Stan Greenberg, also pointed out the same, arguing that Bosnia-Herzegovina was a case where public opinion could be shaped.[39] In this regard, a decision to send ground troops for peace enforcement in Bosnia-Herzegovina could perhaps in itself have created more public support for this action. Elisabeth Drew, one of Clinton's biographers, confirms Simms on this point, but writes that Greenberg also warned Clinton that there was no support for unilateral military action.[40]

---

36 Powell's scepticism is well-documented. See, for example, Carole Rogel, *The Breakup of Yugoslavia and its Aftermath*, Greenwood Press, Westport, 2004, p. 60; Power, 2002, pp. 285 and 304, see *supra* note 19; Burg and Shoup, 1999, pp. 250–251, see *supra* note 28; Elisabeth Drew, *On the Edge: The Clinton Presidency*, Simon and Schuster, New York, 1994, p. 149.

37 Jurek Martin, "Clinton Keeps Up Pressure On Serbs", in the *Financial Times*, 4 May 1993. See also Pilita Clark: "Clinton's Tough Stand Puts Pressure On New Administration", in *The Age*, 7 May 1993.

38 Power, 2002, p. 306, see *supra* note 19.

39 Simms, 2002, p. 57, see *supra* note 23.

40 Drew, 1994, p. 150, see *supra* note 36.

The fact remains that the US public opinion was consistently low for sending US ground troops to enforce a peace throughout the war.[41] In response to the question of whether "the U.S. should take military action" against the Serbs, support was low in early 1993 (27 percent) but grew to 40 percent by April, as the war and Clinton's rhetoric escalated.[42] Support for the use of US ground troops for combat to end the civil war in Bosnia-Herzegovina varied between one-fourth and one-third throughout the war, while opposition varied from half of the respondents to two-thirds.[43] In addition, there was consistently very little support for the United States acting alone, but much more when acting with European allies against Serb aggression.[44] In this regard, the negative stance by the British Government was significant.

There were, therefore, strong reasons for the both United Kingdom and the United States not to go ahead with progressive implementation of the Vance–Owen plan. For the United States, these reasons are so strong that it is difficult to argue that the Clinton administration could plausibly have decided to support progressive implementation. On the other hand, because the counterfactual antecedent is based on a choice, it cannot be completely ruled out either. The conclusion seems to be that the altered antecedent should be regarded as implausible, although not impossible.

8.2.2. Plausibility of the Consequent: Effects of 'Progressive Implementation'

Gow does not explicitly refer to generalisations or analogous situations. The plausibility of the consequents of the hypothesis must therefore be found elsewhere. In the following, I discuss briefly Gow's arguments regarding a positive effect on relations between Russia and the United States and on the Muslim–Croat war. The main discussion is on the argument that a progressive implementation would have pressured the Bosnian Serbs to make peace.

---

41 Richard Sobel, "Trends: United States Intervention in Bosnia", in *The Public Opinion Quarterly*, 1998, vol. 62, no. 2, p. 257.

42 *Ibid.*, p. 253.

43 *Ibid.*, p. 255.

44 Paul A. Papayoanou, "Intra-Alliance Bargaining and U.S. Bosnia Policy", in *The Journal of Conflict Resolution*, 1997, vol. 41, no. 1, p. 102; Sobel, 1998, p. 253, see *supra* note 41.

8.2.2.1. Relations between Russia and the United States

Gow argues that progressive implementation would have led to improved relations between Russia and the United States when compared with factual history. Others seem to agree, in the sense that the relations were characterised by a gradual deterioration. Mike Bowker, for example, has argued that the Russian co-operation in the Vance–Owen process and the Contact Group Plan was gradually replaced by a more pro-Serb – and thus more deviant – Russian stance.[45]

It does not follow from this, however, that US–Russian relations would have been better if the counterfactual progressive implementation had been pursued. Although an immediate positive effect in the relations is likely, it seems impossible to argue convincingly about the longer-term effects. If co-operation on progressive implementation had been successful, Gow's point of view might be plausible. But since the success of this counterfactual operation would have been far from assured, it is difficult to say how the bilateral relationship would have evolved.

8.2.2.2. The Muslim–Croat War

The main problem with Gow's argument that progressive implementation could have helped to stop the Muslim–Croat War is the timing. The branching point of the hypothesis is mid-May 1993, but at this time the two parties were already engaged in military conflict. The statement by Gow that this war was "coming" is in fact not correct, as the war had already begun.[46] From April 1993, there were significant clashes between the ArBiH and the HVO in Bosnia-Herzegovina.[47]

As mentioned, the co-chairmen got Tuđjman and Izetbegović to agree to a ceasefire on 18 May 1993, but this was never implemented.[48] Any deployment of international troops would therefore be deployed in a situation where there was no agreed peace, nor a reliable ceasefire. The

45 Mike Bowker, "The Wars in Yugoslavia: Russia and the International Community", in *Europe-Asia Studies*, 1998, vol. 50, no. 7, p. 1257. According to Lukic and Lynch one important reason for Russian support to Serbs was the need for Russia to re-establish a recognisable "Russian profile" in international affairs following the collapse of the Soviet Union, see Reneo Lukic and Allen Lynch, *Europe from the Balkans to the Urals: The Disintegration of Yugoslavia and the Soviet Union*, Oxford University Press, Solna, 1996, p. 329.

46 Gow, 1997, p. 250, see *supra* note 1.

47 Schrader, 2003, p. 83, see *supra* note 33.

48 Stoltenberg and Eide, 1996, pp. 70 and 72, see *supra* note 1.

troop presence would have had to be substantive in terms of numbers, mandate and equipment for it to be plausible that it could have stopped the Muslim-Croat war.

One may argue that in 1994, the US engagement in Bosnia-Herzegovina led to reconciliation between the Muslims and the Croats. Therefore, this could also have worked a year before. However, the situation was different in 1994. Particularly important is that the Croats felt increasingly isolated internationally and that the HVO was losing ground to ArBiH militarily.[49] This again indicates that for an international force to have plausibly ensured an end to the Muslim-Croat war in mid-1993, it would have had to involve a major commitment. And as described above, the US and UK were profoundly critical to participate in such a mission at that time. If one evaluates the consequent independently of the plausibility of the antecedent, however, Gow's argument could have some plausibility. However, this plausibility would depend on the scale of commitment: A large scale peace enforcement mission with sizeable troop contributions from the United States, and perhaps the United Kingdom, could have served to quell the Muslim–Croat war. But importantly, a larger counterfactual force commitment would diminish the plausibility of the antecedent, as decision-makers would have been even more reluctant to decide in favour of progressive implementation.

8.2.2.3. Coercing the Bosnian Serbs to Make Peace

How many troops would be needed to coerce the Bosnian Serbs to make peace? Karadžić's estimate that 5,000 NATO troops around Brčko would have broken the back of the Bosnian Serb military campaign seems implausible at first glance.[50] All evaluations of the Bosnian Serb military capability suggest that the VRS was at this time the most well-equipped and well-trained army in Bosnia-Herzegovina, albeit smaller in numbers than its adversaries.

In late February 1993, the European Community Monitoring Mission estimated that the active Bosnian Serb units were 70,000–80,000 strong, with 300 tanks and 600 artillery pieces. In comparison, the HVO's overall

---

49 Lukic and Lynch, 1996, p. 217, see *supra* note 45.

50 As previously mentioned, Silber and Little refer to Karadžić as having said that 10,000 troops in Zvornik and the Posavina corridor was all it would take to neutralise the Serbs, in Silber and Little, 1997, p. 278, see *supra* note 12.

strength was estimated to be 45,000–55,000 men, relatively well-equipped in both armour and artillery, and the ArBiH was estimated to be about 50,000–60,000 strong, but with an unspecified number of militia and paramilitary units.[51] A different and later estimate, from June 1993, claimed that the ArBiH had 40 tanks and 30 APCs (captured) and a larger number of artillery pieces, while Croats in Bosnia had 50 tanks and more than 100 artillery pieces.[52] A third estimate suggests that in June 1993, the ArBiH included 120,000 active troops, 80,000 reserves, 40 tanks and one aircraft, while the VRS included only 60,000 troops, but those being supplemented by up to 20,000 Yugoslav army troops, 350 tanks and 35 aircraft.[53]

The VRS had 'inherited' the most of both material and personnel from the old Yugoslav People's Army.[54] This is not to say that the Bosnian Serb armed forces did not include 'bullies', whose primary interest was to wreak destruction, earn money and build private armies. But by any measure, the VRS was the best equipped and probably the best trained force of the three parties in the conflict in Bosnia-Herzegovina in mid-1993. In addition, it received aid from Milošević' Serbia.[55] It was for these reasons that the Bosnian Serbs could expand and hold their occupied territory through military force for the most part of the war.

In other words, an international peace enforcement mission would have faced a considerable challenge in the VRS should it get entangled in open-ended fighting. And there should be no doubt that there was a risk of getting into this kind of situation if NATO forces had been deployed in areas where they would threaten Bosnian Serb interests – particularly in the Northern Corridor in Province 3, as Gow suggests. Karadžić may have had

51 Schrader, 2003, pp. 21–22, see *supra* note 33.

52 Lukic and Lynch, 1996, p. 298, note 61, see *supra* note 45.

53 Sabrina P. Ramet, *Balkan Babel: The Disintegration of Yugoslavia from the Death of Tito to the Fall of Milošević*, Westview Press, Boulder, 2002, p. 213.

54 Barbara Ekwall-Uebelhart and Andrei Raevsky, *Managing Arms in Peace Processes: Croatia and Bosnia-Herzegovina*, United Nations Institute for Disarmament Research (UNIDIR), Disarmament and Conflict Resolution Project, Geneva, 1996, pp. 13–15; General Rupert Smith, *The Utility of Force: The Art of War in the Modern World*, Alfred A. Knopf, New York, 2007, p. 352; Stephen John Stedman, "The Former Yugoslavia", in Richard N. Haass (ed.), *Economic Sanctions and American Diplomacy*, Council of Foreign Relations, New York, 1998, p. 185; Rogel, 2004, p. 58, see *supra* note 36.

55 Serb aid to the VRS is well documented. See, for example, Sabrina P. Ramet, *The Three Yugoslavias: State-Building and Legitimation, 1918–2005*, Woodrow Wilson Center Press, Washington, D.C., 2006, p. 441.

his reservations about getting into a fight with NATO forces, but that is probably less the case with the Bosnian Serb hard-liners, such as General Mladić.[56]

Gow claims that progressive implementation could have been based on NATO planning for a force to implement the Vance–Owen plan. He cites a source indicates that NATO was planning for up to 150,000.[57] This figure is too high, although the planning estimates did vary. And it must also be factored in that a peace enforcement mission would likely have required a more substantial troop commitment than a mission mandated to implement a peace plan that was agreed to by all parties.

US Secretary of Defence Les Aspin is reported to have considered 75,000–100,000 men as a realistic amount of troops needed to implement the Vance–Owen plan, if all parties agreed. At a working dinner arranged by the Italian Minister of Defence during a Eurogroup seminar in Washington, D.C., on 5 May 1993, Aspin had strongly encouraged the others to participate with personnel in a NATO force for implementation of the Vance–Owen plan in Bosnia-Herzegovina, should the Bosnian Serb Assembly accept it. Aspin explained that they planned for a force of between 75,000–100,000 men, depending on the level of resistance. Covering the throughways in the North would require an additional 25,000 men, meaning that the number of troops would be at least 100,000. Furthermore, Aspin also explained that the Clinton administration would be "in deep trouble" in the US public opinion if the American contribution would make up more than one-third of the total force.[58]

One could argue that Aspin may have exaggerated the disapproval of US public opinion in order to attain more commitment from the Europeans. Still, considering both that the statements were made in a closed and high-level working dinner and that the opinion polls cited above seem to confirm the remarks, Aspin is likely to have been fairly precise in regard to the actual US position. If he was, his statements show that implementing the Vance–Owen plan after a rejection would require considerable troop contributions from many other countries.

56 Laura Silber and Allan Little, *The Death of Yugoslavia*, Penguin, London, 1995, p. 316.

57 Gow, 1997, p. 257, see *supra* note 1. Gow's source is the *New York Times*, 11 March 1993, p. A1.

58 Norwegian Embassy in Washington, D.C., *Bosnia-Herzegovina. Uttalelser av Les Aspin* [Bosnia-Herzegovina. Statements by Les Aspin], 7 May 1993, p. 2.

The number of troops needed for a progressive implementation after the Bosnian Serbs had rejected the plan will remain a theoretical matter. Barry R. Posen has speculated that based on the experiences of the British in Northern Ireland, between 90,000 and 200,000 troops would be needed to enforce a peace in Bosnia-Herzegovina.[59] Harold H. Switzer has suggested that peace enforcement would have required 100,000 troops.[60]

The initial British calculations were much higher. In August 1992, Major asked his military chiefs of staff how many troops it would take to force the parties to cease fighting, the answer to which was 400,000 – nearly three times as many as the whole British Army. Moreover, the commitment would be long-term.[61] In retrospect, this number seems clearly exaggerated, but it does provide insight in the perceived choices confronting the British cabinet at that time.

Still, enforcing peace in Bosnia-Herzegovina would probably have required a substantial number of troops, and certainly more than the then nearly 23,000-strong UNPROFOR presence.[62] This is problematic for the plausibility of 'progressive implementation', because it would require a more massive mobilisation than Gow seems to believe. Even if one supposes that the United States could have supported implementation and argued strongly in favour to the other states, it would have taken some time to convince them to participate. It was difficult enough to get NATO countries (and some other states) to contribute troops to implementing a fully ratified Vance–Owen plan, but without ratification, it could prove close to impossible.[63]

59 Barry R. Posen, "A Balkan Vietnam Awaits 'Peacekeepers'", in the *Los Angeles Times*, 4 February 1993; Barry R. Posen, "Military Responses to Refugee Disasters", in *International Security*, 1996, vol. 21, no. 1, pp. 105–106.

60 Switzer, 2001, p. 287, see *supra* note 22.

61 Major, 1999, p. 535, see *supra* note 20.

62 Figure from Larry Minear, Jeffrey Clark, Roberta Cohen, Dennis Gallagher, Iain Guest and Thomas G. Weiss, *Humanitarian Action in the Former Yugoslavia: The U.N.'s Role 1991–1993*, *Occasional Paper #18*, Thomas J. Watson Jr. Institute for International Studies and Refugee Policy Group, Brown University, Providence, 1994, p. 89.

63 The countries most firmly committed to participating in the peace-keeping operation seem to have been USA, UK, France, Russia, the Netherlands, Belgium, Norway and Sweden. See Ian Black, David Fairhall and Martin Walker, "Clinton Sceptical on Bosnia Peace", in *The Guardian*, 4 May 1993.

One could perhaps interject that being progressive, the implementation could start with a limited number of troops, for example a US contingent of 10,000. But this would break completely with the assessment that US public opinion would not approve a unilateral American deployment in Bosnia-Herzegovina at that time, thus further reducing the plausibility of the antecedent. It seems, therefore, that the United States and its NATO allies would have had difficulties in coming up with a number of troops that would be sufficient to enforce the peace along the lines of the Vance–Owen plan.

Would military enforcement of the Vance–Owen plan have brought peace to Bosnia-Herzegovina? The question is of course impossible to answer precisely. Gow suggests that progressive implementation would have restrained the fighting and saved lives. In fact, implementation would have been risky and have had an open-ended outcome. The worst-case scenario would have involved serious Bosnian Serb attacks on the international force. In this case, it could have led to an escalated international military presence in Bosnia-Herzegovina – an operation that might have been far too similar to Vietnam for many Americans to accept, including many senior advisers in the Pentagon.[64] The other option would have been to withdraw. Had the international force withdrawn after having been attacked, the use of force in Bosnia-Herzegovina would have lost credibility for the foreseeable future.

What of the best-case scenario? The doves among the Bosnian Serb officials, perhaps including Karadžić, would have gone back to the negotiating table with real will to make peace and accept the Vance–Owen plan as it was, or with minor modifications. They would also have been able to restrain the hard-liners in political and military leadership.

This may not be an implausible outcome, but the risks of the worst-case scenario were still too great to be ignored. The Bosnian Serbs knew that the Americans had withdrawn earlier that same year from Somalia, another country in which the United States had no strong national interest. The Bosnian Serb leadership may have reasoned that the Americans could be driven out of Bosnia-Herzegovina in the same fashion as Somalia, or even Vietnam. One Bosnian Serb Member of Parliament, General Subotic, said to the press after the Pale decision that "if the Vietnamese could survive

64 Pilita Clark, "Clinton's Tough Stand Puts Pressure On New Administration", in *The Age*, 7 May 1993.

a war conducted by the Americans, we can too".[65] It is difficult to say how many Bosnian Serb political and military leaders agreed with this statement. As argued above, however, the various statements made during and directly after the Pale meeting, seen in isolation, do indicate that a significant number of Bosnian Serb politicians and officers believed war with the United States would be preferable to accepting the Vance–Owen plan.

8.3. Conclusions

The discussion above leads to the conclusion that the progressive implementation-hypothesis has low plausibility. This applies to both the antecedent and the consequents. A counterfactual decision to go ahead with progressive implementation on part of the Clinton administration and the British government seems unlikely, considering the problematic issues relating to historical values and minimal rewrite (military advice and public opinion, particularly). Furthermore, in suggesting a *progressive* implementation, the hypothesis suggests a scenario with consequents in the n-order, which are difficult to falsify. These factors lead to the conclusion that the hypothesis seems implausible. Finally, even if a decision in favour of progressive implementation had been taken, there is also reason to doubt that the size of the force to be deployed would have been sufficient to assure the three consequents that Gow claims would have incurred.

The issue of the number of required troops is interesting also because it illustrates the close relationship between the plausibility of the antecedent and the plausibility of the consequent. In Gow's account, three counterfactual consequents follow from the one changed antecedent. Through deeper scrutiny of the hypothesis, however, it appears that a simple decision on progressive implementation might not have led to these consequents. The consequent of stopping the Muslim–Croat war, for example, requires that the antecedent would probably have had to entail a decision to deploy a greater number of troops than Gow supposes. However, that is less plausible than deploying a smaller number of troops. In this way, the assessment of the plausibility of the consequent leads to a revision of the antecedent, and this revised antecedent is less plausible than the original counterfactual antecedent.

---

65 "Bosnian Serb MPs oppose Vance–Owen peace map", Agence France-Presse, 26 April 1993.

9

Early Air Strikes

The hypothesis that early air strikes would have ended the war is in some accounts tied together with the hypothesis that lifting the arms embargo for the Bosnian Government would have had a similar effect. The reason is that the Clinton administration argued in favour of introducing both these measures in 1993. For this reason, I will in this chapter also comment on the counterfactual measure of lifting the arms embargo for the Bosnian Government, although the chapter is mainly concerned with the hypothesis of early air strikes.

Two of the clearest advocates for a hypothesis that early air strikes would have shortened the war are Warren Zimmermann (*Origins of a Catastrophe*, 1996) and Brendan Simms (*Unfinest Hour*, 2002). Zimmermann's account of the war includes very specific counterfactual propositions, particularly this hypothesis: "Had the North Atlantic Treaty Organisation (NATO) met that [Serb] aggression [against Muslims] with air strikes in the summer of 1992, I believe that a negotiated result would soon have followed. From July 1992 I urged that course without success".[1] Further, he argues that in not adopting the option of air strikes, the United States "wasted the opportunity to prevent over a hundred thousand deaths".[2] Zimmerman also writes that he regrets not having suggested air strikes even earlier, in response to JNA's shelling of Dubrovnik in late 1991.[3] He is, however, more critical to lifting the arms embargo in 1993, arguing that it could have left the Bosnian Government worse off.[4]

---

1 Warren Zimmermann, *Origins of a Catastrophe: Yugoslavia and Its Destroyers – America's Last Ambassador Tells What Happened and Why*, Random House, New York, 1996, pp. xi–xii.

2 *Ibid.*, p. 216.

3 *Ibid.*, p. 158.

4 *Ibid.*, p. 225.

Simms argues that it was wrong not to both lift the arms embargo for the Bosnian Government and initiate early air strikes.[5] He argues that both measures "should have been tried earlier", and that the success of NATO's Operation Deliberate Force in 1995 is evidence to this fact.[6] He argues that the only significant factors for the Dayton agreement were US support of Croat and Muslim advances and NATO air strikes.[7] Finally, he places the blame for obstructing the forceful approach preferred by the Americans on the French and the British, but particularly on the latter, arguing that the United Kingdom played a "disastrous role" in the destruction of Yugoslavia.[8]

9.1.1. A Brief History of 'Lift and Strike'

As described above, the Clinton administration came into office in January 1993 preferring to approach the Bosnian crisis with a policy of 'lift and strike': arming the Muslims (*lift* the arms embargo) and using air force against Bosnian Serb military positions (*strike*). Involved parties and advisors would often support one of these options while opposing the other. Lift and strike was meant to "level the playing field", as Secretary of State Christopher put it, by removing the Serb military advantage. [9] The British government, which opposed the policy, responded by saying that it would only "level the killing field".[10] Lift and strike would involve backing the Bosnian Government against the Bosnian Serbs, which would be very different from using air strikes in a tactical manner to protect UN forces or civilians.

There were disagreements on the wisdom of lift and strike in the American foreign policy leadership. General Colin Powell – who was popular in the United States after the successful military intervention in the Persian Gulf in 1991 – for the longest time opposed the use of air power in

5 Brendan Simms, *Unfinest Hour: Britain and the Destruction of Bosnia*, Penguin, London, 2002, p. 80.

6 *Ibid.*, pp. 342 and 335–337.

7 *Ibid.*, p. 335.

8 *Ibid.*, p. xvii.

9 See "Serbs Reject Vance–Owen Peace Plan", *Agence Europe*, 6 April 1993.

10 Foreign Minister Hurd said this, the quote is taken from Reneo Lukic and Allen Lynch, *Europe from the Balkans to the Urals: The Disintegration of Yugoslavia and the Soviet Union*, Oxford University Press, Solna, 1996, p. 296. See also Douglas Hurd, *Memoirs*, Little, Brown, London, 2003, p. 460.

Bosnia-Herzegovina.[11] Bush's Secretary of Defence, Lawrence Eagleburger, said to Warren Zimmermann in mid-1992 that he believed the Gulf War victory vindicated Powell's view that military intervention should be avoided in Bosnia-Herzegovina, including air strikes.[12] Powell continued to influence US policy on Bosnia-Herzegovina under the Clinton administration. Les Aspin, Clinton's Secretary of Defence, was also sceptical of getting involved militarily in Bosnia-Herzegovina, and argued against an American military intervention.[13]

On the other side of the debate were particularly the Chief of Staff of the Air Force, General Merrill McPeak, and Admiral Jeremy Michael Boorda, chief of NATO's Southern Command (and later Navy Chief).[14] National Security Adviser Tony Lake also argued for a more forceful approach, and Vice President Al Gore consistently argued in favour of using air strikes.[15] President Clinton thus had to struggle with contradictory advice from the beginning.[16]

In addition to the Clinton administration's internal debate about the lift and strike option, the opposition from its European allies was also important. London regarded lifting in particular as counterproductive. Clinton criticised the British in the *Washington Post* on 6 April 1993 for their resistance to a partial lifting of the UN arms embargo.[17] Air strikes would also involve risks for the British, French and other nations' troops, which comprised the UNPROFOR mission in Bosnia-Herzegovina. Both the United Kingdom and France were major troop-contributing countries in UNPROFOR, which made their opinions matter more both to Washington and to the members of the UN Security Council. In fact, the Bush administration had suggested lifting the arms embargo in December 1992, but the

11 Powell wrote an article on this in *Foreign Affairs* in the winter of 1992, see Jeffrey Record, *Making War, Thinking History: Munich, Vietnam, and Presidential Uses of Force from Korea to Kosovo*, Naval Institute Press, Annapolis, 2002, pp. 30–31.

12 Zimmermann, 1996, p. 214, see *supra* note 1.

13 Elisabeth Drew, *On the Edge: The Clinton Presidency*, Simon and Schuster, New York, 1994, p. 142.

14 Simms, 2002, pp. 67–68, see *supra* note 5; Drew, 1994, p. 152, see *supra* note 13.

15 Drew, 1994, pp. 142 and 155, see *supra* note 13.

16 See also Wayne Bert, *The Reluctant Superpower: United States' Policy in Bosnia, 1991–95*, Houndsmills, Basingstroke, 1997, pp. 170–175.

17 James Gow, *Triumph of the Lack of Will: International Diplomacy and the Yugoslav War*, Hurst, London, 1997, pp. 175 and 178.

British worried about safety of troops in face of Serb retaliation. According to John Major, "the Americans soon saw this point".[18]

There were also doubts in ICFY. Lord Owen, who at times supported 'striking', objected to arming the Muslims, arguing that it could fuel the escalating conflict between Muslims and Croats.[19] This problem diminished after a ceasefire between these parties was achieved after American brokering in late February and early March 1994.[20]

The Europeans and others resisted attempts to lift the embargo in the UN Security Council. A notable effort in this regard was the introduction of draft resolution S/25997 on 29 June 1993, which would have lifted the arms embargo for the Bosnian Government. The ensuing debate in the UN Security Council is evidence to the different parties' positions. France, Russia and the UK opposed the draft resolution, with the representative for the latter country (David Hannay) calling it "a solution of despair".[21] In the end, the draft resolution was not passed. Of the Council's 15 members, six voted in favour and there were nine abstentions.[22] A leaked Foreign and Commonwealth Office memorandum from 1993 stated that on 29 June, a Russian veto would have been forthcoming if the UN Security Council had given its majority vote to draft resolution S/25997. The same memo described 'lift and strike' as a "lunatic idea".[23] Hurd also argues that the Russians would never have accepted a resolution in the UN Security Council that would have lifted the arms embargo.[24]

Certain developments in the war in Bosnia-Herzegovina also made lifting the arms embargo difficult. This is best illustrated by the events surrounding the Contact Group Plan. When the Bosnian Serbs rejected the plan in July 1994, Milošević announced that he would to cut all links with the Bosnian Serbs. This made any moves from the West to lift the arms em-

---

18 John Major, *The Autobiography*, HarperCollins Publishers, London, 1999, p. 538.

19 David Owen, *Balkan Odyssey*, Harcourt Brace, London, 1995, pp. 150–151.

20 CIA, Office of Russian and European Analysis, *Balkan Battlegrounds: A Military History of the Yugoslav Conflict, 1990–1995*, vol. 1, CIA, Washington, D.C., 2002, p. 227.

21 Daniel Bethelehem and Marc Weller (eds.), *The 'Yugoslav' Crisis in international Law: General Issues, Part I*, in series *Cambridge International Documents Series*, vol. 5, Cambridge University Press, Cambridge, 1997, pp. 335–336.

22 *Ibid*., p. 338.

23 Lukic and Lynch, 1996, p. 299, see *supra* note 10.

24 Hurd, 2003, p. 459, see *supra* note 10.

bargo for Bosnia-Herzegovina seem inappropriate. According to Gow, Milošević' decision tipped the military balance more in favour of the Croats and Muslims, since the Bosnian Serbs had relied heavily on support from Belgrade in logistics and military assistance.[25] In fact, however, supplies continued to flow from Serbia to the Bosnian Serbs clandestinely.[26] Still, the propaganda effect in regard to efforts to lift the embargo was achieved.

Meanwhile, the arms embargo did not, in any case, prevent large-scale weapons smuggling into Bosnia-Herzegovina, to all parties. The Bosnian Government was particularly reliant on co-operation with the Croats, due to its lack of access to ports. Over time, it was able to bring in large amounts of small arms and light weapons from Croatia, Iran, Turkey and Saudi Arabia, and with the tacit support of the US.[27] The Bosnian Government, however, struggled to attain heavy weapons.[28] Still, over time, the clandestine weapons trade put the Bosnian Government in a better position. One scholar argues that "ironically, it was the very failure of the international arms embargo through smuggling that helped to bring the war to an end".[29] The Americans announced on 11 November 1994, that they would unilaterally lift the arms embargo. This was greatly protested by European NATO members.

NATO used air force to enforce the UN's no-fly zone in Bosnia-Herzegovina. Tactical air strikes against VRS positions in Bosnia-Herzegovina were deployed from 10 April 1994 and onward, but only after a mortar attack on the Sarajevo market place on 28 August 1995, did NATO launch a large-scale operation with strategic characteristics against the VRS.[30] NATO began a sustained bombing campaign to force the Bosnian Serbs to

---

25 Gow, 1997, p. 264, see *supra* note 17.

26 Sabrina P. Ramet, *Balkan Babel: The Disintegration of Yugoslavia from the Death of Tito to the fall of Milošević*, Westview Press, Boulder, 2002, pp. 217–218 and 234.

27 Stephen John Stedman, "The Former Yugoslavia", in Richard N. Haass (ed.), *Economic Sanctions and American Diplomacy*, Council of Foreign Relations, New York, 1998, p. 185.; Warren H. Switzer, "International Military Responses to the Balkan Wars: Crises in analysis", in Branka Magas and Ivo Zanic (eds.) *The War in Bosnia-Herzegovina 1991–1995*, Frank Cass, London, 2001, p. 297.

28 Switzer, 2001, p. 298, see *supra* note 27.

29 Peter Andreas, "The Clandestine Political Economy of War and Peace in Bosnia", in *International Studies Quarterly*, 2004, vol. 48, no. 1, p. 42.

30 CIA, 2002, vol. 1, p. 231, see *supra* note 20.

withdraw heavy weaponry from around Sarajevo, as well as in other areas of Bosnia-Herzegovina.

In this sense, one could say that lift and strike option was eventually implemented, but only in the later stages of the war. The question, however, is whether intervention of a similar kind could have brought peace at an earlier stage.

9.1.2. Specification of the Hypothesis

I have argued, in the theory section, that counterfactuals are more likely to attain plausibility when they are based on a single changed antecedent. Drawing up a scenario by changing more than one antecedent is less in compliance with the criterion of minimal rewrite. A counterfactual 'lift and strike'-hypothesis, therefore, presents some methodological difficulties. Such a hypothesis involves more than one changed antecedent. Lifting the arms embargo would be one possible changed antecedent, and using air strikes would be another. However, lifting the arms embargo could also have been done in a number of ways and at a number of different times. The most obvious would be a resolution by the UN Security Council, because this was the only agency that by international law could have lifted the embargo. However, several factors, which have been described above, suggest that such a hypotheses would breach the minimal rewrite rule: The clear-cut opposition to such a resolution from the United Kingdom and France, the fact that only a minority of six members of the Security Council actually voted to lift the embargo in the mentioned session in June, and the possibility that a Russian veto could have been forthcoming if the Security Council swayed in the direction preferred by the Americans.

Another possible counterfactual antecedent in regard to the arms embargo would be an American unilateral decision not to adhere to the embargo. Such a decision was actually made at a later stage, and conceivably could have been done also in, say, mid-1993. But in the Clinton administration's thinking at that time, the lifting of the arms embargo was closely tied with the concept of air strikes. In this line of thinking, air strikes would not be a direct instrument in coercing the Bosnian Serbs in itself, but a measure to protect the Bosnian Government from attacks up to a point when it was ready to defend itself with new arms.[31] This scenario therefore requires that the counterfactual analysis does take into account the possibility of using air strikes, because it was an integral part of the policy of 'lift'.

As for the air strikes hypothesis, one could imagine several different counterfactual versions: Tactical air strikes to aid UNPROFOR on the ground, tactical air strikes to allow time for the Bosnian Government to arm itself, or strategic air strikes against both Bosnian Serbs and the Serbs to coerce them into signing a peace agreement, to mention some. The many possible antecedents require that a choice must be made. I believe that the hypothesis that would most likely be fruitful is one where the antecedent is a decision to initiate early strategic air strikes. This hypothesis is the one that is perhaps the closest to Zimmermann's line of reasoning, and it also falls within the scope of the counterfactual options that Simms calls for. In the following, therefore, I will concentrate on this approach (with further specifications that will be clarified below). This is not to say, however, that the other counterfactual antecedents are not worthy of study. I do believe, however, that the chosen approach is the most apt for undergoing a clarifying evaluation and the most likely to provide interesting results.

9.1.3. Zimmerman and Simms on Early Air Strikes

Zimmermann presents five arguments in favour of why the United States should have used air strikes early in the war:

1. It would be possible to wage only a limited war by using air strikes against the Serbs in Bosnia (that is, without deploying ground forces).
2. The Bosnian Serbs did not have the fanatical determination and discipline of the North Vietnamese.
3. Modern precision bombs could be potent even without ground forces.
4. A doctrine precluding any military engagement except an absolute sure thing would keep American power on the sidelines of almost every imaginable future crisis.

31 Drew, 1994, pp. 151–152 and 155, see *supra* note 13. This was the compromise policy that was decided upon in a meeting of the Clinton administration principals on 1 May 1993, after much debate about different options.

5. There was a clear moral, perhaps even legal, obligation to intervene, because Serb actions were clearly acts of aggression.[32]

Those familiar with the American military leadership's line of thinking at the time, will see that Zimmermann's arguments 1, 3 and 4 run contrary to the so-called Weinberger–Powell doctrine. This requires, among other criteria, that any American military intervention should involve the use of overwhelming force – an argument against limited military involvements.[33] Argument 2 is a criticism of those contemporaries who drew the analogy to Vietnam in arguing that the United States should not intervene in Bosnia-Herzegovina. The final argument is the only real argument in favour of intervention, since the other four are in fact criticisms of other opinions on air strikes.

Zimmerman further argues that the United States had three major interests at stake in the war. None of them were vital, but all were important when seen as a whole:

1. Sub-regional stability was at stake, particularly there was a risk that the war would affect Greece, Turkey and Italy.
2. The war was a test of the United States' global leadership and resolve, and the US response sent signals to other parts of the world.
3. Morally, the United States has an interest in promoting and protecting multiethnic societies.[34]

In what seems to be a reference to a limited generalisation, Zimmerman also points out that after only two weeks of NATO bombing in 1995, the Serbs agreed to negotiate the end of the war.[35]

Simms's argumentation in favour of air strikes is primarily based on three assumptions: (1) that US public opinion was conducive to a more forceful American military intervention, (2) that the British government erred in their judgement of the war, and (3) that what happened toward the

---

32 Zimmermann, 1996, p. 216, see *supra* note 1.

33 See, for example, James Kurth, "First war in the Global Era: Kosovo and the U.S. Grand Strategy", in Andrew J. Bacevich and Eliot A. Cohen (eds.), *War over Kosovo: Politics and Strategy in a Global Age*, Columbia University Press, New York, 2001, p. 82; Record, 2002, p. 31, see *supra* note 11.

34 Zimmermann, 1996, pp. 217–218, see *supra* note 1.

35 *Ibid.*, p. 232.

end of the war proves that lift and strike should have been implemented before.

The two former arguments, in effect, strengthen the plausibility of the antecedent. However, in Simms account, there are at least two counterfactual antecedents, as he claims both that the United States should have advocated its policy more whole-heartedly – thus winning over their European allies – and that the British should have seen the wisdom of lift and strike. Simms is in this account clearly counterfactual, but does not explicitly base his hypotheses on counterfactual theory. Perhaps for this reason, he does not explain whether he believes that both antecedents would have had to be realised, or just one, in order for the counterfactual consequent to follow.

As regards the argument that the US could have advocated their own policy more strongly, Simms argues that the US public opinion did at times favour air strikes against the Bosnian Serbs, for example, in August 1992, when a *Newsweek* poll showed a 53 percent support for the United States to take a lead in UN-sponsored air strikes against the Bosnian Serbs.[36] He explains further, however, that there was never more than a bare majority for such an approach, and that the support evaporated in October 1993 after the events involving US military in Mogadishu.[37] Still, he argues, there are grounds to believe that the US public would have supported military action in Bosnia if the President had taken the lead.[38] This gives reason to argue that the Clinton administration could have presented more forceful arguments when gathering support for their policy among the Europeans. Simms believes Clinton and Christopher made a mistake in only half-heartedly seeking support for lift and strike in 1993. This was "far from confidence-inspiring", according to Simms.[39]

As regards the other antecedent, British acceptance of the use of air strikes, Simms claims the actual British policy in part was the result of an error of judgement.[40] The British motivations for opposing air strikes were threefold, he argues: (1) The British feared that air strikes would antagonize the Serbs and encourage the Bosnian Government too much, and generally

---

36 Simms, 2002, p. 56, see *supra* note 5.

37 *Ibid.*, p. 56.

38 *Ibid.*, p. 57.

39 *Ibid.*, p. 339–340.

40 *Ibid.*, p. 343.

damage the peace talks; (2) they thought air strikes would expose British forces on the ground to Serb reprisals; and (3) they held the belief that air power alone could not coerce the Bosnian Serbs.[41]

Simms also argues that the British Government's "unsustainably narrow" concept of national interest is a reason for the failure to see the benefits of air strikes. In Simms' opinion, British politicians did not see that Bosnia could escalate to a bigger problem and that a military solution was quicker and less costly.[42] In this way, the British policy on Bosnia-Herzegovina was "disastrous", according to him.[43]

As regards the consequent in Simms' hypothesis – that the Bosnian Serbs would have been coerced to make peace – Simms points to the success of Operation Deliberate Force in 1995 as evidence. As a consequence of the bombing, Serb defences collapsed and ArBiH and HVO forces filled the vacuum, he argues.[44] Meanwhile, he dismisses the argument that the successful ground offensives in Croatia, Operations Flash and Storm, had a decisive effect, although they were contributing factors.[45] He argues that the only significant factors for the Dayton Agreement were US support of Croat and Muslim advances and NATO air strikes.[46]

In addition to NATO's Operation Deliberate Force, Simms also argues that the threat of air strikes had been effective also on other occasions throughout the war: "On no fewer than three occasions between July 1993 and April 1994, the threat of massive NATO air action was brought to bear on the Bosnian Serbs, and in each case it was effective".[47] The three occasions Simms' has in mind were the Bosnian Serb withdrawals from Sarajevo in August 1993 and February 1994 and from Gorazde in April 1994.[48]

---

41 *Ibid.*, p. 68–69.

42 *Ibid.*, p. 343.

43 *Ibid.*, p. xvii and 51.

44 *Ibid.*, p. 333.

45 *Ibid.*, p. 333–334.

46 *Ibid.*, p. 335.

47 *Ibid.*, p. 116.

48 *Ibid.*, pp. 116–119.

9.2. The Scientific Coherence of Early Air Strikes

9.2.1. Logical Consistency

The hypothesis that air strikes could have ended the war sooner is logically consistent, as it is does not break with any logical factors on which it depends.

9.2.2. Pragmatism

The pragmatic advantage of the hypothesis should be obvious. If it is plausible that using air strikes would have brought peace to Bosnia-Herzegovina earlier than the Dayton Peace Agreement, this can be taken as an argument in favour of similar measures in comparable crises. Therefore it is not unreasonable to argue that the lessons of the 'early air strikes' hypothesis are relevant to future conflict management.[49] Furthermore, the hypothesis has the potential to shed light on the levels of power of the decision-makers of involved foreign powers, particularly the United States and the United Kingdom, to end the conflict sooner.

9.2.3. Falsifiability

There is plenty of evidence in regard to the dispositions of the decision-makers in the US and British governments and in other involved countries in regard to air strikes, which can be used to evaluate the plausibility of the antecedent. However, the plausibility of the consequent of an early strategic air campaign in Bosnia-Herzegovina in mid-1993 is difficult to falsify. It relies heavily on the analogy to the events in 1995. Strategic air strikes in 1993, however, would have been implemented throughout a period of operations. In this period, a number of unknown responses and/or policy changes could have been decided upon by all the parties involved in the war. This limits the falisifiability of the scenario, but not sufficiently for it to be labelled as 'scientifically incoherent'. However, the limitations in falsifiability warrants caution as to the lessons that can be drawn from the conclusions.

[49] For example, in March 2011, there is a debate in the international community about the use of NATO air strikes against the regime of Muammar Qaddafi in Libya, including whether the aim of such strikes should be the protection of civilians or regime change.

9.2.4. Conclusions on Scientific Coherence

'Early Air Strikes' does have some constraints in regard to falsifiability, but generally should not be said to break with the criteria of scientific coherence. The clear pragmatism of the hypothesis, especially, is an argument in favour of further exploration.

9.3. The Plausibility of Early Air Strikes

9.3.1. The Plausibility of the Antecedents

Discussing the plausibility of the antecedent is in this case somewhat problematic because the starting points in Zimmermann's and Simms' theories involve different antecedents, particularly changes in US and British policies. The two are, however, connected. In the following, I discuss these antecedents together when possible, and separately when necessary.

9.3.1.1. Subjectively Possible

There is no doubt that early air strikes was subjectively possible. It was supported by significant advisers to President Clinton, such as McPeak, and before that by former US ambassador to Yugoslavia Warren Zimmermann.

9.3.1.2. Specified Branching Point

Simms mentions two possible branching points: February 1993 and April–May 1993, but does not elaborate very much on the specific timing.[50] Zimmermann suggests two: In late 1991 and in the summer of 1992.[51] Zimmermann's suggestions, however, should be interpreted as the earliest chances for air strikes, but not as the only possible branching points.

For the purposes of this discussion, I choose a branching point in May 1993, after the Vance–Owen plan failed to get acceptance from the Bosnian Serbs. There are two reasons for this. First, it was primarily after the Clinton administration came into office that air strikes was pursued by the United States as an approach to the war in Bosnia-Herzegovina. Zimmermann proposed the policy to the Bush administration in 1992, but was met with resistance from those he talked with, including Secretary of State Eagleburger

50 Simms, 2002, pp. 68–69, see *supra* note 5. In addition, he argues that Britain "sabotaged" American initiatives for air strikes in the two years following May 1993.

51 Zimmermann, 1996, pp. xi–xii and 158, see *supra* note 1.

and National Security Adviser General Brent Snowcroft.[52] He also writes that the Defence Department and the Joint Chiefs of Staff were consistently opposed to military intervention in Bosnia-Herzegovina in 1992.[53] For this reason, it seems that one would have greater chances of establishing plausibility of the antecedent when operating with a branching point in the time of the Clinton administration, which actively advocated the use air strikes.

Second, Simms' discussion of US policy is focussed on the time of the Clinton administration, and he specifically mentions April–May 1993 as a point in time when Britain sabotaged what he argues was an American initiative for using air strikes, although he does not elaborate much on this point.[54] The Clinton administration did make an effort to convince its European allies to adopt a more forceful approach to the conflict in May 1993. Although its preferred approach was lifting the arms embargo, with supplementing air strikes, this time might still be one when a counterfactual joint position on air strikes might have been possible.

President Clinton confirmed publicly on 16 April 1993, that air strikes were under consideration.[55] On 1 May, Secretary of State Christopher was dispatched on a high-profile, six-day tour of five European capitals – London, Paris, Brussels, Bonn and Moscow – to rally support for the 'lift and strike' option.[56] This American policy of late April should be seen in the light of the peace negotiations of the Vance–Owen process. At this time, the Vance–Owen plan was still being negotiated, and it would have been very difficult to go ahead with lift and strike when the Vance–Owen process seemed so close to its conclusion. Lifting the arms embargo or using air strikes before May 1993 would have been answered by protests not only from Russia, but also France and the United Kingdom. However, the air strikes option was more agreeable to the British, although they had serious reservations.[57] In light of the discussions on Christopher's trip and the failure of the Vance–Owen plan just days after, this time seems one that

52 *Ibid.*, pp. 214–215.

53 *Ibid.*, pp. 219–220.

54 Simms, 2002, pp. 68–69, see *supra* note 5.

55 Bill Gertz, "U.S. Considers Airstrikes", in *The Washington Times*, 17 April 1993.

56 Barry Schweid, "Christopher Holds New Talks with Allies on Bosnia", in *Associated Press*, 17 May 1993; Drew, 1994, p. 155, see *supra* note 13.

57 Hurd, 2003, p. 461, see *supra* note 10.

decisions could have been made to favour air strikes against the Bosnian Serbs.

The decision to *implement* the air strike policy would in the counterfactual scenario have been most relevant directly after the rejection of the peace plan in Pale. This seems the most relevant time because it was commonly held at the time that the referendum would not approve of the peace plan, but was set up to give the rejection by the Bosnian Serb Assembly more legitimacy. In any case, it would be the decision in early May to use air strikes that would serve as the branching point.

This branching point serves the further purpose of narrowing the general *target* for early air strikes to the Bosnian Serbs, that is, not including targets in Serbia. After Milošević' support for the Vance–Owen plan and his attempts to convince the Bosnian Serbs to accept it, an aerial campaign that would also be directed at Serbia proper seems to have been out of the question in the discussions in the Clinton administration.[58]

9.3.1.3. Minimal Rewrite Rule

As explained above, the Clinton administration did not argue in favour of strategic air strikes against the Bosnian Serbs in 1993. At this time, 'lift and strike' entailed the use of tactical air strikes while the Bosnian Government received new arms. However, it does not seem to break with the minimal rewrite criterion to suppose that the US government could have decided to use air strikes against the Bosnian Serbs at this time. As mentioned, there were central members of the Clinton team, such as Al Gore, who argued consistently in favour of air strikes, and McPeak gave Clinton an optimistic assessment of the possibilities of such strikes.[59] Major writes that Clinton told had him that he opposed the use of air strikes as a stand-alone option in April 1993, but also made it clear that he had received conflicting advice.[60] It seems that in this situation, with uncertainty and conflicting advice, it would have been possible for the President to have decided to use air strikes strategically in May 1993.

Before discussing the minimal rewrite rule in regard to a counterfactual British decision, there is a need to ask whether the assumption that an altered British policy could have been a decisive factor for the use of early

58 Bert, 1997, p. 172, see *supra* note 16.

59 Drew, 1994, pp. 142, 154 and 155, see *supra* note 13.

60 Major, 1999, pp. 540–541, see *supra* note 18.

air strikes. Put in another way, how many countries would have had to change their position in order for early air strikes to have been implemented? At the one end, could the United States have done this unilaterally? At the other, would it have required support from the members of the UN Security Council, or European NATO allies other than the United Kingdom?

It seems to me that the one extreme – US unilateral air strikes – is fairly implausible. One reason is that unilateral air strikes would have been met with uncertain – and probably negative – reactions in the American general opinion. In-depth polling by Steve Kull and Clay Ramsay showed that although an average of 60 percent favoured *multilateral* intervention in Bosnia-Herzegovina, around 60 percent of Americans were against *unilateral* American intervention.[61] Other pollsters have come to the same conclusion: There was at times a majority in favour of multilateral military action in Bosnia-Herzegovina, and in favour of the use of air power to protect peace-keepers, but consistent opposition to unilateral military action.[62] In addition there were also grave doubts in the US military leadership about the effectiveness of air strikes, and there was also significant opposition to unilateral military action in Congress.[63]

At the other end is the option of full multilateral action, in this case meaning air strikes with the approval of the UN Security Council. This also seems to be fairly unfeasible, given Russia's negative view on air strikes. If a resolution had been tabled in the Security Council, even with the support of the other permanent members (the United Kingdom, France and China), the Clinton administration risked facing a Russian veto. There is evidence that the Russians on 29 June 1993 were ready to veto a draft resolution that would have lifted the arms embargo.[64] One can assume that a draft resolution in favour of air strikes at the same time would have faced a

61 See Gow, 1997, pp. 214–216, see *supra* note 17. Gow refers to Steve Kull and Clay Ramsay, *US Public Opinion on Intervention in Bosnia*, Program on International Policy Attitudes, CISSM, School of Public Affairs, University of Maryland, College Park, 1993, pp. 1, 5 and 6.

62 Richard Sobel, "Trends: United States Intervention in Bosnia", in *Public Opinion Quarterly*, 1998, vol. 62, no. 2, pp. 253 and 257; Paul A. Papayoanou, "Intra-Alliance Bargaining and U.S. Bosnia Policy", in *The Journal of Conflict Resolution*, 1997, vol. 41, no. 1, p. 102.

63 See, for example, Pilita Clark, "Clinton's Tough Stand Puts Pressure On New Administration", in *The Age*, 7 May 1993; Drew, 1994, pp. 149–150, see *supra* note 13.

64 Lukic and Lynch, 1996, p. 299, see *supra* note 10.

similar Russian stance.[65] John Major has argued that one of the reasons why air strikes did work in 1995, as opposed to earlier, was that the Bosnian Serbs had lost the support of both Milošević and the Russians.[66] Zimmermann also acknowledges that Russian support for the Serbs was an obstacle for the implementation of lift and strike.[67]

What is left, then, is the possibility of joint air strikes by the United States and one or more key allies in Europe. Among the countries that Christopher attempted to sway in May 1993, France was opposed to air strikes, but would go along if the United States agreed to commit ground troops – which the French knew was unlikely.[68] The United Kingdom was open for discussion about this option.[69] Douglas Hurd writes in his memoirs that the UK might have agreed to air strikes, but not to lifting the arms embargo at this time.[70] Germany was reluctant to support air strikes (for constitutional and historical reasons).[71] Russia, as mentioned, was opposed.[72] Among other NATO members, Turkey was the only country

65 Regarding the relationship between Russia and the former Yugoslavia and the international community, respectively, see Mike Bowker, "The Wars in Yugoslavia: Russia and the International Community", in *Europe-Asia Studies*, 1998, vol. 50, no. 7, pp. 1245–1261; Lukic and Lynch, 1996, p. 329, see *supra* note 10.

66 Major, 1999, p. 545, see *supra* note 18.

67 Zimmermann, 1996, p. 225, see *supra* note 1.

68 Drew, 1994, p. 156, see *supra* note 13; John M. Broder and Doyle McManus, "Clinton's Bosnia Plan Expected On Saturday", in *The Los Angeles Times*, 30 April 1993. Major writes that Mitterand was strongly opposed to air strikes when the two spoke about the option in April 1993, Major, 1999, pp. 540–541, see *supra* note 18.

69 Drew, 1994, p. 156, see *supra* note 13. See also "Hurd Rules Out Use Of Troops in Bosnia Conflict – Bosnia Debate", *The Times*, 30 April 1993.

70 Hurd, 2003, pp. 452 and 461, see *supra* note 10.

71 "Germany Holds Out Hopes For Bosnia Peace Plan", *Reuters News*, 26 April 1993. German chancellor Helmut Kohl argued publicly for a lifting of the arms embargo long before the Christopher tour in May, see Bill Clinton, *My Life*, Hutchinson, London, 2004, pp. 511–512; Susanne M. Schafer, "Aspin urges U.S., allies to end Bosnian conflict White House may offer plan", in *Associated Press*, 7 February 1993.

72 Bowker, 1998, p. 1257, see *supra* note 65; Simon Tisdall, John Palmer and Ian Black: "Clinton Backs Away From Bosnia Action", in *The Guardian*, 11 May 1993.

clearly in favour of both lifting and striking, although the Dutch also indicated that they were sympathetic.[73] Italy was negative, while Canada and took a position similar to that of the United Kingdom.[74]

In this case, it seems that support from the United Kingdom would be particularly important. This is the case because the United Kingdom, along with France, was the most important European contributor to both NATO and UNPROFOR in Bosnia. Furthermore, in Operation Deliberate Force, these three did by far the most heavy lifting, with US planes having flown 65.9 percent of the total sorties, the United Kingdom 9.3 percent and France 8.1 percent.[75] This indicates that a joint US–British position might have been significant enough to pressure France and the other NATO members to accept air strikes against Bosnian Serb positions. But how does a counterfactual British policy comply with the heuristic of minimal rewrite?

A problem for all countries participating in UNPROFOR was the danger to their troops on the ground in Bosnia-Herzegovina in the event of NATO air strikes. Gow has argued that there were not enough UNPROFOR soldiers on the ground to withstand any dedicated VRS retaliation.[76] More important than mere numbers, however, was that the mandate and the mission had been set up for peace-keeping and not peace enforcement. UNPROFOR operated in Bosnia-Herzegovina on a mandate for humanitarian assistance and peace-keeping, not for fighting a war. And retaliation against UNPROFOR was by no means improbable.

The United Kingdom had 2,500 peace-keepers in the former Yugoslavia in mid-1993, while the French had 5,000. In reference to the danger to the UNPROFOR troops, Foreign Secretary Douglas Hurd declared in Parliament on 29 April 1993 that "[w]e would not agree to action which would put British forces at risk".[77] This sentiment was echoed a few days

73 On Turkey, see, for example, Schweid, "Christopher Holds New Talks With Allies on Bosnia", 17 May 1993. On the Netherlands, see Drew, 1994, p. 156, see *supra* note 13.

74 On Italy, see Drew, 1994, p. 156, see *supra* note 13. On Canada, see, for example, Broder and McManus, 1993, see *supra* note 68.

75 NATO, "AFSOUTH Fact sheet: Operation Deliberate Force" (on file with the author).

76 Gow, 1997, p. 145, see *supra* note 17.

77 "Hurd Rules Out Use Of Troops In Bosnia Conflict – Bosnia Debate", *The Times*, 30 April 1993 ('The Times Hurd').

later by French Foreign Minister Alain Juppé, who argued that the US proposal for division of labour was unfair in that it suggested that Americans bombed and the Europeans on the ground had to run for cover.[78]

Indeed these fears for the UNPROFOR troops were later shown to be justified when peace-keepers were in fact taken hostage in 1995 in response to NATO air strikes.[79] In the event of air strikes, the UN troops were likely to be caught in the crossfire. Evacuation of UNPROFOR in the high-risk areas of Bosnia-Herzegovina was also problematic, as the humanitarian effort would likely suffer as a consequence, which Hurd pointed out to the press in late April 1993.[80]

In what has been called "a passionate debate" in the House of Commons on 29 April 1993, the British Foreign Policy leadership expressed their views on the situation in Bosnia-Herzegovina.[81] Foreign Secretary Hurd argued fiercely against lifting of the arms embargo, but wanted to keep the air strikes option open even in spite of clear risks. Shadow foreign secretary Jack Cunningham expressed his support for air strikes backed by UN resolutions, but underscored that "[t]here are no risk-free options".[82] Some of Hurd's colleagues in the Conservative party were more critical than Hurd, arguing that air strikes should only be thought of as a last resort if all else failed.[83]

It is clear that the air strikes option was considered by key British politicians in 1993. Hurd also confirms this in his memoirs.[84] This sentiment also seems to have a degree of support not only in the Conservative cabinet, but also among the leaders of the opposition. The conclusion seems to be that it would have been possible for the British politicians to side with the Clinton administration on the issue of air strikes in mid-1993.

---

78 "U.S. Poised To Help Keep Bosnia Peace 30,000 Ground Troops May Join NATO Force", *The Record*, 4 May 1993.

79 Sabrina P. Ramet, *The Three Yugoslavias: State-Building and Legitimation, 1918-2005*, Woodrow Wilson Center Press, Washington, D.C., 2006, p. 457; NATO, "AFSOUTH Fact sheet: Operation Deliberate Force", see *supra* note 75.

80 Broder and McManus, 1993, see *supra* note 68.

81 The Norwegian Embassy in London, *Bosnia-debatt i Underhuset* [Debate about Bosnia in the House of Commons], 30 April 1993, p. 1 ('Norwegian Embassy in London Report').

82 The Times Hurd, see *supra* note 77.

83 Norwegian Embassy in London Report, p. 2, see *supra* note 81.

84 Hurd, 2003, p. 452, see *supra* note 10.

9.3.1.4. Historical Values

Much of what was argued in regard to historical values in discussing 'progressive implementation' above also applies here. The memory of Vietnam in the United States military and political leadership created a fear of getting involved in an escalating and open-ended military conflict, which was a major reason for opposition also to air strikes in the US military.[85] However, since the Clinton administration did favour air strikes, it is not possible to argue that historical values rendered air strikes impossible or even implausible, although this factor may partly explain why the air strikes option at times was only supported half-heartedly. In the United Kingdom, conservative ideology may have played some part, as Simms has suggested, but considering that there was a debate considering air strikes among the political leaders, one can also conclude that this ideology cannot be said to rule out a counterfactual British policy.

In conclusion, it should be considered plausible that both the United States and the United Kingdom could have chosen to use strategic air strikes in Bosnia-Herzegovina.

9.3.2. Plausibility of the Consequent

Would early air strikes have led to an earlier peace settlement? Zimmermann's and Simms' arguments rely heavily on analogies, and above all on the comparison with NATO's Operation Deliberate Force in 1995. An assessment of similarities and differences between 1995 and 1993 is therefore necessary in order to evaluate the plausibility of the consequent.

9.3.2.1. Reference to Generalisations or Analogous Situations

As mentioned, Simms and Zimmermann argue that the success of Operation Deliberate Force in 1995 show that air strikes should have been used earlier. The analogy initially seems well-founded, because the experiences from the NATO air campaign in Bosnia in 1995 may indicate some of the countermeasures that might have been used by the Bosnian Serbs in 1993 – notably the use of the Yugoslav-era aerial defence system and the taking of UNPROFOR hostages.

---

85 Samantha Power: *A Problem from Hell: American and the Age of Genocide*, Basic Books, New York, 2002, p. 284; Zimmermann, 1996, pp. 214 and 216, see *supra* note 1; Switzer, 2001, p. 284, see *supra* note 27.

Operation Deliberate Force lasted from 30 August to 14 September 1995. During the operation, NATO flew 3,515 sorties and dropped a total of 1,026 bombs. The multinational air force included contributions from the United States, the United Kingdom, France, Germany, Italy, the Netherlands, Spain and Turkey.[86] Most of the 56 primary ground targets were assessed to have been destroyed.[87] NATO declared the mission objectives met on 20 September. As described above, the operation immediately preceded the start of the peace negotiations that led to the Dayton Peace Agreement.

Could an analogous operation in mid-1993 have led to serious peace talks? Or would this have been impossible at this stage in the war? Answering these questions require that one considers the main similarities and differences in the two historical situations. A number of arguments on either side of the debate have been put forth.

At the time in 1993, a number of arguments against air strikes concentrated on the problem of limited effectiveness of air strikes, due to unfavourable geographical and meteorological conditions. Those military advisers who opposed air strikes both in the United States and the United Kingdom presented such arguments to the political decision-makers, arguing both that strikes would be largely ineffective and lead to sizeable losses.[88] After 1995, there are still those who have argued that air strikes were generally ineffective, such as General Sir Michael Rose.[89] However, the fact that the operation succeeded in hitting most of its primary targets and suffered almost no losses, indicate that the arguments from 1993 were too pessimistic.[90] And of course, it would be difficult to argue that the weather and terrain conditions were significantly different in 1993 and 1995. Hence, for the purposes of evaluating the feasibility of the analogy, the arguments of weather and terrain are of little consequence.

---

86 NATO, "AFSOUTH Fact sheet: Operation Deliberate Force", see *supra* note 75.

87 CIA, 2002, vol. 1, p. 394, see *supra* note 20.

88 Major, 1999, p. 541, see *supra* note 18; Bert, 1997, pp. 172–173, see *supra* note 16; Thomas E. Ricks, "US Joint Chiefs oppose Air Strikes against the Serbs: Leaders of Armed Forces Tell Clinton There Aren't Any Good Military Options", in the *Wall Street Journal*, 28 April 1993.

89 Michael Rose, *Fighting for Peace: Bosnia 1994*, The Harvill Press, London, 1998, p. 6. Simms contradicts Rose on this point in Simms, 2002, p. 333, see *supra* note 5.

90 See the evaluation in CIA, 2002, vol. 1, pp. 394–396, see *supra* note 20.

John Major, defending his decision not to support early air strikes, has argued that the conditions in 1995 were different from 1993 in a number of ways. His list may serve as a good starting point for evaluating the differences and similarities between 1995 and 1993:

1. The Bosnian Serbs had lost the support of Russia and Milošević.
2. The sanctions were beginning to bite.
3. The Americans were significantly more heavily engaged diplomatically.
4. The Croats had built an army and armed it.
5. The Croat–Muslim Federation was attacking in Western Bosnia.
6. The Bosnian Serbs faced much stronger opposition in the UN Rapid Reaction Force around Sarajevo.
7. A political solution acceptable to all parties had been tabled.[91]

Major uses these points to justify why his government changed their position on air strikes between 1993 and 1995. The points are also arguments for why the air strikes bore results in 1995 and might not have in 1993. It is in this way I use them in the following discussion, as a basis for evaluating the plausibility of the consequent, that is, how air strikes affected the peace process.

As regards the first factor on the list, is seems clear that Milošević' relationship with the Bosnian Serbs was more important than the Russian relationship with them. Russia leaned toward the Bosnian Serbs' and Milošević' position, but did not support the Bosnian Serbs when this was not also in line with Belgrade policy. The split between Milošević and the Bosnian Serbs that was deepening between 1993 and 1995 has been seen by some as an important factor in bringing about a peace settlement, in line with Major's perception.[92] Simms, however, argues that the split was not of high significance, pointing to the fact that it began in May 1993 and was complete in Mid-1994.[93] It is indicative that the Bosnian Serbs were also in disagreement with Milošević in the Vance-Owen peace process – and importantly at the Pale meeting – without this leading to a peace settlement. This split was, however, not a lasting rupture, as Milošević continued to

91 Major, 1999, p. 545, see *supra* note 18.

92 Stedman, 1998, p. 190, see *supra* note 27.

93 Simms, 2002, p. 335, see *supra* note 5.

pay VRS officers' salaries without interruption and later resumed arms transfers to the VRS.[94] The greater division later between Milošević and the Bosnian Serbs must have been at least a contributing factor leading to Dayton, because of the Serb assistance to the Bosnian Serb war effort. However, the fact that the two had disagreed over signing a peace agreement before, indicates that this factor should not be regarded as *decisive* in increasing the probability of a peace settlement.

As regards point two on the list – the effectiveness of the sanctions – there has been an extensive debate on whether these were effective in contributing to a peace settlement in 1995. The available evidence is in my opinion inconclusive. I shall make no attempt to settle the issue in these pages, but limit my comment to confirm that there is no consensus on the effectiveness of the sanctions in regard to the peace process.[95]

At any rate, if the sanctions were significant, the effects of this are likely to have been present also in 1993. The development and state of the Serb economy was poor already then: According to one estimate, it contracted by 26 percent in 1992 and by 28 percent in 1993. Real income declined 50 percent across the board, and industrial production fell by 22 percent in 1992 and by 37 percent in 1993. Officially, the unemployment rate reached 23 percent in 1993, but estimates from private economists claim that the rate was actually closer to 40 percent. The portion of the population defined as 'poor' rose from 14 percent to 44 percent.[96]

These economic indicators reveal little of the psychological effect of the sanctions on the Serbs. Adam LeBor has argued that, initially, the sanctions did not weaken Milošević, as the Serbs got a version of the "blitz spirit" of wartime Londoners.[97] However, the sanctions were not new in mid-1993, and their economic consequences, at least, would have been foreseeable for the Serb leadership. It therefore seems difficult to argue that

---

94 Ramet, 2006, p. 441, see *supra* note 79.

95 See, for example, Stedman, 1998, pp. 177–178, see *supra* note 27. Stedman concludes that sanctions were not very effective, as do Lukic and Lynch, 1996, p. 300, see *supra* note 10. For examples of arguments in favour of the effectiveness of sanctions on the peace process, see Louis Sell, *Slobodan Milošević and the Destruction of Yugoslavia*, Duke University Press, Durham, 2002, p. 208; David Cortright and George A. Lopez (eds.), *The Sanctions Decade: Assessing UN Strategies in the 1990s*, Lynne Rienner Publishers, Boulder, 2000, pp. 63 and 77.

96 Cortright and Lopez (eds.), 2000, p. 73, see *supra* note 95.

97 Adam LeBor, *Milošević: A Biography*, Bloomsbury, London, 2002, p. 210.

the changes in the effectiveness of sanctions as an incentive to engage in the peace process had changed to a great extent between 1993 and 1995.

Simms refutes the third argument on Major's list, that the Americans were significantly more heavily engaged diplomatically in 1995 than in 1993, implying that this argument is an excuse to place blame on the Americans for why success was not achieved earlier.[98] The argument that the Americans' increased engagement in the diplomatic talks was a key factor leading to the Dayton Peace Agreement resembles the line of argumentation that forms the basis for the hypothesis of 'Increased US Diplomatic Pressure'. I have argued that there is little to indicate that a change in the American diplomatic pressure was decisive for the peace process. Certainly, it was a difference that the United States took the lead in the international peace negotiations leading to Dayton, whereas ICFY was clearly in the lead in 1993. As explained in chapter 6, however, there was considerable American pressure on the Bosnian Serbs also in May 1993, at the time of the Athens conference and the Pale meeting, without this leading to the desired outcome. This makes it difficult to argue that US diplomatic engagement – as separate from American willingness to use force – should be seen as a decisive factor in the peace process.

In regard to points six and seven on Major's list, the reference to the UN Rapid Reaction Force and an acceptable peace solution, it should be noted that Rose has presented much the same arguments. Rose's opinion is that the NATO air campaign against the Serbs in 1995 was followed by successful peace talks only because it was part of a series of tactical offensives, including "the use of artillery and mortar by the UN Rapid Reaction Force to neutralise the Bosnian Serb heavy weapons around Sarajevo, the Croat–Muslim Federation ground offensive in the west of Bosnia-Herzegovina, and most important of all, the emergence of a political settlement acceptable to all sides".[99]

Rose was the UNPROFOR commander in Bosnia-Herzegovina in 1994, and approved some NATO air strikes against Bosnian Serb positions during his time in charge. For the most part of his time in command in Bosnia, however, he held back in regard to air strikes. In his account of the war he devotes a great amount of space to the discussion of whether air

98 Simms, 2002, p. 335, see *supra* note 5.

99 Rose, 1998, p. 238, see *supra* note 89.

strikes could have been used in 1994 to increase the chances of a peace settlement – a question that he answers in the negative.

The argument that the tabling of an acceptable peace deal was a key change in 1995 as compared with previous years 1993 is partly also supported by Burg and Shoup. They argue that in general it is futile to project power into an ethnic conflict without tying its use to a political solution devised in advance.[100]

One could argue that the idea of strategic air strikes at an earlier stage would primarily have been to get the Bosnian Serbs to the negotiation table with real will to reach a settlement. An air campaign could theoretically have aided in changing the military balance on the ground without being tied to a specific peace plan. If air strikes had brought the Bosnian Serbs to the negotiating table with real will to make peace in 1993, one could also have argued that an alternative peace process and a counterfactual peace plan would have been the result. Still, it is a central difference between the situations in 1993 and 1995 that the peace process had evolved to a point at which not only were the Western states more in alignment in facing the Bosnian Serbs, but at which the Bosnian Serbs had also agreed to let Milošević represent them in the peace negotiations. This happened just before Operation Deliberate Force commenced.[101]

The creation and deployment of the UN Rapid Reaction Force was approved by the UN Security Council on 16 June 1995.[102] It was planned as a two-brigade force, composed of British, French and Dutch troops. After some delays, it became an operational in Bosnia-Herzegovina in August 1995, and was significantly involved in the offensive against Bosnian Serb positions around Sarajevo, in coordination with NATO air strikes, during Operation Deliberate Force.[103]

It is difficult to estimate the impact of the Rapid Reaction Force separately from the air strikes, as the two were put to use at the same time. As a whole, both efforts signalled that the international community, and par-

---

100 Steven L. Burg and Paul S. Shoup, *The War in Bosnia-Herzegovina: Ethnic Conflict and International Intervention*, M.E. Sharpe, Armonk, 1999, p. 404.

101 CIA, 2002, vol. 1, pp. 395–396, see *supra* note 20.

102 UN Security Council resolution 998, S/RES/998(1995), 16 June 1995 (http://www.legal-tools.org/doc/408c24/).

103 CIA, 2002, vol. 1, pp. 567–568, see *supra* note 20.

ticularly the NATO countries, was now willing to use force against the Bosnian Serbs, thus moving from peace-keeping to peace enforcement. In this regard, the Rapid Reaction Force and the NATO aerial campaign were two sides of the same coin. If a strategic aerial campaign had been launched in 1993, some form of regrouping of UNPROFOR to prepare for this would have taken place. But there was no advanced planning for such a scenario that indicates that a restructuring would have involved the creation of a Rapid Reaction Force of the same kind as was deployed in 1995. Rather, it seems more likely that UNPROFOR would have been in a weaker position in 1993 than in 1995 to contribute to a strategic air strikes campaign. With the absence of the UN Rapid Reaction Force, the effect of the international use of force might also have been somewhat more limited than it was in 1995, although there would almost certainly still have been a considerable effect.

This leaves points four and five on Major's list, regarding the military build-up and alliance of the Croat and Muslim forces against the Bosnian Serbs. These are central arguments in regard to the plausibility of the analogy and thus of the consequence of 'early air strikes'. The military situation and relative strength of the parties was different in 1993 and 1995, as has no doubt been made clear above. In May 1993, the Bosnian Croats and Bosnian government were fighting each other, whereas in 1995 they were united against the Bosnian Serbs. Meanwhile, the strength of both the Croatian Army and the two forces of the Federation had increased by 1995. *Jane's Defence Weekly*'s estimate, for example, was that the ArBiH forces had doubled in size between November 1993 and November 1994, to 164,000 troops.[104] It was also better equipped, particularly in regard to its growing arsenal of heavy weapons. Could air strikes have been effective in getting the Bosnian Serbs to agree to a peace settlement before the military build-up of the Croat and Bosnian Government forces had come to the point that it was in 1995?

There are those who doubt that the military build-up and advances of the Croat, Bosnian Croat and Bosnian Government Forces in 1995 was central in the process leading to the Dayton Agreement. And there is certainly no consensus on whether the change in the relative military strength of the ground forces in Bosnia-Herzegovina was decisive in bringing about the peace settlement. At the one end of the debate is Simms, who writes that

[104] Ramet, 2002, p. 230, see *supra* note 26.

the argument that the Croatian and Federation military advances were decisive has "something to it", but that it is "designed to undermine the retrospective credibility of 'lift and strike'.[105] Gow takes a similar view in *The Serbian Project and its Adversaries* (2003), arguing that it was the air strikes – not the Croatian and Bosnian ground forces – that brought an end to the war.[106] Many accounts of the war, however, hold the belief that both the air strikes and the changed military balance on the ground were decisive in bringing the peace negotiations to a successful conclusion at Dayton.[107] Even the CIA, which assesses Operation Deliberate Force to be "in almost all respects […] an unqualified success", argues that it was mainly the combined ground offensives of HV, HVO and ArBiH forces that finally drove the Bosnian Serbs to the negotiating table with real will to make peace.[108] It argues further that the effect of the air strikes was not as significant as it might have appeared, and that the VRS still functioned as a coherent military force throughout its operational area, even at the height of the aerial campaign. Another study, on the effectiveness of aerial bombing campaigns from 1917-1999, takes the position that Operation Deliberate Force was a success in getting concessions from the Serbs in the peace negotiations, but underscores the synergy with the HV, HVO and ArBiH advances on the ground.[109]

Of course, one may argue that it was the psychological effect of the fact that the international community was now militarily engaged against the Bosnian Serbs that brought about the crucial change, more than the actual damage inflicted by the aerial campaign. However, it seems to me that the changes in the military balance cannot be ignored. The territorial advances that the HV, HVO and ArBiH forces made in 1995 were extensive. These represented the greatest changes in military and territorial control since 1993 and immediately preceded the peace talks in Dayton. I therefore

105 Simms, 2002, pp. 333–334, see *supra* note 5.

106 James Gow: *The Serbian Project and its Adversaries*: *A Strategy of War Crimes*, Hurst, London, 2003, pp. 197–198.

107 See, for example, Stedman, 1998, p. 178, see *supra* note 27; Cortright and Lopez (eds.), 2000, pp. 80–81, see *supra* note 95; Clinton, 2004, p. 512, see *supra* note 71; Switzer, 2001, pp. 302–303, see *supra* note 27; Hurd, 2003, p. 476, see *supra* note 10 (Hurd does not draw a strong conclusion in this regard, but seems to believe the changed military balance – including the effect of air strikes and a re-enforced UNPROFOR – was the most important).

108 CIA, 2002, vol. 1, pp. 395–396, see *supra* note 20.

109 Michael Horowitz and Dan Reiter, "When Does Aerial Bombing Work?: Quantitative Empirical Tests, 1917-1999", in *The Journal of Conflict Resolution*, 2001, vol. 45, no. 2, p. 167.

find it difficult to accept that this did not contribute significantly to bringing about the Dayton peace negotiations.

The conclusion seems to be that there are enough differences between the situations in 1993 and 1995 that an analogy in regard to the effectiveness of air strikes cannot be drawn without qualifications. The existence of a unified and militarily strong Croat–Muslim front against the Bosnian Serbs and the build-up of Croat forces are particularly significant differences. However, the analogy seems to be plausible as far as military effectiveness is concerned. The arguments of 1993 that air strikes would not have been effective in terms of hitting their targets, and that they would result in considerable losses, were put to the test in 1995. Only one plane was in fact shot down in Operation Deliberate Force.[110]

Certainly, an air campaign in 1993 would have differed from 1995, and would not have been risk free. There would for example have been a high probability that Bosnian Serb forces would have taken UNPROFOR personnel as hostages, as they did in 1995. And in the absence of a militarily strong Croat-Muslim alliance and a built up Croatian military, strategic air strikes might not have been immediately followed by a negotiated peace deal, as was Operation Deliberate Force.

9.4. Conclusion on the Plausibility of the Consequent

Although the effects of counterfactual air strikes in Bosnia in 1993 are impossible to measure exactly, a case can be made to say whether it would have increased the chances of peace or not. From the discussion above, it seems to follow that air strikes in 1993 would have involved more risk than in 1995, and that there would have been no certainty of outcome. However, as there seems to be a strong case for arguing that the changes in the military balance were decisive to the success of the Dayton process, a case can be made for arguing that air strikes in 1993 would have increased the chances of successful peace negotiations at an earlier stage.

110 NATO, "AFSOUTH Fact sheet: Operation Deliberate Force", see *supra* note 75; CIA, 2002, vol. 1, p. 394, see *supra* note 20.

10

Conclusions and Reflections: Counterfactuals in the Historiography of the War in Bosnia-Herzegovina

10.1. Theory Awareness and Use of Counterfactuals in the Historiography of the Conflict

The hypotheses discussed in the case study are but a few examples of the many counterfactual hypotheses that have been put forth in the historiography of the war in Bosnia-Herzegovina. With a basis in the discussion above, there should be no doubt that counterfactuals are integral to the body of historiography of this conflict.

The counterfactuals discussed here are not only theoretically interesting. The pragmatic advantages of the hypothesis of early air strikes, for example, include lessons for future conflict management. In this way, counterfactuals in historiography may affect present and future policy planning. Arguing that the politicians should have used air strikes earlier in Bosnia-Herzegovina can lead to arguments for similar courses of action in other situations.

I believe that the discussions in the case study also show that counterfactuals in historiography are used with a varying degree of awareness of counterfactual theory. Many of the hypotheses I have discussed have been advocated by scholars and diplomats who do not explain how their hypotheses are counterfactual, or what methodological challenges this implies. It may be that counterfactuals are so integrated into our common sense thinking about history that they are not seen to be out of order. But, as I have attempted to show, the lack of a clear theoretical foundation may lead to deficient, and even misleading, conclusions.

In this regard, the hypotheses I have selected for study are probably not the most revealing, because I have attempted to select those that seem sufficiently thorough to warrant deeper scrutiny. There are many other works that present counterfactual hypotheses almost without any of the specifications that would be necessary to establish scientific coherence and plausibility. An example is the common notion that the war could have been avoided if state recognition of Slovenia and Croatia had been delayed. Former ICFY Co-Chairman Stoltenberg brings up this hypothesis in his book about the war, but fails to provide any significant evidence.[1] Such use of counterfactuals may be deceptively convincing to the readers, while also being difficult to disprove. Certainly an explicit reflection on the actual evidence for such a hypothesis would be useful.

Among the hypotheses I have discussed in the preceding chapters, there are also examples of how lack of theory informed use of counterfactuals lead to doubtful conclusions. The shortcomings sometimes seem quite basic. Gow's first hypothesis, about increased US pressure, fails to specify a branching point. Had he done so, it would have increased the clarity of the hypothesis, and consequently also the possibility of measuring its plausibility. Without a specified branching point, Gow leaves the reader guessing as to what his exact purpose has been, and makes it all the more difficult to judge whether the hypothesis has merit or not.

The second hypothesis, about 'progressive implementation' of the Vance–Owen plan, also has basic shortcomings. For example, Gow's and Owen's accounts do not mention the limitations in setting up a hypothetical historical development involving incremental deployment of troops. At the very least, a theory informed approach would have increased the clarity of these limitations, particularly in regard to the level of certainty of the conclusions drawn.

10.2. Pragmatism of the Three Counterfactual Hypotheses

I have already discussed the pragmatic advantages of the three hypotheses in the preceding chapters, and will not repeat those conclusions here. In general, however, it is worth mentioning that all three hypotheses deal, at least implicitly, with two pragmatic advantages that I have drawn up in the theory section under the category 'knowledge about the past'. These are (1) clarification of the level of necessity of historical events and (2) measuring the levels of power held by the historical decision-makers to make different choices and affect the course of history.

All three hypotheses are based on the notion that the course of the war could have been altered if key international political actors had adopted

---

1 See Thorvald Stoltenberg and Kai Eide, *De tusen dagene: Fredsmeklere på Balkan* [The One Thousand Days: Peace Negotiators in the Balkans], Gyldendal, Oslo, 1996, p. 49.

different policies. Depending on one's evaluation of the hypotheses' scientific coherence and plausibility, they do therefore shed light over some of the options the historical actors were confronted with, and the possibilities for having made different choices. For example, if a policy of strategic air strikes in 1993 realistically could have been adopted and plausibly could have served to shorten the war, this clarifies the opportunities that international actors had to influence the course of the war. The extent of actual clarification, however, depends on the quality of the hypothesis and the available evidence. In the case of all three hypotheses discussed here, I have argued that there are limitations as to how definitively one can establish plausibility for either one. The hypotheses may thus serve to provide insight into the history of the war, but they do so with obvious limitations as to the strength of the conclusions that can be drawn. Through the informed use of counterfactual theory, these limitations can be clarified.

It is also worth reflecting on the fact that all three hypotheses also seem to have pragmatic advantages in the category I have labelled 'Social Pragmatic Advantages I, Understanding The Present'. All three have the function of assigning a sort of responsibility for the tragedies of the war in Bosnia-Herzegovina to specific historical decision-makers. Historiography often portrays decision-makers as heroes or villains. Recent war historiography, including on Bosnia-Herzegovina, is certainly no exception.

Owen places the responsibility on the Clinton administration for the fact that the Vance–Owen plan did not bring peace to Bosnia-Herzegovina. Gow echoes this accusation. Zimmermann also holds the US government responsible for not acting sooner, but for different reasons. Simms accuses the British government for not seeing the wisdom of the American call for a more forceful approach. Because the history of Bosnia-Herzegovina is still recent, an effect of these hypotheses is to cast in doubt the United States' (or the United Kingdom's) general willingness to make sacrifices in the pursuit of peace and putting an end to human suffering, even when opportunities present themselves. In this sense, the three counterfactual hypotheses I have discussed are not only historiographically interesting, but they also serve political purposes in our present time.

Finally, all three hypotheses also include pragmatic advantages in the form of 'Lessons for the Future'. I have already mentioned this in the preceding chapters. In particular, the hypothesis 'Early Air Strikes' seems to be one that has informed the policy decisions of Western leaders in confronting large-scale conflicts, and probably still does. I hope to have shown here that such lessons should be applied with caution, because there is a risk of making false analogies.

10.3. Should Counterfactuals Generally be Avoided?

The fact that counterfactuals provide imprecise answers and can be misleading begs the question of whether they should be used by historians at all. One could argue that the counterfactuals discussed in this case study do little to increase our knowledge of history, but instead provide us with hypothetical questions to which no definitive answers can be found. The counterfactuals that have been discussed have not provided historiography with facts that could not otherwise be uncovered, so perhaps the counterfactual approach is a mere exercise in futility?

A practicing historian could take this view and, as a consequence, try to avoid those hypotheses that seem to lead only to speculative answers. However, there is no reason to believe that counterfactuals will be, or even could be, eliminated from historiography at any time in the future. Imprecise instruments are also useful, and can sometimes be necessary.

The 'anvil' may be an apt metaphor for counterfactual theory. Skilled metal workers will use a number of different instruments for their work, the anvil being one of them. The anvil, by itself, is a useless and blunt object, but when used with skill and right material, and when the right amount of force is applied, a number of useful items can be made. Similarly, the historian can and will use counterfactuals to form theories about the significance of different causes and events in history. Without counterfactuals, the historian will have one less tool to hammer out those analyses that seem to be integral to historiography. I have attempted to show that such hypotheses are certainly integral to the historiography of the war in Bosnia-Herzegovina. Little can be gained by ignoring this fact.

At the same time, there is no doubt that counterfactual hypotheses can be used carelessly, or with lack of skill. The quality of the anvil is irrelevant, if the material applied is clay instead of metal, or if the metal worker is unskilled. Historiography, as well as political debates, includes many examples of sweeping counterfactual theories that are unfounded or misleading. When encountering such theories, it should be the duty of the historian to reveal the flaws inherent. And only by familiarising oneself with the theoretical foundations of counterfactual analysis will it be possible to point out the specific shortcomings in counterfactual hypotheses. Only then can there be increased awareness about what the possible lessons from history are, and what they are not. The conclusions are not trivial, because they are part of the foundations for present and future policy formation.

Index

TOAEP TEAM

OTHER VOLUMES IN THE PUBLICATION SERIES

Morten Bergsmo, Mads Harlem and Nobuo Hayashi (editors):
Importing Core International Crimes into National Law
Torkel Opsahl Academic EPublisher
Oslo, 2010
FICHL Publication Series No. 1 (Second Edition, 2010)
ISBN: 978-82-93081-00-5

Nobuo Hayashi (editor):
National Military Manuals on the Law of Armed Conflict
Torkel Opsahl Academic EPublisher
Oslo, 2010
FICHL Publication Series No. 2 (Second Edition, 2010)
ISBN: 978-82-93081-02-9

Morten Bergsmo, Kjetil Helvig, Ilia Utmelidze and Gorana Žagovec:
The Backlog of Core International Crimes Case Files in Bosnia and Herzegovina
Torkel Opsahl Academic EPublisher
Oslo, 2010
FICHL Publication Series No. 3 (Second Edition, 2010)
ISBN: 978-82-93081-04-3

Morten Bergsmo (editor):
Criteria for Prioritizing and Selecting Core International Crimes Cases
Torkel Opsahl Academic EPublisher
Oslo, 2010
FICHL Publication Series No. 4 (Second Edition, 2010)
ISBN: 978-82-93081-06-7

Morten Bergsmo and Pablo Kalmanovitz (editors):
Law in Peace Negotiations
Torkel Opsahl Academic EPublisher
Oslo, 2010
FICHL Publication Series No. 5 (Second Edition, 2010)
ISBN: 978-82-93081-08-1

Morten Bergsmo, César Rodríguez Garavito, Pablo Kalmanovitz and Maria Paula Saffon (editors):
Distributive Justice in Transitions
Torkel Opsahl Academic EPublisher
Oslo, 2010
FICHL Publication Series No. 6 (2010)
ISBN: 978-82-93081-12-8

Morten Bergsmo, César Rodriguez-Garavito, Pablo Kalmanovitz and Maria Paula Saffon (editors):
Justicia Distributiva en Sociedades en Transición
Torkel Opsahl Academic EPublisher
Oslo, 2012
FICHL Publication Series No. 6 (2012)
ISBN: 978-82-93081-10-4

Morten Bergsmo (editor):
Complementarity and the Exercise of Universal Jurisdiction for Core International Crimes
Torkel Opsahl Academic EPublisher
Oslo, 2010
FICHL Publication Series No. 7 (2010)
ISBN: 978-82-93081-14-2

Morten Bergsmo (editor):
Active Complementarity: Legal Information Transfer
Torkel Opsahl Academic EPublisher
Oslo, 2011
FICHL Publication Series No. 8 (2011)
ISBN print: 978-82-93081-56-2
ISBN e-book: 978-82-93081-55-5

Morten Bergsmo (editor):
Abbreviated Criminal Procedures for Core International Crimes
Torkel Opsahl Academic EPublisher
Brussels, 2017
FICHL Publication Series No. 9 (2018)
ISBN print: 978-82-93081-20-3
ISBN e-book: 978-82-8348-104-4

Sam Muller, Stavros Zouridis, Morly Frishman and Laura Kistemaker (editors):
The Law of the Future and the Future of Law
Torkel Opsahl Academic EPublisher
Oslo, 2010
FICHL Publication Series No. 11 (2011)

ISBN: 978-82-93081-27-2

Morten Bergsmo, Alf Butenschøn Skre and Elisabeth J. Wood (editors):
Understanding and Proving International Sex Crimes
Torkel Opsahl Academic EPublisher
Beijing, 2012
FICHL Publication Series No. 12 (2012)
ISBN: 978-82-93081-29-6

Morten Bergsmo (editor):
Thematic Prosecution of International Sex Crimes
Torkel Opsahl Academic EPublisher
Beijing, 2012
FICHL Publication Series No. 13 (2012)
ISBN: 978-82-93081-31-9

Terje Einarsen:
The Concept of Universal Crimes in International Law
Torkel Opsahl Academic EPublisher
Oslo, 2012
FICHL Publication Series No. 14 (2012)
ISBN: 978-82-93081-33-3

莫滕·伯格斯默 凌岩(主编):
国家主权与国际刑法
Torkel Opsahl Academic EPublisher
Beijing, 2012
FICHL Publication Series No. 15 (2012)
ISBN: 978-82-93081-58-6

Morten Bergsmo and LING Yan (editors):
State Sovereignty and International Criminal Law
Torkel Opsahl Academic EPublisher
Beijing, 2012
FICHL Publication Series No. 15 (2012)
ISBN: 978-82-93081-35-7

Morten Bergsmo and CHEAH Wui Ling (editors):
Old Evidence and Core International Crimes
Torkel Opsahl Academic EPublisher
Beijing, 2012
FICHL Publication Series No. 16 (2012)
ISBN: 978-82-93081-60-9

YI Ping:
戦争と平和の間——発足期日本国際法学における「正しい戦争」の観念とその帰結
Torkel Opsahl Academic EPublisher
Beijing, 2013
FICHL Publication Series No. 17 (2013)
ISBN: 978-82-93081-66-1

Morten Bergsmo and SONG Tianying (editors):
On the Proposed Crimes Against Humanity Convention
Torkel Opsahl Academic EPublisher
Brussels, 2014
FICHL Publication Series No. 18 (2014)
ISBN: 978-82-93081-96-8

Morten Bergsmo (editor):
Quality Control in Fact-Finding
Torkel Opsahl Academic EPublisher
Florence, 2013
FICHL Publication Series No. 19 (2013)
ISBN: 978-82-93081-78-4

Morten Bergsmo, CHEAH Wui Ling and YI Ping (editors):
Historical Origins of International Criminal Law: Volume 1
Torkel Opsahl Academic EPublisher
Brussels, 2014
FICHL Publication Series No. 20 (2014)
ISBN: 978-82-93081-11-1

Morten Bergsmo, CHEAH Wui Ling and YI Ping (editors):
Historical Origins of International Criminal Law: Volume 2
Torkel Opsahl Academic EPublisher
Brussels, 2014
FICHL Publication Series No. 21 (2014)
ISBN: 978-82-93081-13-5

Morten Bergsmo, CHEAH Wui Ling, SONG Tianying and YI Ping (editors):
Historical Origins of International Criminal Law: Volume 3
Torkel Opsahl Academic EPublisher
Brussels, 2015
FICHL Publication Series No. 22 (2015)
ISBN print: 978-82-8348-015-3
ISBN e-book: 978-82-8348-014-6

Morten Bergsmo, CHEAH Wui Ling, SONG Tianying and YI Ping (editors):
Historical Origins of International Criminal Law: Volume 4
Torkel Opsahl Academic EPublisher
Brussels, 2015
FICHL Publication Series No. 23 (2015)
ISBN print: 978-82-8348-017-7
ISBN e-book: 978-82-8348-016-0

Morten Bergsmo, Klaus Rackwitz and SONG Tianying (editors):
Historical Origins of International Criminal Law: Volume 5
Torkel Opsahl Academic EPublisher
Brussels, 2017
FICHL Publication Series No. 24 (2017)
ISBN print: 978-82-8348-106-8
ISBN e-book: 978-82-8348-107-5

Morten Bergsmo and SONG Tianying (editors):
Military Self-Interest in Accountability for Core International Crimes
First Edition
Torkel Opsahl Academic EPublisher
Brussels, 2015
FICHL Publication Series No. 25 (2015)
ISBN print: 978-82-93081-61-6
ISBN e-book: 978-82-93081-81-4

Wolfgang Kaleck:
Double Standards: International Criminal Law and the West
Torkel Opsahl Academic EPublisher
Brussels, 2015
FICHL Publication Series No. 26 (2015)
ISBN print: 978-82-93081-67-8
ISBN e-book: 978-82-93081-83-8

LIU Daqun and ZHANG Binxin (editors):
Historical War Crimes Trials in Asia
Torkel Opsahl Academic EPublisher
Brussels, 2016
FICHL Publication Series No. 27 (2015)
ISBN print: 978-82-8348-055-9
ISBN e-book: 978-82-8348-056-6

Mark Klamberg (editor):
Commentary on the Law of the International Criminal Court
Torkel Opsahl Academic EPublisher
Brussels, 2017

FICHL Publication Series No. 29 (2017)
ISBN print: 978-82-8348-100-6
ISBN e-book: 978-82-8348-101-3

Stain Nordengen Christensen:
Possibilities and Impossibilities in a Contradictory Global Order
Torkel Opsahl Academic EPublisher
Brussels, 2018
Publication Series No. 31 (2018)
ISBN print: 978-82-8348-104-4.
ISBN e-book: 978-82-8348-105-1

All volumes are freely available online at http://www.toaep.org/ps/. For printed copies, see http://toaep.org/about/distribution/. For reviews of earlier books in this Series in academic journals and yearbooks, see http://toaep.org/reviews/.

CPSIA information can be obtained
at www.ICGtesting.com
Printed in the USA
BVHW04*0850110718
521382BV00005B/11/P

9 788283 481020